CATHOLICISM

Facilitator Guide

Facilitator Guide written by
PEGGY PANDALEON

WORD
on FIRE

FOURTH EDITION

CATHOLICISM

Facilitator Guide Table of Contents

Study Program Checklist

This is a summary of all the key steps Word on Fire recommends for the CATHOLICISM Study Program. You can use it in your planning and program administration. Additional detail for each phase is provided in the remainder of this guide.

PHASE ONE: PLANNING

____ Pray your way through all planning and put your trust in the Holy Spirit. As St. Paul tells us in First Thessalonians, "Rejoice always. Pray without ceasing."

____ At least three months ahead, the Program Coordinator should meet with the Pastor or Group Director to secure program approval and to plan the dates of the program, including the pre-program Leader's Orientation session.

____ Identify and reserve the room where the program will be held. This room should include:

1. Video player with large enough screen to be viewed by whole class. If you have a large group, it is often helpful to have the screen raised for easier viewing.

2. Chairs to accommodate all participants

3. Break-out rooms or secluded areas for small group discussion – a separate space for each group. Many participants enjoy gathering around tables during the discussion, so they can spread out their materials

____ Recruit other members of the leadership team: Program Administrator and Group Discussion Leaders. You should have one Group Discussion Leader for every 8-10 participants.

____ Order Study Program Leader Kit about two months ahead, so the Program Coordinator can review the materials and begin to plan the Leader's Orientation session.

____ Determine if the cost of the program materials will be passed through to the participants. Don't forget to include shipping, handling, applicable tax and any other expenses your program will incur in the total cost to be allocated and assigned as a registration fee.

____ Publicize the *CATHOLICISM* program with free, downloadable posters and flyers found at *www.wordonfire.org/catholicism-support-materials/*

____ Place an announcement in the Sunday Bulletin that includes a registration form (also available at *www.wordonfire.org/catholicism-support-materials/*). Ask for the registration form and fee to be submitted at least three weeks ahead of the start of the program, so you can order the right number of Study Guides for your group. You should order a few extra for late registrants and walk-ins. If they have not been opened, you can return them within 90 days for a full refund.

___ Right before the Leader's Orientation Session, the Program Administrator should compile a roster that includes names and contact information of all those registered.

___ Assign each participant on the roster to a Group Discussion Leader (to be announced at Leader's Orientation). Try to balance age, gender and adult formation experience, so each group has a mix. Also, if you know many of the registrants, try to balance the "talkers" with the "listeners" and assign close friends or spouses to different groups.

___ Hold the Group Leaders Orientation Session 1-2 weeks ahead of the start of the program. See details in the Program Planning section on page 5.

PHASE TWO: HOSTING THE PROGRAM

___ Pray your way through the program and put your trust in the Holy Spirit. As St. Paul tells us in First Thessalonians, "Rejoice always. Pray without ceasing."

___ First session: *Welcome and Orientation.* Create an atmosphere where people can comfortably get oriented to the program and start to get to know others in their small groups.

___ Begin Leadership Team Meetings before the second session. Meet to pray, discuss leaders' own responses to Questions for Understanding and to cover any administrative issues.

___ Make sure there is a way for participants to ask questions that might still remain after the group discussion. If you have a priest involved, questions should be directed to him.

___ Encourage the Group Leaders to email or contact each of their group members regularly outside of the program sessions. Group Leaders can call, email, or connect with participants in person. This contact is important to build fellowship among the small groups, to uncover any concerns, and to promote trust and openness. Remember, evangelization starts with a loving relationship.

PHASE THREE: EVALUATION AND NEXT STEPS

___ Pray your way through the program and put your trust in the Holy Spirit. As St. Paul tells us in First Thessalonians, "Rejoice always. Pray without ceasing."

___ Revise and/or hand out the survey (available at *www.wordonfire.org/catholicism-support-materials/*) two or three sessions before the program ends. Encourage all participants and leaders to complete the survey, so you can continuously improve your Adult Formation ministry.

___ Share any comments or suggestions with Word on Fire by emailing: *CatholicismStudyProgram@WordOnFire.org*

___ Discuss options for your next Adult Formation Program. Word on Fire offers other study programs based on Bishop Barron's video lectures.

For more information on these program, please go to: *www.wordonfire.org/study-programs*

Program Materials

Everyone will need to have a Catholic Bible and access to the *Catechism of the Catholic Church* to complete the questions in each lesson.

Catholic translations of the Bible are encouraged. These include:

> **Revised Standard Version Catholic Edition**: a more literal translation used for serious Scripture study
>
> **New American Bible**: used in the liturgy and easier to read
>
> **New Jerusalem Bible**: more contemporary language, but still true to the original meaning

To look up references in the *Catechism of the Catholic Church*, you can purchase a copy of the *Catechism* or go to this website and enter the paragraph number to display the text: *www.scborromeo.org/ccc.htm*

Each person must have his/her own Study Guide so everyone can write answers to the questions and take notes individually. Copying of lessons, without permission, is forbidden by copyright laws. It is suggested that each small group leader have a Leader Guide, complete with the Facilitator Guide and Answer Key.

Every lesson follows the same format:

> **Outline**: Follows the video presentation, so it can be useful for taking notes.
>
> **Commentary**: Expands on and captures much of the content presented in the video. Contains information that is useful in answering the *Questions for Understanding*.
>
> **Questions for Understanding**: Answers can be found in the commentary, the Bible and the *Catechism of the Catholic Church*. Participants should be encouraged to write down their answers as research has shown that the simple act of writing something down actually increases retention significantly. Each discussion session (ex. Streamline structure) should cover all of the *Questions for Understanding*, so please budget your time accordingly.
>
> **Questions for Application**: Each discussion should include at least two *Questions for Application*. Group leaders can assign specific questions the week before, so participants can prepare those that will be discussed. If some of the questions seem too personal, please still encourage your group to think about them and to pray and reflect on them privately. The study program provides many opportunities for enrichment of each person's spiritual life, whether in a group or individually.
>
> **Terms and Names**: Defines theological and other terms used, and provides a brief description of the people referenced in the lesson.

Additional materials included in the Study Program Leader Kit can be used to enrich and supplement the videos and Study Guides. These additional materials include:

- CATHOLICISM: *A Journey to the Heart of the Faith* (published by Random House/Image)

One copy of this book is recommended for each study program, so that the group leaders can resource additional details about the video content. Details in the book provide depth and insight above and beyond the commentary in the Study Guide.

Bishop Barron wrote the book based on the scripts for the video episodes—one chapter for each episode. He also included many of the visual images that appear in the video series, with the name and location of each image noted.

Your participants might like to borrow or buy this book to learn more about the program's theological and artistic content. While we would like to recommend that each participant purchase the book, we realize that this might be cost prohibitive, so we have included one in the Study Program Leader Kit, so your group will still have access to this rich, expansive text.

- Prayer Cards

These cards can be distributed before the program begins as part of your promotional efforts, and/or they can be given to the Study Program participants. We recommend using the *Prayer for the New Evangelization*, which comes from selected texts written by Pope Emeritus Benedict XVI, as a closing prayer for each session of the Study Program. It will be easy for participants to pray along if they have one of these cards in their Study Guides.

- Faith Clips: 50 Theological and Spiritual Questions about the Catholic Faith

This popular DVD from Word on Fire has been an aid to catechesis for many parishes, schools, and individuals. Bishop Barron provides short answers to key questions on a diverse range of topics from God, Jesus, and the Trinity to the sacraments, prayer, and the spiritual life.

Faith Clips is an additional tool to help discussion leaders address questions that might come up. This DVD is easy to use with menus that allow you to view an entire topic, such as "Jesus," or view each individual question separately within the topic, such as "Why did Jesus have to die the way he did?"

- Extended Answer Key

Provided as additional commentary, this resource is intended to provide the facilitator with an in-depth reflection on each *Question for Understanding*. It is not intended to be a "black-and-white, right-or-wrong" checklist against which all participants' responses are judged. Therefore, please be cautious when sharing this information, as some may become discouraged if they perceive that they   should produce the same answer.

Program Planning

Set up the dates and times for the program according to procedures in your parish or group. Make sure to discuss the program plans with your Pastor or community leader.

It is helpful to publish a complete calendar for the program that includes each session's date and what will be covered in that session. The session schedule for each program option is listed in the Program Structure section, beginning on page 11.

Announce the program in the parish or group. FREE support materials are available at *www.wordonfire.org/catholicism-support-materials/* and include:

- -Registration Form
- -Poster
- -Flyer
- -Bulletin/Pulpit Announcement
- -Evaluation Survey
- -Certificate of Completion

Strive to have one Sunday set aside where the program can be announced from the pulpit at all Masses and parishioners can register as they leave Mass.

Set up a table in the vestibule and have the Study Guide there for review and registration forms available. If possible, run the *CATHOLICISM* series trailer on a laptop, so parishioners can experience the visual impact of the study. The trailer can be found at *http://catholicism.wordonfire.org/#watch*.

Run an announcement in the Bulletin, which can include a registration form. Provide a deadline for registration that is at least three weeks before your first session, so you can order Study Guides for each participant. Study Guides can be returned within 90 days for a full refund as long as they are not used. You might want to order a few more than you think you will need, as most groups have walk-in registrants at the first session.

Supply and collect registration forms, so you know how many will participate and can order enough Study Guides. You also can collect a registration fee to cover the materials. A registration form template can be downloaded at *www.wordonfire.org/catholicism-support-materials/*

Leadership Team

The three key roles on the Leadership Team are:

- **Program Coordinator**
- **Program Administrator**
- **Group Discussion Leader**

Program Coordinator:

- Manages the overall program and is the key contact for the Pastor and parish
- Plans and executes the promotion of the study program
- Begins each session with prayer and announcements when all are assembled as one group
- Recruits Group Discussion Leaders with the approval of the Pastor or supervisor of the community
- Addresses participant issues and concerns, if they arise

Program Administrator:

- Manages the registration process, including finances for the group
- Orders and distributes materials
- Develops a roster that lists all participants and their contact info
- Makes nametags for each participant and group leader

Group Discussion Leader:

- Facilitates discussion of study guide questiosn with group of 8-10 participants
- Takes attendance each session and contacts members who miss frequently to uncover any issues
- Contacts each member each week outside of class via phone, email, or in person
- The Program Coordinator and Administrator can also serve as Group Discussion Leaders

Leadership Preparation

Leaders' Orientation: A few weeks before the start of your *CATHOLICISM* program, plan to host an orientation for the leaders. This can be accomplished in about two hours and should include the following:

- **Prayer and Spiritual Enrichment:** Invite a priest or experienced speaker to lead a 45-60 minute spiritual enrichment session. This could be on any facet of the Church and should include some assigned reading from Scripture or specific writings. The purpose of this time is to grow spiritually and prepare for the mission of adult formation and evangelization.

- **Program Overview:** Explain the structure of the *CATHOLICISM* program, including the leadership meetings before each session and the unique activities that will be part of the Orientation Session. Give each Group Discussion Leader his/her own Leader Guide, which contains this Facilitator Guide, all the lessons and the Extended Answer Key. Ask the leadership team to briefly review the materials before the program starts.

- **Group Discussion Leader's Role:** Review the section of this guide that explains the role of a Group Discussion Leader. Reinforce that the leader is a *facilitator*, not a teacher or expert.

- **Group Assignment:** Give each leader a list of his/her members and contact information. Word on Fire suggests that you pre-assign groups, so friends and spouses do not sit together. It is important that each member comes as an individual and forms new bonds within this discussion group. Pre-existing relationships have certain communication patterns and "inside connections" that could create a clique-like atmosphere, which will work against group cohesion.

- Once the groups are assigned, ask each leader to contact his or her members for a friendly introduction and to provide a reminder about the first session's date and time.

- **Administrative Tasks:** You can enlist your leadership team to help with tasks that are necessary to prepare for the first session (e.g., making name tags; unpacking study guides; preparing "get to know you" exercises for the first small group discussion, etc.)

Leadership Prep Meeting: Begin regular preparation meetings with the leadership team before the *second* session. This meeting should be held before each general session to pray together and also to help the Group Discussion Leaders prepare to facilitate their groups by going through the *Questions for Understanding* together. During each Leadership Prep Meeting (60 minutes) plan to:

- Pray as a team for the program as a whole and for any individual intentions. These meetings should begin and end with prayer. Often, the leadership team will bring the needs of individuals in their small groups to prayer at these meetings.

- Review the *Questions for Understanding*. When the Leaders spend some time discussing their own responses and all the resources they uncovered to answer the questions, they will be much better prepared to facilitate their own small groups.

- Discuss any administrative or participant issues.

CATHOLICISM

Group Discussion Leader Guidelines

ROLE:

You are Christ's representative to your small group. As a Leader, people will look to you to model Christ's attitudes and behavior and to also be loyal and true to the teachings of his Church. During the study, enrich your own spiritual life by spending more time in prayer, attending Mass more frequently, and receiving the Sacraments regularly.

You are a facilitator, not a teacher or expert. You are called to facilitate discussion of the study guide questions in the small groups, not to teach the material or give your own answers to the questions. Use the resources provided in the Leader Kit, especially the Study Guide Commentary and the Extended Answer Key, to guide your group to more fully understand the content of each lesson. The philosophy of this approach is that we are all adults learning together with Bishop Barron as our "teacher," under the guidance of the Holy Spirit. Group Leaders facilitate this learning without becoming experts or teachers themselves. If there are outstanding questions at the end of the group discussion, you should first seek a priest or deacon for guidance. In addition, Word on Fire can help with questions when emailed to StudyPrograms@WordOnFire.org. However, it may take up to three weeks to receive a response as our qualified staff is small. Another great resource for questions is the *Catholic Answers* forum (*forums.catholic.com*)

You are the shepherd of the group. Help each member feel comfortable. Keep discussion focused on the material for that lesson. Lead with love and a positive attitude of accepting each person's worth in Christ.

Your goal is to create and maintain positive group dynamics in the discussion. Some groups may have one or more challenging people that you will have to manage within the group discussion or talk to privately. Please review the *Managing Challenging Personalities* document on our website at: *www.wordonfire.org/catholicism-support-materials/*

Responsibilities:

1. Outside the session, **pray for your group** collectively and as individuals. Also, before beginning the discussion of the lesson, say a short prayer with the group.

2. **Be watchful for "contrary spirits."** Increase your own prayer time and reception of the Sacraments, especially the Eucharist, to access God's grace to fortify your leadership.

3. **Create a relaxed, warm atmosphere of acceptance and eagerness to learn from one another.**

    *   Get to know your members. Contact them frequently during the program to build relationships and answer any questions they may have.
    *   Maintain eye contact with each person in the group.
    *   Reassure that "we are all learning together."
    *   Encourage the use of nametags.

4. **Establish that you are the facilitator and leader of the discussion.**

   - If your group is assembled around a table, sit at the head of the table If seated at a round table or in a circle of chairs, sit in the chair facing the door and leave the spot opposite you open (i.e., in a horse-shoe-type pattern).
   - If possible, face the door so you can welcome late-comers.
   - To ensure positive group dynamics, manage personalities within the group or by talking to the person privately. Some helpful tips can be found in the *Managing Challenging Personalities* summary at *www.wordonfire.org/catholicism-support-materials/*

5. **Act as a facilitator, not as a teacher or expert.**

   <u>Draw answers from your group; refrain from teaching</u>. Refrain from sharing your own opinions or answers to the questiosn. Remain neutral as much as possible, so members feel they can express differing thoughts and not look for the leader's answer as affirmation. Be patient when there is silence. Don't jump in with answers, but you can rephrase the question or probe to foster dialogue.

   <u>Use discernment in handling misconceptions</u>. Try to tactfully bring out the truth according to the Church's teaching. It is useful to ask for other opinions around the circle if an answer seems confusing or does not reflect the truth of God's word.

   <u>Keep track of time</u>. Lessons should be completed during your allotted time. Avoid getting off the subject—stick with the lesson. In each discussion session, the Leader is responsible for finishing ***all*** of the *Questions for Understanding* and as many *Questions for Application* as possible (except under the Stream-line Program Structure, in which only the questions that have been pre-assigned need to be completed).

   <u>Use the Extended Answer Key carefully</u>. It will add insight to the group discussion. Do not present the Extended Answer Key as the standard to which the group is supposed to attain in their written work. The Answer Key is called "Extended" because it is much more detailed than any one participant's answers and brings in information from sources not available to the group. Please do not photocopy and hand out the Answer Key as this can set up unrealistic expectations for each participant's contributions.

   All the questions can be answered from the Study Guide Commentary and from the scripture and *Cathechism* references provided. It is not necessary to view the video to answer the questions adequately. The small-group discussion will be much more fruitful if participants prepare and complete the questions in writing before the discussion.

6. **Promote participation by all group members**

   During the first session, develop some ground rules for participation. It's helpful to prepare your group with an understanding of the overall program. Please set expectations at a high level so the participants can truly commit to grow into better disciples and evangelists.

Some suggestions to share with the participants for setting expectations and ground rules for discussion:

- **Pray:** Ask for guidance from the Holy Spirit and then keep an open mind.

- **Commit to the study:** Plan to come each time and stay for the whole session. Obviously emergencies come up, but the goal is to begin the study with an attitude of commitment to attend all sessions.

- **Everyone participates:** The Group Discussion Leader may say something like, "If you tend to talk a lot, please listen more. If you prefer to listen, please pick at least one of your answers to share with the group each time. Questions are welcome – don't feel you have to have an answer to talk."

- **Be Prepared:** Stress the importance of reading the Commentary and writing down answers to the questions; however, tell them to come even if they didn't have time to prepare. They will still benefit from hearing others discuss the questions and from watching the video.

  Encourage members to complete their lessons when they are absent so they can keep up with the study. You may want a second set of videos to lend when someone misses a session. Or participants can economically rent the episode they missed at: *https://wordonfiredigital.vhx.tv/products*

- **Guarantee confidentiality:** All things discussed in the group are to be kept confidential. This is very important, especially for the *Questions for Application* in each lesson.

Program Structure Options

	FOUNDATIONAL 20 SESSIONS	**INTENSIVE** 11 SESSIONS
Participant Profile	• All laity • Approach for those new to adult formation • RCIA • Mature teens and college students	• Laity who have more experience with adult formation • Teachers/catechists for certification or enrichment • Willing to spend 2-3 hours in preparation
Session Time	**90 MINUTES** (30 minute video + 60 minute discussion)	**2 - 2.5 HOURS** (60 minute video + 60 to 90 minute discussion)
Approach	• Ten episodes, each broken into two parts with a lesson for each part • Allows time to truly absorb each lesson	• Full episode video (both parts) and discussion of study guide questions for both parts of lesson in each session • Requires full preparation (both parts) of study guide questions before watching
Preparation	• Read commentary and complete study guide queestions for *one part* of lesson before each session • Finish each session with group discussion of *one part* of lesson	• Read commentary and complete study guide questions for *both parts of each lesson* before each session • Finish each session with group discussion of *both parts* of lesson

FOUNDATIONAL SESSION PLAN

Number of sessions: 20
Duration of each session: 90 minutes
Lesson flow: Each session covers either Part 1 or Part 2 of a video episode. After the first session, preparation for each succeeding session includes reading the study guide commentary and answering the *Questions for Understanding* and *Questions for Application* in the Study Guide.

Session 1: **Orientation (30 minutes)**
- Registration of walk-ins
- Distribute Study Guides
- Overview of Program Structure

Lesson 1, Part 1 (60 Minutes)
- Watch Episode 1, Part 1 video: *Tracks 1-4* (12 minutes)
- Meet in small groups for introductions and to learn how to complete lessons. Give participants five minutes to read commentary and then start working through Lesson 1, Part 1 *Questions for Understanding* & *Application*. Complete at home.
- Assign Lesson 1, Part 2 Reading and *Questions for Understanding* & *Application*.

Session 2: **Lesson 1, Part 2**
- Watch Episode 1, Part 2 video: *Tracks 5-8*
- Discuss Lesson 1, Part 2 *Questions for Understanding* & *Application*
- Assign Lesson 2, Part 1 Reading and *Questions for Understanding* & *Application*

Session 3: **Lesson 2, Part 1**
- Watch Episode 2, Part 1 video: *Tracks 1-3*
- Discuss Lesson 2, Part 1 *Questions for Understanding* & *Application*
- Assign Lesson 2, Part 2 Reading and *Questions for Understanding* & *Application*

Session 4: **Lesson 2, Part 2**
- Watch Episode 2, Part 2 video: *Tracks 4-6*
- Discuss Lesson 2, Part 2 *Questions for Understanding* & *Application*
- Assign Lesson 3, Part 1 Reading and *Questions for Understanding* & *Application*

Session 5: **Lesson 3, Part 1**
- Watch Episode 3, Part 1 video: *Tracks 1-4*
- Discuss Lesson 3, Part 1 *Questions for Understanding* & *Application*
- Assign Lesson 3, Part 2 Reading and *Questions for Understanding* & *Application*

Session 6: **Lesson 3, Part 2**
- Watch Episode 3, Part 2 video: *Tracks 5-9*
- Discuss Lesson 3, Part 2 *Questions for Understanding* & *Application*
- Assign Lesson 4, Part 1 Reading and *Questions for Understanding* & *Application*

Sessions 7-20: *Continue as above with Lessons 4-10. Track listings for each lesson part on pg. 16-17.*

INTENSIVE SESSION PLAN

Number of sessions: 11
Duration of each session: 2 - 2.5 hours
Lesson flow: Participants read the entire study guide commentary (both lesson parts) and prepare/ write down answers to all questions before each session. Each session begins with the video (50-55 minutes) and concludes with 60-90 minutes of discussion of the *Questions for Understanding* and *Questions for Application.*

Session 1:
- Registration of walk-ins
- Distribute Study Guides/Workbooks
- Overview of Program Structure
- Meet in small groups for introductions and "get to know you"
- Assign preparation for Lesson 1 (both parts). Prepare includes reading commentary and preparing *Questions for Understanding* and *Questions for Application* for each part.

Session 2:
- Watch video Episode 1
- Discuss Lesson 1
- Assign reading and question prep for Lesson 2

Session 3:
- Watch video Episode 2
- Discuss Lesson 2
- Assign reading and question prep for Lesson 3

Session 4:
- Watch video Episode 3
- Discuss Lesson 3
- Assign reading and question prep for Lesson 4

Session 5:
- Watch video Episode 4
- Discuss Lesson 4
- Assign reading and question prep for Lesson 5

Session 6:
- Watch video Episode 5
- Discuss Lesson 5
- Assign reading and question prep for Lesson 6

Sessions 7-12: - Continue as above with Lessons 7-11

Session Overview

Gathering and Opening (10 minutes)

> The coordinator should begin the session promptly. It is very important to start and finish on time out of respect for participants.
>
> Many groups offer refreshments and encourage their participants to come a few minutes early for some time of fellowship. You can also sing a hymn together to set a reverent tone.
>
> If you have a priest or deacon participating, he can lead the Opening Prayer and offer a few words related to the session topic. Try to avoid another lecture here — the video itself serves as the "lecture" and teaching part of the program.
>
> The *Prayer to the Holy Spirit* is an appropriate prayer to use to begin each session. You can copy this prayer so everyone may pray along:
>
>> *Come Holy Spirit. Fill the hearts of your faithful*
>> *And kindle in them the fire of your love.*
>> *Send forth your spirit, and they shall be created*
>> *And you shall renew the face of the earth.*
>>
>> *O God, who by the light of the Holy Spirit,*
>> *Did instruct the hearts of the faithful,*
>> *Grant that by the same Holy Spirit*
>> *We may be truly wise and ever enjoy His consolations*
>> *Through Christ, our Lord. Amen.*
>
> Also, the *Prayer to St. Michael the Archangel* has been used by some groups to seek spiritual protection:
>
>> *St. Michael the Archangel defend us in battle.*
>> *Be our protection against the wickedness and snares of the Devil.*
>> *May God rebuke him, we humbly pray,*
>> *And do thou, O Prince of the heavenly hosts, by the power of God,*
>> *Cast into hell Satan, and all the evil spirits*
>> *Who roam through the world*
>> *Seeking the destruction of souls. Amen.*
>
> During the first session, the Program Coordinator should present the ground rules and expectations for participation. Each Group Discussion Leader should discuss these ground rules and adapt or add to them as they and their small-group members see fit.

Video Viewing (~ 25 minutes)

- Entire group of participants views the video in one location
- Use the menu in the next section to select tracks for Parts 1 and 2
- Can use outline in Study Guide to take notes as the video is playing

Discussion Groups (30-60 minutes)

- Break into small groups for discussion of questions that participants have prepared at home.

- Use the menu in the next section to skip to sections within each lesson's video, so parts of the lesson can be reviewed as needed to answer questions or clarify issues.

- After or during the discussion, you can verbally share information from the Extended Answer Key provided at the back of this Leader Guide.

Closing Prayer (held in small groups)

Prayer for the New Evangelization (on *CATHOLICISM* prayer cards)

Lord Jesus Christ, you have given your Church the mission to proclaim the Gospel to all the nations. May our efforts to fulfill this mission be guided by the Holy Spirit so that we might be a leaven of new life, salt of the earth and a light of the world – worthy missionaries and faithful to You.

Make us valiant witnesses to the Faith of the Church, and inspire us to speak the truth with love. Help us to communicate to others the joy that we have received.Permit us to be united, but not closed; humble, but not fearful; simple, but not naive; thoughtful, but not overbearing; contemporary, but not superficial; respectful of others, but boldly your disciples.

May we bear into the world the hope of God, which is Christ the Lord, who rose from the dead and lives and reigns with the Father and the Holy Spirit, one God forever and ever. Amen.

DVD Set Contents

Use this menu to select chapters within each video so that you can break the videos into two parts to match the lessons, if desired.

EPISODE 1

Lesson 1, Part 1
1.   Introduction (1:50)
2.   Both God and Human (2:00)
3.   Jesus is Lord (2:40)
4.   Amazed and Afraid (5:10)

Lesson 1, Part 2
5.   1st Task: Gathering the Tribes (3:40)
6.   2nd Task: Cleansing the Temple (6:14)
7.   3rd Task: Dealing with the Enemies (18:12)
8.   4th Task: Reigning as Lord (7:36)

EPISODE 2

Lesson 2, Part 1
1.   Intro (0:58)
2.   The Teachings of Jesus (4:42)
3.   The Beatitudes (17:06)

Lesson 2, Part 2
4.   The Path of Non-Violence (9:15)
5.   The Prodigal Son (7:28)
6.   Matthew 25 (11:16)

EPISODE 3

Lesson 3, Part 1
1.   The Atheist (1:59)
2.   The Mystery of God (5:19)
3.   Arguments for God's Existence (7:24)
4.   Argument from Intelligibility (4:30)

Lesson 3, Part 2
5.   Naming God (5:16)
6.   The Provident Creator (4:56)
7.   The Problem of Evil (9:28)
8.   The Trinity (8:08)
9.   The Meaning of It All (1:43)

EPISODE 4

Lesson 4, Part 1

1. Intro (2:38)
2. The Annunciation (6:14)
3. Mary & Zion (5:09)
4. The Mother of God (4:03)

Lesson 4, Part 2

5. The Immaculate Conception (10:38)
6. The Assumption (3:08)
7. Mother of the Church (7:34)
8. Mother of the New Covenant (6:31)

EPISODE 5

Lesson 5, Part 1

1. The Indispensable Men (4:10)
2. Peter (7:40)
3. Peter's Confession (10:03)

Lesson 5, Part 2

4. Paul (3:30)
5. Conversion and Mission (11:53)
6. Resurrection (6:11)
7. Participation in Christ (11:53)

EPISODE 6

Lesson 6, Part 1

1. Intro (1:47)
2. The Mystery of the Church (6:50)
3. Ekklesia (8:17)
4. The Church is One (6:41)

Lesson 6, Part 2

5. The Church is Holy (3:30)
6. The Church is Catholic (3:26)
7. The Church is Apostolic (4:03)
8. Papal Infallibility (9:16)

EPISODE 7

Lesson 7, Part 1

1. Intro (1:06)
2. Communion with the Lord (3:02)
3. The Gathering (11:34)
4. The Telling of Stories (6:10)

Lesson 7, Part 2

5. The Offering (7:58)
6. The Real Presence (12:14)
7. Communion and Sending (4:15)

Online Resources

The following resources can be found online at: *www.wordonfire.org/catholicism-support-materials/*

ADVERTISING

- Poster
- Flyer
- Bulletin/Pulpit Announcement

STUDY PROGRAM SUPPORT

- Registration Form
- Bishop Robert Barron's biography
- Certificate of Completion
- Evaluation Survey
- *Managing Challenging Personalities for Effective Group Discussion*

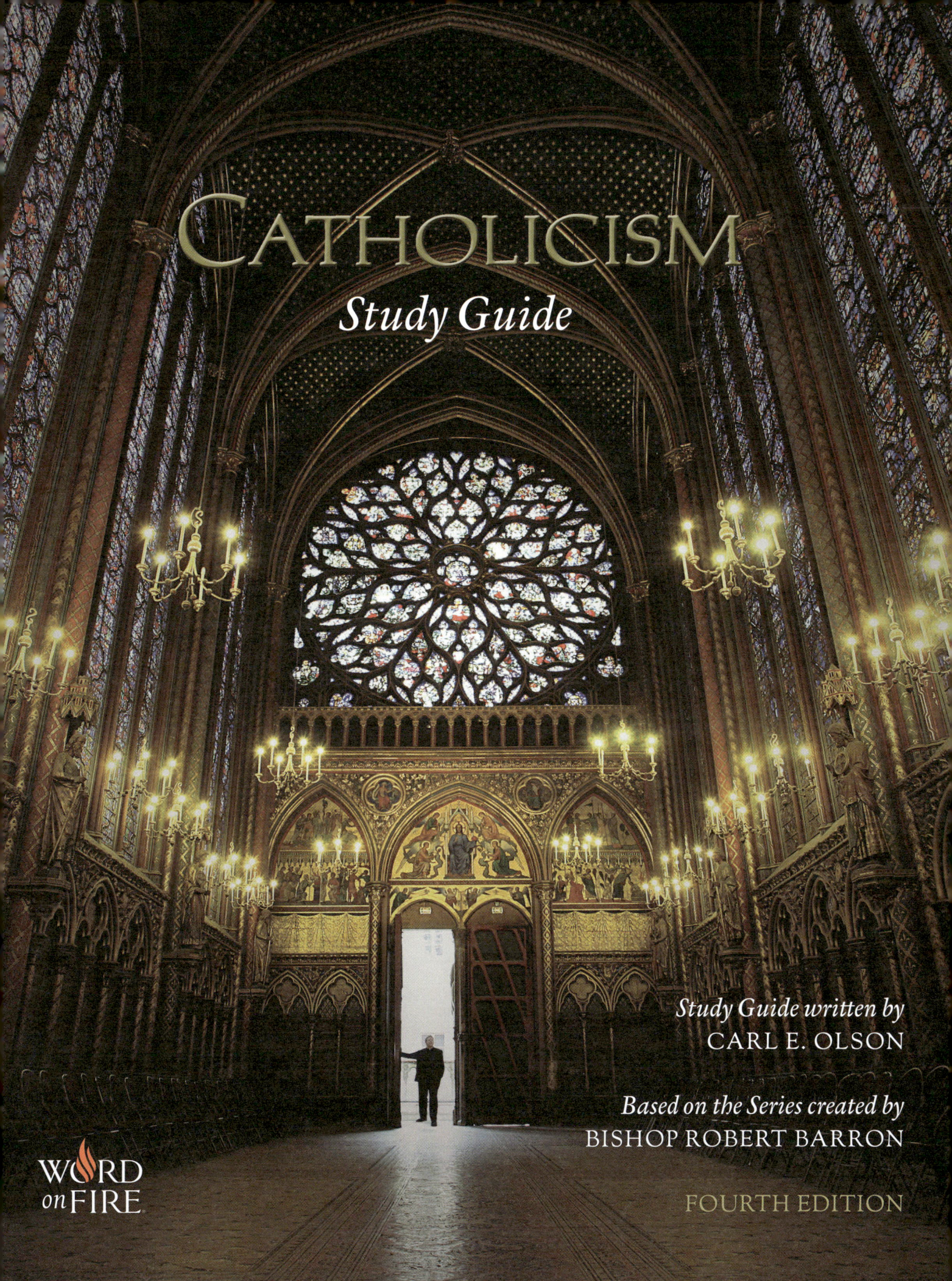

Catholicism

Study Guide

Study Guide written by
CARL E. OLSON

Based on the Series created by
BISHOP ROBERT BARRON

WORD
on FIRE

FOURTH EDITION

CATHOLICISM
Study Guide Table of Contents

Introduction to
CATHOLICISM

"Catholicism speaks through powerful words," states Bishop Robert Barron in his introduction to this adult formation series, mentioning the New Testament, the *Confessions* of St. Augustine, the *Summa Theologiae* of St. Thomas Aquinas, Dante's *Divina Commedia*, the sermons of Bl. John Henry Newman, and St. Thérèse of Lisieux's autobiography, *The Story of a Soul*. "It also communicates through beauty," he remarks, mentioning the splendid fourteenth-century Orvieto Cathedral in central Italy, the Sistine Chapel in Vatican City, Bernini's breathtaking sculpture, *Ecstasy of St. Teresa*, and the Church of the Holy Sepulchre in Jerusalem.

This dual focus is at the heart of Catholicism. There are the powerful words of Jesus Christ, the Apostles, Church Fathers and Doctors, popes, bishops and priests, saints and martyrs, mystics and theologians, poets and novelists, and others. Through inspired Scripture, theological study, philosophical reflection, sermons, autobiographies, poems, novels, and essays, these men and women have declared and described the Faith from within the heart of the Church. Throughout this program, viewers encounter many of the most profound thinkers and significant writers of the Church.

In a different but complementary way, artists, architects, sculptors, painters, and musicians have used their talents to express and convey the beauty of God and his creation, the glory of the Gospel, and the mystery of the Church. "The function of all art," wrote Pope Pius XII, "lies in fact in breaking through the narrow and tortuous enclosure of the finite, in which man is immerged while living here below, and in providing a window to the infinite for his hungry soul." This program seeks to provide a window to the infinite by showing and reflecting on some of the most splendid churches, sculptures, and places of Catholicism. "Souls ennobled, elevated, and prepared by art," Pius XII noted, "are thus better disposed to receive the religious truths and the grace of Jesus Christ" ("The Function of Art" April 8, 1952).

Jesus Christ reveals the truth of God because he is God. In this respect, Christ is the living source and ultimate end toward which all creation is moving. Christ has revealed that the movement toward him finds its proper trajectory though the Church – the inspired, finite reality that beckons and leads the soul to share communion with the Lord, who is the Truth Itself. *CATHOLICISM* presents the truth and beauty of the Faith so that all may discover for themselves the Truth and Beauty of the Lord.

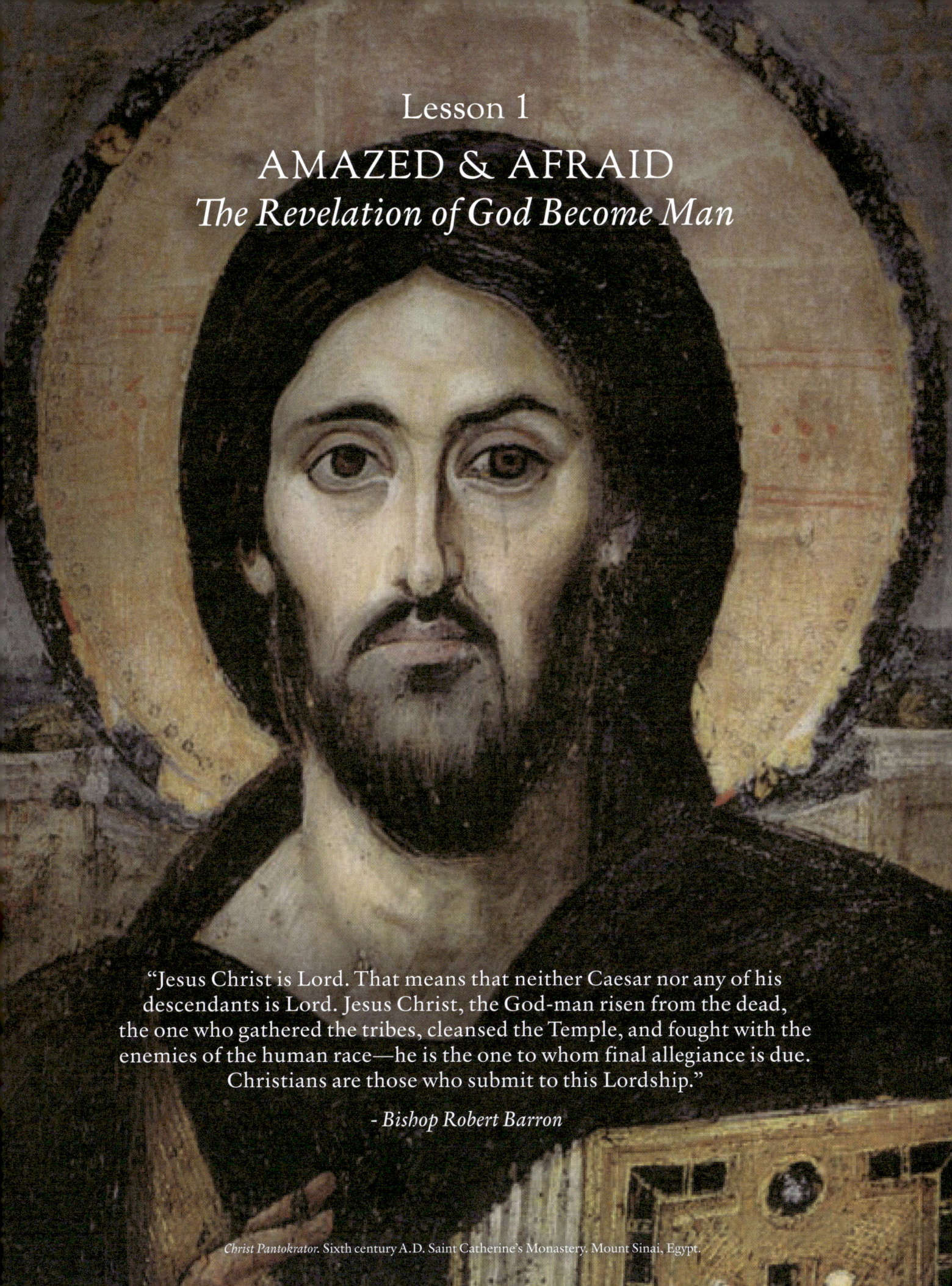

Lesson 1

AMAZED & AFRAID
The Revelation of God Become Man

"Jesus Christ is Lord. That means that neither Caesar nor any of his descendants is Lord. Jesus Christ, the God-man risen from the dead, the one who gathered the tribes, cleansed the Temple, and fought with the enemies of the human race—he is the one to whom final allegiance is due. Christians are those who submit to this Lordship."

- Bishop Robert Barron

Christ Pantokrator. Sixth century A.D. Saint Catherine's Monastery. Mount Sinai, Egypt.

AMAZED & AFRAID
Episode 1, Part 1

OUTLINE *(Tracks 1-4 on DVD)*

I. Both God and Human

  A. Christ is the privileged door (Chesterton)

  B. The divine humor (Dante's *Divine Comedy*)

  C. "And on that sacred jest/the whole of Christianity doth rest" (Chesterton)

  D. Jesus emerged as a deeply disconcerting and subversive figure

II. Jesus is Lord

  A. The Incarnation is the central "hinge" of Christianity

  B. The question: "Who do men say that the Son of man is?" (Mt. 16:13)

  C. Buddha, Mohammed, and Confucius did not claim to be divine

  D. Jesus compels a choice

  E. Jesus is either God or he is a bad man; there is no middle ground

  F. "...and they were amazed, and those who followed were afraid" (Mk. 10:32)

AMAZED & AFRAID: Lesson 1, Part 1

Both God and Human

Jesus Christ is unique, fully human and fully divine; he is the privileged door by which man can be restored to right relationship with God. Yet the story of God becoming man is not abstract or academic, but is instead bursting with deep mystery, heavenly joy, and rich humor. It is what G. K. Chesterton called "that sacred jest" upon which "the whole of Christianity doth rest." The Incarnation is at the heart of the divine comedy, as the great Italian poet, Dante Alighieri, put into verse in one of the world's greatest literary works, the *Divina Commedia*.

The uniqueness of Jesus is captured by the Evangelists in numerous passages in the Gospels. One such passage, which is rarely commented on, is found in the tenth chapter of the Gospel of Mark: "And they were on the road, going up to Jerusalem, and Jesus was walking ahead of them; and they were amazed, and those who followed were afraid" (Mk. 10:32).

Why the amazement? Why the fear? St. Mark describes several other similar reactions of amazement and fear by the disciples, each the result of divine actions by Jesus, as when he calmed the raging storm on the Sea of Galilee (Mk. 4:35-41), when he cast out demons (Mk. 5:1-15), when he was transfigured on the mount (Mk. 9:1-6), when he spoke prophetically about his death and Resurrection (Mk. 9:30-32), and when his Resurrection was announced by the angel at the tomb (Mk. 16:1-8). The fear was that of human beings in the presence of God, as when Moses and the people were afraid at Mount Sinai amidst the blazing, thundering glory of the Lord (Ex. 3:6; 20:18). The amazement and fear were not due to Jesus being a mere teacher or human leader, but because he was God.

Buddha, Mohammed, Confucius, and other religious founders and leaders did not claim to be God, the Son of God, or divine. They did not say they were the Way, the Truth, and the Life (Jn. 14:6). Instead, they pointed toward truth, toward a path, toward a way of living. That is quite different from the words and actions of Jesus, who never presented himself as one of many viable options, but as The One. The shocking and singular nature of Jesus' identity was summarized and articulated adeptly in *Dominus Iesus*, the Congregation for the Doctrine of the Faith's August 6, 2000, document on the "unicity and salvific universality of Jesus Christ and the Church":

> *The doctrine of faith must be firmly believed which proclaims that Jesus of Nazareth, son of Mary, and he alone, is the Son and the Word of the Father. The Word, which "was in the beginning with God" (Jn 1:2) is the same as he who "became flesh" (Jn 1:14). In Jesus, "the Christ, the Son of the living God" (Mt 16:16), "the whole fullness of divinity dwells in bodily form" (Col 2:9). He is the "only begotten Son of the Father, who is in the bosom of the Father" (Jn 1:18), his "beloved Son, in whom we have redemption... In him the fullness of God was pleased to dwell, and through him, God was pleased to reconcile all things to*

himself, on earth and in the heavens, making peace by the blood of his Cross"
(Col 1:13-14; 19-20). (sec.10)

It was not by accident or coincidence that Jesus asked his disciples about what they and others thought of him and his identity in "the district of Caesarea Philippi" (Matt. 16:13). A mostly pagan area almost twenty-five miles north of the Sea of Galilee, the region originally named "Panion" or "Paneas" after the Greco-Roman deity Pan, an ancient diety of the natural world. It was eventually renamed by Philip, the son of Herod the Great, in honor of Tiberius Caesar and himself. There at the base of Mount Hermon––which marked the northern border of Israel–– water flowed underground and surfaced in a cave at the base of a high limestone cliff. At the time of Christ it was a place of devoted pagan worship (especially to Baal), with niches cut into the cliff holding statues of numerous deities. Pagans believed it marked the spot where the netherworld met the material world. At the top of this cliff stood a temple in honor of Caesar.

It was, in other words, a veritable and visually arresting display of "Who's Who" among the pagan gods. "Who," asked Jesus of his disciples, "do men say that the Son of Man is?" After hearing the responses—John the Baptist, Elijah, Jeremiah, or one of the prophets—Jesus asked the question he asks of every man: "But who do you say that I am?" He stands before the false gods of this world and asks for our decision; he compels a choice. He is either God or a bad man—a liar or a lunatic.

†

"Jesus Is Lord!"

"To confess that Jesus is Lord is distinctive of Christian faith."
– Catechism of the Catholic Church, par. 202.

The word *kyrios* was used in ancient Greece and the larger Hellenistic world to refer to a superior or someone in authority. It was employed by the Romans for their emperors and was used by some pagans for their gods. While St. Paul's use of the term for Jesus had an eye toward the pagan world, it was grounded in Jewish tradition and usage. First-century Jews largely refused to pronounce the Hebrew name for God (*Yahweh*), instead substituting other names. The most common substitute was *adonai*, meaning "Lord," which was translated to *kyrios* in the Septuagint, the Greek translation of Scripture used by Greek-speaking Jews living in Egypt, Rome, and other parts of the Mediterranean world.

The term was a favorite of St. Paul, who calls Jesus *Kyrios* some 180 times in his letters. For example:

> ... IF YOU CONFESS WITH YOUR LIPS THAT JESUS IS LORD AND BELIEVE IN YOUR HEART THAT GOD RAISED HIM FROM THE DEAD, YOU WILL BE SAVED. (ROM. 10:9)

> THEREFORE I WANT YOU TO UNDERSTAND THAT NO ONE SPEAKING BY THE

SPIRIT OF GOD EVER SAYS "JESUS BE CURSED!" AND NO ONE CAN SAY "JESUS IS LORD" EXCEPT BY THE HOLY SPIRIT. (1 COR. 12:3)

And, from St. Paul's epistle to the Philippians, a hymn likely used in early Christian worship:

THEREFORE GOD HAS HIGHLY EXALTED HIM AND BESTOWED ON HIM THE NAME WHICH IS ABOVE EVERY NAME, THAT AT THE NAME OF JESUS EVERY KNEE SHOULD BOW, IN HEAVEN AND ON EARTH AND UNDER THE EARTH, AND EVERY TONGUE CONFESS THAT JESUS CHRIST IS LORD, TO THE GLORY OF GOD THE FATHER. (PHIL. 2:9-11)

In another striking passage, from his first letter to the Christians in Corinth, St. Paul rejects any polytheistic understanding of Jesus and the Father—a commonplace belief in the ancient pagan world—instead writing that "yet for us there is one God, the Father, from whom are all things and for whom we exist, and one Lord, Jesus Christ, through whom are all things and through whom we exist" (1 Cor. 8:6). In his book, *Lord Jesus Christ: Devotion to Jesus in Earliest Christianity* (Eerdmans, 2003), New Testament scholar Larry W. Hurtado writes:

In this astonishingly bold association of Jesus with God, Paul adapts wording from the traditional Jewish confession of God's uniqueness, known as the Shema, from Deuteronomy 6:4:, "Hear, O Israel: The Lord our God is one Lord" (Kyrios heis estin [LXX], translating Heb. Yahweh 'echad). (p. 114)

Jesus, in other words, is one with the Father in such an astounding way that he and the Father are separate persons, yet God is one in nature.

QUESTIONS FOR UNDERSTANDING — Part 1:

1. Bishop Barron says that the "essence of humor is the coming together of opposite—the meeting of incongruous things." How is "divine humor" or "sacred jest" revealed in the Incarnation? (CCC 461, 463)

2. What is the significance of St. Paul and other New Testament writers describing Jesus as Lord? What are the Old Testament roots of that title? How would most first century Greeks or Romans respond to the statement, "Jesus is Lord"? (CCC 446, 448, 450)

3. What place does the Incarnation have in the beliefs of the Catholic Church? How does the Incarnation distinguish Jesus Christ from men such as Buddha, Mohammed, or Confucius? What options are available when one has to decide who Jesus Christ is? (CCC 423, 430-445)

QUESTIONS FOR APPLICATION — Part 1:

1. How can I demonstrate, in both my public and private actions, my belief that Jesus is Lord? Are there some areas of my life that I need to relinquish more to his lordship?

Praying in day to day life before Meals and on my own personal time

CATHOLICISM

2. Do I sometimes doubt the Church's techings about the Incarnation? What questions do I have about the person, actions, or teachings of Jesus? How can I go about addressing those doubts and questions?

3. How does sin undermine and harm my spiritual life? Do I need to go to confession more regularly, read Scripture more often, or spend more time in prayer? What are some steps I might consider taking in growing in my relationship with the Lord?

by giving me guilt and fault

AMAZED & AFRAID
Episode 1, Part 2

OUTLINE *(Tracks 5-8 on DVD)*

I.   The Work of Jesus, the Messiah

   A. Described in the Torah (Law), Prophets, and Psalms

   B. The Messiah, the Anointed One, called to four tasks (N. T. Wright)

   C. Jesus accomplished the four tasks in the strangest way

II. The First Task: Gathering the Tribes of Israel

   A. This gathering is for the sake of the world

   B. The Kingdom of God is the call to be gathered and reunited

   1. Man is scattered due to sin

   2. God desires man to be gathered together into a people

   C. Jesus shepherded the people of Israel, forming the New Israel, the Church

III. The Second Task: Cleansing the Temple of God

   A. Adam was the first priest; the Garden of Eden was the first temple

   1. Adoration is perfect, proper alignment to God

   2. Original sin is the adoration of the wrong thing(s)

   B. Israel was a temple, created to teach right praise and to offer sacrifices

   1. Sacrifice is the act of giving something of creation back to the Creator

   2. The prophets spoke of God's presence leaving the Temple and looked forward to a new and perfect Temple

   C. The cleansing of the Temple by Jesus

   1. Not an act of rebellion, but of rebuilding

   2. The Temple to be rebuilt, however, was the temple of his body

   3. Jesus is the dwelling-place of God, the perfect sacrifice

IV. The Third Task: Dealing with the Enemies of Israel

    A. The Davidic Warrior

      1. Israel was constantly oppressed by other peoples: the Egyptians, Babylonians, Assyrians, Philistines, Romans

          i. This oppression was the result of Israel's sin

          ii. Liberation from this oppression could come only from God

      2. Jesus is a "Davidic Warrior"

          i. The power of God is revealed in a baby in a manger

          ii. The baby Jesus was "behind enemy lines" (C. S. Lewis)

      3. Godly humility vs. worldly power

          i. Worldly power: Quirinius, governor of Syria, and Caesar Augustus

          ii. Heavenly power: the True Emperor, Jesus Christ

          iii. The true emperor is not fed, but feeds (the Eucharist)

    B. Dealing with the Enemies of Israel: Palm Sunday and Holy Week

      1. Jesus took on "all forms of human dysfunction"; the sins of the world

      2. He embodied the Sermon on the Mount while on the Cross

    C. The Resurrection

  1. Completed the first three tasks of the Messiah

      2. The only good explanation for the early Christian movement, which logically should have died with Christ Jesus

      3. Not a symbol, metaphor, or fable

      4. "Shalom, peace": Jesus shows his wounds to the disciples in the Upper Room

V. The Fourth Task: Reigning as Lord of the Nations

    A. "Iesus Kyrios" ("Jesus is Lord")

      1. Pilate, by putting the sign over the crucified Christ, was, ironically and unwittingly, the first evangelist

      2. The words "Jesus is Lord" were fighting words in the first century, leading to direct confrontation with Rome and Caesar

    B. However, it was through Rome that Christ and his Church would go out to all the world.

    C. "Glad Tidings" was an imperial greeting; the good news (Gospel) was not about Roman rulers, but about the King of Kings

    D. The Cross taunts Rome and its successors

AMAZED & AFRAID: Lesson 1, Part 2

The Tasks of the Messiah

In the face of numerous false gods, Peter responded, "You are the Christ, the Son of the living God" (Matt. 16:16). Jesus is the Messiah (*Christós* is Greek for "the Messiah"), the Anointed One. "It became the name proper to Jesus," explains the *Catechism of the Catholic Church*, "only because he accomplished perfectly the divine mission that 'Christ' signifies" (par. 436). That mission, as Bishop Barron explains, involves four tasks: gathering the tribes of Israel, cleansing the Temple of God, dealing with the enemies of Israel, and reigning as Lord of the nations. Each of these four tasks is described, in varying ways, in the Torah (the Law), the Prophets, and the Psalms. While most first-century Jews would be quite familiar with those tasks, they were surprised, even scandalized, by how Jesus went about fulfilling them.

†

Gathering the Tribes

"Save us, O LORD our God," wrote the Psalmist, "and gather us from among the nations, that we may give thanks to thy holy name and glory in thy praise" (Psa. 106:47). "At that time Jerusalem shall be called the throne of the LORD," stated the prophet Jeremiah, "and all nations shall gather to it, to the presence of the LORD in Jerusalem, and they shall no more stubbornly follow their own evil heart" (Jer. 3:17). These are just two of the numerous instances where psalmists and prophets spoke with hope and longing for a future gathering by God of his people and a restoration of the holy city, Jerusalem.

Because of their failure to keep the Law and to observe the commandments, the Israelites had been scattered far and wide by war, persecution, and exile. When the Law was given and the Mosaic covenant established, the people of Israel were warned of the curses that would fall upon them if they strayed from the Torah's precepts and commands. If the Israelites turned away from the covenant, made graven images to worship, and did evil in the sight of God, they would be destroyed, scattered "among the peoples, and you will be left few in number among the nations where the LORD will drive you" (Deut. 4:23-27; 28:58-68). But what if they repented and came back to God?

AND WHEN ALL THESE THINGS COME UPON YOU, THE BLESSING AND THE CURSE, WHICH I HAVE SET BEFORE YOU, AND YOU CALL THEM TO MIND AMONG ALL THE NATIONS WHERE THE LORD YOUR GOD HAS DRIVEN YOU, AND RETURN TO THE LORD YOUR GOD, YOU AND YOUR CHILDREN, AND OBEY

HIS VOICE IN ALL THAT I COMMAND YOU THIS DAY, WITH ALL YOUR HEART AND WITH ALL YOUR SOUL; THEN THE LORD YOUR GOD WILL RESTORE YOUR FORTUNES, AND HAVE COMPASSION UPON YOU, AND HE WILL GATHER YOU AGAIN FROM ALL THE PEOPLES WHERE THE LORD YOUR GOD HAS SCATTERED YOU. (DEUT. 30:1-3)

This was, for first-century Jews, a central task of the Messiah: to bring about the gathering and reunification of the people of Israel. When Jesus announced the Kingdom of God, listeners heard a promise of national restoration, Davidic in nature and scope. Jesus, however, went deeper, to the root of the problem: sin. Because of sin, men were alienated from God (removed from the Garden of Eden), divided amongst themselves (Cain killing his brother Abel), and scattered far and wide (the Tower of Babel). The term sin comes from a German word (*Sünde*) for sundering and division. As Bishop Barron explains in his book, *The Priority of Christ: Toward a Postliberal Catholicism* (Brazos Press, 2007):

> So when Jesus of Nazareth said, "The time is fulfilled, and the kingdom of God has come near; repent, and believe in the good news" (Mark 1:15), he was not calling attention to general, timeless spiritual truths, nor was he urging people to make a decision for God; he was telling his listeners that Yahweh was actively gathering the people of Israel and, indirectly, all people into a new salvific order, and he was insisting that his hearers conform themselves to the new state of affairs. In this gathering, he was implying, the forgiveness of sins—the overcoming of sundering and division—would be realized. In a word, the proclamation of the kingdom was tantamount to an announcement that the Gatherer of Israel had arrived and had commenced his work. (p.72)

This work was oriented toward the formation of the new Israel, the Church. "So likewise the new Israel which while living in this present age goes in search of a future and abiding city is called the Church of Christ... God gathered together as one," stated the fathers of the Second Vatican Council, "all those who in faith look upon Jesus as the author of salvation and the source of unity and peace, and established them as the Church that for each and all it may be the visible sacrament of this saving unity" (*Lumen Gentium* 9). In the Church, all the tribes, nations, and peoples of the earth are united in the love of the Father, the life of the Son, and the power of the Holy Spirit.

†

Cleansing the Temple of God

Israel was a type of temple, created to praise God, to offer Him sacrifices, and proclaim His name among the nations. King David desired a permanent temple, and his son Solomon eventually built the Temple in Jerusalem, one of the great glories of the ancient world. In the Old Testament, the Temple was often referred to as "the house of the Lord." Sometimes, in association with the city of Jerusalem, it was called "Zion" (Psa. 48), which in turn represented the chosen people of God.

Adam can be understood as a type of priest, and the Garden of Eden as a type of temple. In the Garden, man and woman enjoyed perfect adoration of God. They were in full harmony and communion with God, what the Council of Trent described as a "state of holiness and justice" (Session V). Original sin came about by man's abuse of his freedom, his choosing to adore something (power and prestige) and someone (self) instead of God (see CCC 396-401, 1707). The first priest sinned and was evicted from the idyllic temple God had prepared for him.

The Temple was a barometer of the health of the covenantal relationship between God and the people. Many of the prophets warned that a failure to uphold the Law and the covenant would result in the destruction of the Temple. The prophet Jeremiah declared that having the Temple could not protect the people from the consequences of their sins: "Do not trust in these deceptive words: 'This is the temple of the LORD, the temple of the LORD, the temple of the LORD'" (Jer. 7:4).

Following the exile, the Temple was rebuilt. Shortly before the birth of Christ, Herod undertook a massive expansion of the Temple.

It was there that Jesus was presented by Mary and Joseph and blessed by Simeon (Lk. 2:22-35) and where he, in his youth, spent time talking to the teachers of the Law (Lk. 2:43-50). It was also the setting for the cleansing of the Temple and Jesus' shocking prophecy: "Destroy this temple, and in three days I will raise it up" (Jn. 2:19).

Was Jesus, in cleansing the Temple, attacking the Temple itself? No. Was Jesus, in making his remark, saying he would destroy the Temple? No. But, paradoxically, the love of the Son for his Father and his Father's house did point toward the demise of the Temple in Jerusalem. "This is a prophecy of the Cross," wrote Joseph Cardinal Ratzinger in *The Spirit of the Liturgy* (Ignatius Press, 2000), "he shows that the destruction of his earthly body will be at the same time the end of the Temple." Why? Because a new and everlasting Temple was established by the death and Resurrection of the Son of God. "With his Resurrection the new Temple will begin: the living body of Jesus Christ, which will now stand in the sight of God and be the place of all worship," explains Ratzinger. "Into this body he incorporates men" (p. 43).

The new Temple of God did, in fact, come down from heaven. It dwelt among man (Jn. 1:14). "It" *is* a man, the Messiah, who is the true Temple, through whom Christians become temples of the Holy Spirit. Through baptism we are joined to the one Body of Christ, and that Body, the Church, is the "one temple of the Holy Spirit" (CCC 776, 1197; 1 Cor. 6:19). The destruction of the Temple one generation from the death and Resurrection of Christ was a sign that the beginning of a new era in God's work of salvation had begun. That era is the age of the Church, which is the seed of the Kingdom established by the Messiah.

†

Dealing with the Enemies of Israel

The tiny nation of Israel was, with rare exceptions, constantly fighting for survival, oppressed by a seemingly endless number of enemies: Egyptians, Philistines, Babylonians, Assyrians, and, of course, the Romans. Since the Messiah was to gather together the scattered people, he would also have to take on and destroy the ones doing the scattering. He would need to be a warrior, Bishop Barron notes, "who struggles against all the powers of dissolution, antagonism, and violence that have marred his creation. Jesus the warrior gives concrete expression to the righteous anger of God that is apparent on practically every page of the Old Testament" (*The Priority of Christ*, pp. 90-91).

Oppression by enemies and the scattering of the people of Israel were part and parcel of the same failure to keep the commandments. The people had been warned that breaking the covenant would result in being "struck down before your enemies" and ruled by foreigners (Lev. 26:14-17). God alone could liberate from such oppression, and faithful Israelites looked forward to the day when He would do so. What they didn't expect was how He would bring the fight, engage the enemy, and win the war.

C. S. Lewis, in *Mere Christianity* (1952), argued that Jesus was either a liar, a lunatic, or the Son of God. "Now it seems to me obvious that he was neither a lunatic nor a fiend: and consequently, however strange or terrifying or unlikely it may seem, I have to accept the view that he was and is God. God has landed on this enemy-occupied world in human form." And what was the central purpose, Lewis asked, of this divine invasion behind enemy lines? To simply teach? To punish mankind? No, Lewis wrote, Christians "think the main thing he came to earth to do was to suffer and be killed."

The Gospel of Luke makes a pointed contrast between divine power and worldly power, between the humility of God and the domineering control of rulers such as Herod, the king of Judea; Quirinius, the governor of Syria; and Caesar Augustus, the emperor of Rome (see Lk. 1:5; 2:1-2). St. Luke tells the story of the true Emperor and King, who didn't arrive with the trappings of human glory, but is born in a manger and wrapped in swaddling clothes. He didn't have a human army, military might, or political connections, but came with a host of angels and a band of shepherds (Lk. 2:8-18), revealing his divine origins and reveling in his earthly existence.

G. K. Chesterton, in the opening lines of "A Word," captured in poetic form the wonder, strangeness, and excitement surrounding the coming of the new Davidic warrior:

> *A word came forth in Galilee, a word like to a star;*
> *It climbed and rang and blessed and burnt wherever brave hearts are;*
> *A word of sudden secret hope, of trial and increase*
> *Of wrath and pity fused in fire, and passion kissing peace.*
> *A star that o'er the cited world beckoned, a sword of flame;*
> *A star with myriad thunders tongued: a mighty word there came.*

Divine humanity and demonic power met face-to-face when Jesus went into the desert for forty days before beginning his public ministry (Mt. 4:1-11; Mk. 1:12-13; Lk. 4:1-13). The three temptations presented by Satan to Jesus echo some of the essential tests faced (and failed) by the Israelites during forty years in the wilderness, all of them rooted in rebellion against God and the pursuit of self-centered ends.

Satan tempted Jesus to show his power by turning stones into bread (Mt. 4:3-4). This was a temptation of the most base level—to choose bodily needs and pleasure over spiritual nourishment and God's life. Satan next tempted Jesus to reveal his heavenly glory by throwing Himself from the top of the Temple and having angels carry him to safety (Mt. 4:5-7). Thus the setting moved higher: the target was the ego and the temptation was to seek personal glory over God's will. In the final temptation, the Evil One offered Jesus all the kingdoms of the world if he fell down and

worshipped the fallen angel (Mt. 4:8-10). This took place at the top of a lofty mountain; it was the temptation to choose personal power and dominance over God's power and reign.

Jesus vehemently rejected all three temptations with quotes from the Torah. He knew his kingdom could only be established through suffering and death. He understood that true power comes through love and sacrifice, not fear and coercion. And he knew his glorified body would be revealed and the Kingdom established in rising from the grave, not by avoiding death. His rejection of Satan's overtures showed the heart of the Messiah and Warrior intent on fulfilling the Father's plan of salvation.

†

Reigning as Lord of the Nations

On the cross, Jesus embodied the Sermon on the Mount: "Blessed are the poor in spirit, for theirs is the kingdom of heaven. Blessed are those who mourn, for they shall be comforted. Blessed are the meek, for they shall inherit the earth" (Mt. 5:3-5). In taking on the sins of the world, Jesus took on all forms of human dysfunction, discord, depravity, and despair. "Without a doubt," wrote the Swiss theologian Hans Urs von Balthasar in *A Short Primer For Unsettled Laymen* (Ignatius Press, 1985), "at the center of the New Testament there stands the Cross, which receives its interpretation from the Resurrection... Whoever removes the Cross and its interpretation by the New Testament from the center in order to replace it, for example, with the social commitment of Jesus to the oppressed as a new center, no longer stands in continuity with the apostolic faith. He does not see that God's commitment to the world is most absolute precisely at this point across a chasm" (p. 81).

Christ's Paschal Mystery brought to completion his first three Messianic tasks. Although the Resurrection is beyond human comprehension, it is not symbolic or metaphorical in nature. It "cannot be interpreted as something outside the physical order, and it is impossible not to acknowledge it as an historical fact" (CCC 643). Skeptics have argued the Resurrection was a clever fable or a form of mass delusion. But this simply cannot account for the rise of the early Christian movement and the willingness demonstrated by many of the first Christians to die rather than renounce their belief in the risen Messiah.

How does one explain the sermon given by St. Peter on Pentecost if he had not had a transformative encounter with the risen Lord? The man "Jesus, delivered up according to the definite plan and foreknowledge of God, you crucified and killed by the hands of lawless men," the head apostle told the marveling crowd, "But God raised him up, having loosed the pangs of death, because it was not possible for him to be held by it" (Acts 2:23-24). St. Paul addressed the issue directly: "But if there is no resurrection of the dead, then Christ has not been raised." He wrote to the Christians in Corinth: "if Christ has not been raised, then our preaching is in vain and your faith is in vain" (1 Cor. 15: 13-14).

When Pontius Pilate placed the sign over Jesus on the cross—"Jesus of Nazareth, the King of the Jews" (Jn. 19:19)—he unwittingly became the first evangelist (his wife, according to an ancient tradition, became a disciple of Christ). The irony of the mocking sign, of course, was that it spoke the truth. And when St. Paul described Jesus Christ as "the blessed and only Sovereign, the King of kings and Lord of lords" (1 Tim. 6:15), he was putting forth fighting words. The first three centuries of Christianity witnessed the spilt blood of many martyrs as Rome often sought to destroy the fledgling Church. But, in another example of divine humor, it would be through Rome that Christ and his Church would go forth to all of the world, proclaiming the good news and glad tidings, "Jesus is Lord!"

Dante's Divine Comedy:

Dante Alighieri (c.1265-1321) was a statesman, the father of the Italian language, and one of the world's finest poets. His *Divina Commedia*, the Divine Comedy, is the finest epic poem in Italian literature and one of the great poems in world literature. Its 14,233 lines are divided into three canticles—*Inferno* (Hell), *Purgatorio* (Purgatory), and *Paradiso* (Paradise)—which have a combined total of 100 cantos (33 each, with one as a prologue).

In medieval literature, a comedy was not primarily humorous, as in modern comedies, but described a work with a happy ending. The word comedy comes from Greek words meaning happiness (*komos*) and singer (*aoidos*), thus referring to a work in which a poet would "sing" about a happy story. As Dante explained in a letter, a comedy "begins with harshness in some thing, whereas its matter ends in a good way..."

The Divine Comedy describes Dante's journey from hell through purgatory and to paradise, a journey beginning during Holy Week, on the night before Good Friday, and ending on the Wednesday following Easter. The soul of the Roman poet Virgil guides Dante through hell and on Mt. Purgatory. They are accompanied by Statius, another classical poet, during their ascent of Mt. Purgatory. In the Garden of Eden, Dante meets with Beatrice, who teaches him while guiding him to and through the nine celestial spheres of heaven. The last part of his journey, which culminates in an overwhelming vision of God, is in the company of the mystic St. Bernard.

Beatrice, in Canto VII of *Paradiso*, speaks to Dante about the Incarnation:

> *Whence the whole human race was weak, forlorn,*
> *and through the many centuries they roved,*
> *all lost, until the Word of God came down*
> *Uniting human nature long removed*
> *from its Creator with Himself, one Person,*
> *by the sole act of His eternal Love.* (Dante Alighieri, *Paradise*,
> trans. Anthony Esolen [New York: Random House, 2007], 67)

In her study of Western literature, *In the Light of Christ* (Ignatius Press, 2006), literary critic, novelist, and poet Lucy Beckett writes that reading Dante's epic poem "is an experience, aesthetic, intellectual and spiritual, like no other." She also notes, "The Incarnation is for Dante the very heart of revealed truth, to which he refers again and again in the poem" (pp. 197, 198).

QUESTIONS FOR UNDERSTANDING — Part 2:

1. What were the four central tasks expected of the Messiah by most first century Jews?
    Where did those tasks originate and what are some examples of how they were expressed?

* Gathering the tribes of Israel
* Cleansing the Temple of God
* Dealing with the enemies of Israel
* reighty as lord of the Nations

2. Why did the tribes of Israel need to be gathered? How did Jesus go about doing this?
    (CCC 541, 542)

3. What was the purpose of the Temple within ancient Judaism? How did Jesus identify himself with the Temple? (CCC 2099, 2100, 1179, 1197)

4. What enemies did Jesus conquer and how did he do battle? (CCC 559, 550, 635)

5. Why did Jesus die on the cross? What did he accomplish, fulfill, and embody in being crucified? (CCC 599, 613, 614, 614, 616, 618, 622, 623)

6. Why is the historical and physical nature of the Resurrection so important to Christians? What is an historical argument in favor of the Resurrection? (CCC 638, 639, 643, 644, 645)

AMAZED & AFRAID

7. Who was the first evangelist for the crucified Messiah? What is the irony of that fact? (CCC 306, 307)

QUESTIONS FOR APPLICATION — Part 2:

1. What does the sacrifice of Christ on the Cross mean to you personally?

2. We are all called to be evangelists and to spread the Gospel. How can I be a better evangelist of the good news? What fears or concerns do I have about evangelizing? What can I do about those fears or concerns?

AMAZED & AFRAID

NOTES

✠

TERMS & NAMES

Augustine of Hippo, Saint (354-430). A bishop, Church Father and Doctor, and one of the most significant and influential philosophers and theologians in the Western world. He recounted his dramatic conversion from Manicheanism to Catholicism in his *Confessions*. Other famous works include *The City of God* and *The Trinity*, along with numerous homilies and commentaries.

Caesar Augustus (63 B.C. – A.D. 14). The first emperor of Rome who ruled over what is considered Rome's golden age and brought about *Pax Augusta*, the Augustan peace.

Chesterton, G. K. (1874-1936). An English journalist, apologist, and man of letters who is one of the most quoted authors in the English language. Agnostic in his youth, he was Anglican for many years before becoming Catholic in 1922. His best-known works include *Orthodoxy, The Everlasting Man,* and *What's Wrong With the World.*

Dante Alighieri (c.1265-1321). An Italian statesman, the father of the Italian language, and one of the world's finest poets. His *Divina Commedia*, the Divine Comedy, is the finest epic poem in Italian literature and one of the great poems in world literature.

The Divine Comedy: One of the world's greatest poems, written by Dante Alighieri (c.1265-1321). The *Divina Commedia* is the finest epic poem in Italian literature, depicting the journey from hell to heaven. Its 14,233 lines are divided into three canticles—*Inferno* (Hell), *Purgatorio* (Purgatory), and *Paradiso* (Paradise).

Incarnation: The Christian belief that God the Son, the second person of the Trinity, assumed human nature and became man, Jesus Christ, in order to save man from sin and death.

Kyrios: The Greek word for "lord." It was used to describe human rulers, but was also in the Septuagint, the Greek version of the Old Testament, to refer to God in place of the sacred name, *Yahweh*. It is used some 180 times in the New Testament to refer to Jesus, explicitly asserting belief in his divinity.

Lewis, C. S. (1898-1963). An Anglican author, apologist, and professor who wrote several bestselling and influential works of popular theology and apologetics. Lewis was an avowed agnostic in his early adult years but eventually embraced Christianity, in part through the writings of G. K. Chesterton and the friendship of J. R. R. Tolkien. Among his best-known works are *Mere Christianity*, *The Great Divorce*, and *The Screwtape Letters*.

Messiah: A title of royalty, derived from a Hebrew word meaning "to anoint." It refers to the Lord's anointed one and was used in the Old Testament primarily in reference to kings, who were anointed as part of the ritual of their installation (see 1 Sam. 10:1, 16:13). By the first century, the term (*Messias* in Greek) was used to refer to a coming Davidic king who would, many Jews believed, save Israel from oppression and reestablish a Davidic kingdom.

Newman, John Henry Cardinal (1801-1890). One of the most famous converts to Catholicism of the nineteenth century and a brilliant scholar, preacher, and apologist. As a young man he was a major figure in the Oxford Movement, but his study of early Church history convinced him to become Catholic. His most famous works include *An Essay on the Development of Christian Doctrine*, *Apologia Pro Vita Sua*, and *An Essay on the Grammar of Assent*.

Pontius Pilate: Roman governor, or procurator, of Judea from A.D. 26-36, who condemned Jesus to death by crucifixion.

Torah: The first five books of the Old Testament (Genesis, Exodus, Leviticus, Numbers, Deuteronomy), also called the "five books of Moses" or the Pentateuch. The name comes from the Hebrew word (*tôrâ*) meaning *instruction* or *law*.

Wright, N. T. (b. December 1948). Anglican Bishop and a leading New Testament scholar. Key academic works include *The New Testament and the People of God*, *Jesus and the Victory of God*, and *The Resurrection of the Son of God*.

von Balthasar, Hans Urs (1905-88). A Swiss priest and theologian considered to be one of the most important Catholic intellectuals and writers of the twentieth century and praised by Popes John Paul II and Benedict XVI for his accomplishments. Incredibly prolific and diverse, he wrote over one hundred books and hundreds of articles.

Recommended Reading:

- *The Priority of Christ* by Robert Barron
- *Jesus and the Victory of God* by N. T. Wright
- *The Everlasting Man* by G. K. Chesterton
- *Mere Christianity* by C. S. Lewis
- *Lord Jesus Christ: Devotion to Jesus in Earliest Christianity* by Larry W. Hurtado
- *The Divine Comedy* by Dante

Lesson 2

HAPPY ARE WE
The Teachings of Jesus

"Jesus nailed to the cross is the very icon of liberty, for he is free
from those attachments that would prevent him from attaining the true good,
which is doing the will of his Father."

- *Bishop Robert Barron*

Diego Velázquez. *Christ Crucified*. 1632. Museo Del Prado. Madrid, Spain.

THE TEACHINGS OF JESUS
Episode 2, Part 1

OUTLINE *(Tracks 1-3 on DVD)*

I. Questions About Jesus

A. There are numerous "versions" of Jesus. Which is true?

B. Who was Jesus? What did he do and say? What did he mean?

C. The temptation of the New Age Christ

II. The Path of Joy: The Teachings of Jesus

A. *Dominus Iesus* and the uniqueness of Jesus of Nazareth

B. He alone is the Son and the Word of the Father

C. Jesus' teaching is a central part of his mission

D. Jesus' teaching is the focus of early Christian writings

III. The Beatitudes

A. Joy and freedom for excellence

B. Two versions in the Gospels

   1. Luke 6:17-49

   2. Matthew 5-7

C. Reveals the fullness of the Old Law

D. Expresses the heart of the New Law

E. Intimate connection between Old and New

   1. Jesus is the new Moses

   2. The mountaintop is the new Mt. Sinai

   3. The Sermon is the new Law

   4. Given to the new people of God, the Church

F. The meaning of "happy" or "blessed" is difficult, but essential

G. The Beatitudes

   1. "Blessed are the merciful...": To love with the heart of God

   2. "Blessed are the pure in heart...": Free from distractions

3. "Blessed are those who hunger and thirst for righteousness…": The desire for true justice

4. "Blessed are the peacemakers…": Reconciliation with God and others

5. "Blessed are the poor in spirit…": The need for humility

6. "Blessed are those who mourn…": A proper response to suffering

7. "Blessed are the meek…": Renunciation of power and glory

8. "Blessed are those who are persecuted for righteousness' sake…": Sign of detachment from the world

    i. Charles Lwanga and his companions

H. The Sermon should be understood in light of the Mount of Calvary

    1. Christ crucified is detached from:

        i. Wealth

        ii. Pleasure

        iii. Power

        iv. Honor

    2. Christ crucified loved the will of the Father

    3. Christ crucified is the happiest man

THE TEACHINGS OF JESUS: Lesson 2, Part 1

"The title 'Son of God' signifies the unique and eternal relationship of Jesus Christ to God his Father: he is the only Son of the Father; he is God himself. To be a Christian, one must believe that Jesus Christ is the Son of God."

– *Catechism of the Catholic Church*, par. 454

"Christ as God is the fatherland where we are going, Christ as Man is the way by which we go."

– St. Augustine (Sermon 124, 3)

It has been said, only partially in jest, that there are as many versions of Jesus as there are theologians, Scripture scholars, and historians. The identity of Jesus and the meaning of his teachings have fascinated, inspired, and, yes, frustrated tens of millions. Scholars and ordinary men and women have sought to know and understand the words and works of a first-century Jewish carpenter. Countless books, articles and, in recent decades, documentaries and television programs have been produced in attempts to explain, explore, and, in some cases, deny the deeds and words of Jesus of Nazareth.

Who was he? What did he do? Why did he do it? What did he say? And what did he mean when he said it?

Of course, there are many who argue that Jesus, however interesting he might be, was merely one guide, teacher, or guru among others. A good example of this approach can be found in *The Third Jesus: The Christ We Cannot Ignore* (Harmony Books, 2008), by Deepak Chopra, the prolific and popular New Age author. For Chopra, traditional, orthodox Christianity has not only failed to help people follow Christ, it has created a false Christ who keeps Jesus' true intentions hidden. What Jesus really intended, he writes, was "a completely new view of human nature, and unless you transform yourself, you misunderstand what he had to say...He wanted to inspire a world reborn in God."

Chopra argues that there are three versions of Jesus: the historical Jesus, who really cannot be known; the Jesus of Church dogma and doctrine, "built up over thousands of years of years by theologians and other scholars"; and, finally, the Christ of Chopra, who "taught his followers how to reach God-consciousness" (pg. 2). This Jesus, he claims, was "a savior," but "not the savior, not the one and only Son of God. Rather , Jesus embodied the highest level of enlightenment. ... Jesus intended to save the world by showing others the path to God-consciousness" (pg. 2). This sort of customized Jesus is increasingly popular, for it first removes Jesus from his cultural and historical context, then detaches him from his theological context, and finally places him into whatever subjective context might appeal to those looking for a Christ without a cross.

Chopra is not a Christian, however, so it isn't surprising that he attempts to remake Jesus along non-Christian lines. But many Christians have difficulty fighting the temptation to soften or deny the uniqueness of Jesus. In August 2000, Cardinal Joseph Ratzinger, then head of the Congregation for the Doctrine of the Faith, issued a declaration titled *Dominus Iesus*, "on the unicity and salvific universality of Jesus Christ and the Church." It stated:

> *In contemporary theological reflection there often emerges an approach to Jesus of Nazareth that considers him a particular, finite, historical figure, who reveals the divine not in an exclusive way, but in a way complementary with other revelatory and salvific figures. The Infinite, the Absolute, the Ultimate Mystery of God would thus manifest itself to humanity in many ways and in many historical figures: Jesus of Nazareth would be one of these. More concretely, for some, Jesus would be one of the many faces which the Logos has assumed in the course of time to communicate with humanity in a salvific way.* (sec. 9)

In other words, there are Christian theologians and teachers who present Jesus as just one guide among many possible and equally viable guides when it comes to knowing God. This thesis, Cardinal Ratzinger made clear, is "in profound conflict with the Christian faith":

> *The doctrine of faith must be firmly believed which proclaims that Jesus of Nazareth, son of Mary, and he alone, is the Son and the Word of the Father. The Word, which "was in the beginning with God" (Jn 1:2) is the same as he who "became flesh" (Jn 1:14). In Jesus, "the Christ, the Son of the living God" (Mt 16:16), "the whole fullness of divinity dwells in bodily form" (Col 2:9). He is the "only begotten Son of the Father, who is in the bosom of the Father" (Jn 1:18), his "beloved Son, in whom we have redemption... In him the fullness of God was pleased to dwell, and through him, God was pleased to reconcile all things to himself, on earth and in the heavens, making peace by the blood of his Cross" (Col 1:13-14; 19-20).* (sec. 10)

As we've already seen in the first episode, Jesus is not just another ethical guide, spiritual teacher or personal guru. Jesus cannot be known by picking and choosing whatever facts, actions, or words might be appealing while ignoring everything else. Jesus is the Incarnate Word of God. And precisely as the Word made flesh, he came, "full of grace and truth," to speak to man with words of grace and truth (Jn. 1:14). He came to share the greatest spiritual teaching and most transforming moral wisdom, and to give us power to become children of God (Jn. 1:12-13).

This teaching and wisdom was a central part of Jesus' mission, perfectly aligned and connected to his miracles and his Paschal Mystery. Jesus often referred to himself and accepted the titles of prophet and teacher. There are numerous episodes in the Gospels describing Jesus teaching the crowds and preaching to his disciples. In fact, that teaching and preaching seems to be what Jesus did with most of his time during his three years of public ministry. His wisdom and insight, as well as the often provocative nature of his teachings, were appreciated from the start. Many of the earliest writings about Jesus focus on

his sayings, and many Scripture scholars think these sayings were already being recounted and remembered even before Jesus' crucifixion.

The wisdom of his words seems to have been appreciated right from the beginning. Many of the earliest writings we have about Jesus concern his sayings and aphorisms. These were remembered and passed around even during Jesus' lifetime. Many of those who followed Jesus in the crowds were curious about his miracles. But many were also attracted to his words; he amazed the people as much with his words as with his healings. After Jesus' first public statement in the synagogue, St. Luke recounts, "And all spoke well of him, and wondered at the gracious words which proceeded out of his mouth..." (Lk. 4:22). After the Bread of Life discourse, in which Jesus insisted his disciples must eat his flesh and drink his blood, many of those following Jesus drew back and left him. Jesus asked those remaining, "Will you also go away?" Peter, the head apostle, replied, in words that resonate down through time, "Lord, to whom shall we go? You have the words of eternal life..." (Jn. 6:60-69). The words of Jesus are always challenging, but they are always life giving.

We will now look at Jesus' great discourse, the Sermon on the Mount, and two of his best-known parables, the Good Samaritan and the Prodigal Son.

†

The Sermon on the Mount: The Beatitudes

There are two versions of the Sermon on the Mount recorded in the Gospels. The shorter and lesser known is found in Luke 6; the much longer and better known version is in the fifth, sixth, and seventh chapters of Matthew's Gospel. Those chapters contain what is most likely a compilation, or summary, of Jesus' teaching, the sort of things he would typically say as he traveled to the various villages and towns of Galilee.

The Sermon on the Mount expresses the heart of the New Law. "The New Law or the Law of the Gospel," states the *Catechism of the Catholic Church*, "is the perfection here on earth of the divine law, natural and revealed. It is the work of Christ and is expressed particularly in the Sermon on the Mount" (par. 1965). Elsewhere, the *Catechism* says, "The Law of the Gospel *fulfills the commandments of the Law*." (par. 1968) There is a deeply significant relationship to the Old Law and to the fulfillment of the Law given to Moses and the people at Mt. Sinai:

> *The Lord's Sermon on the Mount, far from abolishing or devaluing the moral prescriptions of the Old Law, releases their hidden potential and has new demands arise from them: it reveals their entire divine and human truth. It does not add new external precepts, but proceeds to reform the heart, the root of human acts, where man chooses between the pure and the impure, where faith, hope, and charity are formed and with them the other virtues. The Gospel thus brings the Law to its fullness through imitation of the perfection of the heavenly Father, through forgiveness of enemies and prayer for persecutors, in emulation of the divine generosity. (par. 1968)*

This intimate connection between the Old and the New can be seen, first, in the location chosen by Jesus to give the sermon: a mountaintop. "Seeing the crowds," writes Matthew, "he went up on the mountain, and when he sat down his disciples came to him" (Mt. 5:1). Throughout the Old Testament, mountains are shown to be places where God is encountered, where God reveals something about himself, his Law, his plan for man. The most prominent of these mountains was Mt.

Sinai, where Moses ascended to receive the Law from God and descended to bring it to the people. Jesus, in going up on the mountain, presents himself as the New Moses, the giver of a new and perfect law. "Jesus sits on the cathedra of Moses," explains Pope Benedict XVI in *Jesus of Nazareth*, "But he does so not after the manner of teachers who are trained for the job in a school; he sits there as the greater Moses, who broadens the Covenant to include all nations." The mountain, then, is "the new and definitive Sinai" (p. 66).

Sitting on that new Sinai, Jesus gathered his disciples around him, evocative of the Church that would take his teachings to the ends of the earth, as well as a larger crowd, evocative of those who would (and will) hear him down through history. The first word he utters is "happy," or "blessed" (*makarios* in Greek; *beatitudo* in Latin). The word "happy" can be a difficult or misleading one for modern readers, as Mark Brumley notes:

> People today often associate happiness with "having a good time"—with pleasure and comfort, the antithesis of suffering and want. But contemporary usage is flawed. True happiness is spiritual and moral, not merely emotional or pleasurable. The saints in heaven are *supremely* happy, because they're with God, the source of all happiness. We call their happiness *beatitude*, and we speak of the *beatific* vision of God, which the saints enjoy. ("The Blessings & Curses of the Beatitudes," *The Catholic Faith* [September/October 2001])

This happiness, then, is joyful, flowing from the life of God. The one thing every person desires is joy—and Jesus, the Incarnate Word, tells us how to find true joy and happiness. Yet his first words are perplexing; they sound negative: "Blessed are the poor in spirit, for theirs is the kingdom of heaven" (Mt. 5:2). Put another way, happy are those who *don't* have something! Whatever does he mean by this?

The answer is found in honestly acknowledging who we are and seeing what we really need. We are made by God and for communion with God. "You stir man to take pleasure in praising you," wrote St. Augustine in the opening paragraph of *Confessions*, "because you have made us for yourself, and our heart is restless until it rests in you." Nothing short of God will fill up the infinite longing within us.

God, who is love (and the source of all love), wills the good of the other. Love is living for the other. To have God, then, is to have one's life completely shaped by love and suffused with love—to become love. "He who does not love," wrote St. John, "does not know God; for God is love" (1 Jn. 4:8). Having received the gift of divine life, we must give it to others as a gift: "Beloved, if God so loved us, we also ought to love one another" (1 Jn. 4:11). This is the glorious paradox of grace: in sharing God's life and love with others, we grow in that very life and love.

With this in mind, let's look at each of the beatitudes.

I. BLESSED ARE THE MERCIFUL, FOR THEY SHALL OBTAIN MERCY (Mt. 5:7)

The words "mercy" and "merciful" are used about 150 times in the Bible. *Hesed,* or tender mercy, is God's greatest characteristic in the Old Testament. The Lord, Moses was told, is "merciful and gracious, slow to anger, and abounding in steadfast love and faithfulness" (Ex. 34:6). "Have mercy on me, O God," cries King David, "according to thy steadfast love;

according to thy abundant mercy blot out my transgressions" (Ps. 51:1). "I will not look on [Israel] in anger," the Lord tells the prophet Jeremiah, "for I am merciful, says the LORD; I will not be angry for ever" (Jer. 3:12). This mercy is a deep compassion; in the New Testament it is called *agape*, which is pure, disinterested love. This love must be everything, for without it, there is no happiness, no joy, no peace. To be merciful is to love with the heart of God. "Be merciful," Jesus said, "even as your Father is merciful" (Lk. 6:36).

II. BLESSED ARE THE PURE IN HEART, FOR THEY SHALL SEE GOD (Mt. 5:8)

This is sometimes translated as "singleness of heart," or "blessed are the single-hearted." Bishop Barron writes, "The single-hearted is the one who, in Augustine's phrase, loves God first and everything else for the sake of God. Such a person's 'heart' or center is uncomplicated, unsullied, pure" (*And Now I See...*, p. 189). The person who is pure in heart knows what his life is about; he is free of distractions. He is entirely given to pursuing holiness, the sort of purity spoken of by the author of Hebrews: "Strive for peace with
all men, and for the holiness without which no one will see the Lord" (Heb. 12:14).
St. Chromatius, in his *Tractate on Matthew*, wrote that the "pure of heart are those who have gotten rid of sin's filth, have cleansed themselves of all the pollution of the flesh and have pleased God through works of faith and justice" (Manlio Simonetti, ed., *Ancient Christian Commentary on Sacred Scripture: Matthew 1-13* [IVP Academic, 2001], 87).

III. BLESSED ARE THOSE WHO HUNGER AND THIRST FOR RIGHTEOUSNESS, FOR THEY SHALL BE SATISFIED (Mt. 5:6)

The theme of righteousness and being righteous is a rich and essential one in Scripture. God's ways are righteous—that is, they are just, holy, and rightly ordered—and those who walk in his love will hunger and thirst for righteousness. But man, fallen and sinful, turns away from righteousness; he grasps at fleeting things he thinks will fill up the God-sized hole in his heart: wealth, pleasure, power, and honor. There must be a disciplined, grace-filled response to this inclination, motivated by a desire to respond to these words, spoken by Jesus a bit later in the Sermon on the Mount: "But seek first his kingdom and his righteousness, and all these things shall be yours as well" (Mt 6:33). St. John Chrysostom noted that Jesus did not say, "Blessed are those who *cling* to righteousness," but blessed are those who thirst and hunger for justice.

IV. BLESSED ARE THE PEACEMAKERS, FOR THEY SHALL BE CALLED SONS OF GOD (Mt. 5:9)

Since the Fall, there has been little peace in the world; peace between tribes and peoples and nations has usually been, at best, fleeting and fragile. St. Augustine, in *The City of God*, explained that true peace is founded and rooted in God's law and is ordered toward the common good:

The peace of the body then consists in the duly proportioned arrangement of its parts. The peace of the irrational soul is the harmonious repose of the appetites, and that of the rational soul the harmony of knowledge and action. The peace of body and soul is the well-ordered and harmonious life and health of the living creature. Peace between man and God is the well-ordered obedience of faith to eternal law. Peace between man and man is well-ordered concord. Domestic peace is the well-ordered concord between those of the family who rule and those who obey. Civil peace is a similar concord among the citizens. The peace of the celestial city is the perfectly ordered and harmonious enjoyment of God, and of one another in God. The peace of all things is the tranquility of order. Order is the distribution which allots things equal and unequal, each to its own place. (Bk. 19, Ch. 13)

Peace with God and with ourselves is established when we are reconciled to God through the new covenant established by Christ's salvific work on the Cross. "For he is our peace," wrote St. Paul to the Christians at Ephesus, "who has made us both one, and has broken down the dividing wall of hostility, by abolishing in his flesh the law of commandments and ordinances, that he might create in himself one new man in place of the two, so making peace, and might reconcile us both to God in one body through the cross, thereby bringing the hostility to an end" (Eph. 2:14-16).

V. BLESSED ARE THE POOR IN SPIRIT, FOR THEIRS IS THE KINGDOM OF HEAVEN (Mt. 5:3)

In order for the divine life to flow (and thus to grow), there must be humility. St. Hilary, in his commentary *On Matthew*, wrote that "the Lord taught by way of example that the glory of human ambition must be left behind when he said, 'The Lord your God shall you adore and him only shall you serve. And when he announced through the prophets that he would choose a people humble and in awe of his words, he introduced the perfect Beatitude as humility of spirit" (*On Matthew*, 4.2). He was referring to the words of the Lord, through the prophet Isaiah: "But this is the man to whom I will look, he that is humble and contrite in spirit, and trembles at my word" (Is. 66:2). Humility is necessary for a proper detachment from the things of this world, so that the divine life can flow into you and through you to the world. "When the soul turns itself into a vacuum, an empty space," wrote Bishop Barron in *And Now I See...: A Theology of Transformation* (Crossroad: New York, 1998, p. 185), "then the divine wine can flow in and intoxicate. And this state of affairs is the Kingdom of God, the coming together that has appeared paradigmatically in Jesus and that is now offered as a power to be shared."

VI. BLESSED ARE THOSE WHO MOURN, FOR THEY SHALL BE COMFORTED (Mt. 5:4)

This might sound to some like the advice of a masochist who seeks out sorrow and pain. But the meaning is very much in keeping with the first beatitude: consider how fortunate you are to not be attached to good feelings, to not rely on emotional crutches for comfort. Good feelings and pleasure can be addictive, just like wealth and power. They distort our view of life and this world, keeping us from seeing the truly sorrowful and fallen nature of man without God. Those who mourn—especially those who mourn for their sins—know that suffering, however intense, can not destroy the divine life. No pain, however deeply felt and experienced, can detach us from the divine love. Our response to pain and suffering should be that of Job: "Naked I came from my mother's womb, and naked shall I return; the LORD gave, and the LORD has taken away; blessed be the name of the LORD" (Job 1:21).

VII. BLESSED ARE THE MEEK, FOR THEY SHALL INHERIT THE EARTH (Mt. 5:5)

This exhortation to meekness certainly runs contrary to our natural instincts. Part of the problem is that meekness is often thought of as weakness and lacking courage. Yet Moses was praised for being meek (Num. 12:3), King David wrote that God will "hear the desire of the meek" (Ps. 10:17), and the prophet Isaiah proclaimed, "The meek shall obtain fresh joy in the LORD..." (Is. 29:19). Jesus described himself as meek, or lowly of heart (Mt. 11:29). To be meek is to be humble, gentle, and patient, especially in the face of distress, provocation, and injustice. It is a renunciation of power, earthly glory, and control; by being willing to let go of it, the doors are opened to the divine life. The perfect example of this sacrificial meekness, of course, is the Incarnate Word of God on the Cross, willingly taking the abuse and accepting the death he did not deserve.

VIII. BLESSED ARE THOSE WHO ARE PERSECUTED FOR RIGHTEOUSNESS' SAKE, FOR THEIRS IS THE KINGDOM OF HEAVEN. BLESSED ARE YOU WHEN MEN REVILE YOU AND PERSECUTE YOU AND UTTER ALL KINDS OF EVIL AGAINST YOU FALSELY ON MY ACCOUNT. (Mt. 5:10-11)

Jesus told his disciples to pursue peace, but he also promised they would often encounter persecution as they preached and lived the gospel. Like the Old Testament prophets, they would be attacked, maligned, and even martyred: "Rejoice and be glad, for your reward is great in heaven, for so men persecuted the prophets who were before you" (Mt. 5:12). Yet this is also, paradoxically, a sign of hope, for it demonstrates, in dramatic terms, the detachment from worldly approval. Persecution, in all of its forms, is more often than not the normal state of affairs for the disciple of Christ. Jesus was quite blunt about this fact, telling the disciples that, "you will be hated by all for my name's sake. But he who endures to the end will be saved" (Mt. 10:22). Hans Urs von Balthasar, in *The Moment of Christian Witness* (Ignatius Press, 1994), wrote that "persecution constitutes the normal condition of the Church in her relation to the world, and martyrdom is the normal condition of the professed Christian. ... Again, this does not mean that every single Christian must suffer bloody martyrdom, but he must consider the entire case as the external representation of the inner reality out of which he lives" (pp. 21, 22).

The Sermon on the Mount can only be fully understood in light of the Mount of Calvary. "He who climbed the first to preach the Beatitudes," wrote Fulton Sheen in his *Life of Christ* (New York, 1958), "must necessarily climb the second to practice what He preached...The Sermon on the Mount cannot be separated from His Crucifixion, any more than day can be separated from night" (p. 115). St. Thomas Aquinas said the beatitudes are best exemplified in Christ crucified, so that you will be happy only if you despise what Jesus despised on the cross and if you love what he loved. What did he despise? Wealth (he was stripped of every belonging), pleasure (he endured intense physical and psychological suffering), power (he was nailed to the cross, immobilized), and honor (he was publicly mocked and taunted). And what did he love? Patience, charity, obedience, and humility.

The message of the sermon is the reformation of man's heart through forgiveness, faith, and Jesus' gift of eternal life. The Son of God not only preached the beatitudes, he lived them out in his Passion. Fully human and fully divine, he showed how the New Law is given and how the divine life is lived.

The Grünewald Crucifixion:

"There is a painting of the awful death of Jesus," writes Bishop Barron in *The Strangest Way: Walking the Christian Path* (Maryknoll, NY: Orbis, 2002), "that the German artist Matthias Grünewald completed ... for the patients and staff at a hospital specializing in diseases of the skin. It is one of the most terribly beautiful depictions of Calvary ever made" (p. 11). Grünewald (c.1470-1528), whose real name was probably Mathis Gothardt Neithardt—and who was known during his lifetime as Mathis der Maler, or "Mathis the Painter"—was an architect and engineer. He was also a contemporary of the great Albrecht Dürer (1471-1528), who is far better known; in fact, several of Grünewald's works—including his *Crucifixion*—were for many centuries attributed to Dürer.

The *Crucifixion* was one of nine images on the twelve panels of the striking Isenheim Altarpiece, which Grünewald painted between 1512 and 1516. Among the handful of surviving paintings by Grünewald, the altarpiece is the largest and greatest. It was originally painted for the Monastery of St. Anthony in Isenheim near Colmar, France, where the monks of the Order of St. Anthony specialized in treating epilepsy, blood diseases, and skin diseases, especially ergotism, the symptoms of which— convulsions and skin eruptions— are seen in the figure of Christ in the painting.

Grünewald's style is unique, a mixture of "old school" two-dimensionality and shocking vividness and nearly gruesome detail. The torment and agony of Christ is palpable, a startling comparison to the iconic rendering of St. John the Baptist, to his left, who holds an open book and points serenely to the misshapen, disfigured, crucified Christ. Behind John is the inscription of his words: *illum oportet crescere me autem minui* ("He must increase, but I must decrease"; Jn. 3:30). On the other side of the cross, St. John the Apostle holds the Blessed Mother, depicted in a Cistercian nun's habit; St. Mary Magdalene kneels, weeping, the agonized arch of her body and distended fingers echoing those of her dying Lord. Below the cross is a lamb, bearing its own cross, with blood from its wounded chest pouring into a chalice.

"Art historians have puzzled over this work for a century and a failed to solve its enigmas," wrote Paul Johnson in *Art: A New History* (New York: HarperCollins, 2003). "Anyone who takes the trouble to journey to Colmar can reach a personal verdict on one of the most enigmatic masterpieces of Western art" (p. 300).

QUESTIONS FOR UNDERSTANDING — Part 1:

1. How does the Catholic Church teach that Jesus is completely unique in his person and work? (CCC 454, 464, 614, 617)

2. Read Luke 6 and Matthew 5-7. In what ways are the two versions of the Sermon on the Mount similar and different?

3. How does the Sermon on the Mount express and fulfill the commandments of the Law? What are some of the key connections between the Sermon on the Mount and the Law? (CCC 1965, 1968)

4. What is the meaning of "happy" or "blessed" as used in the Sermon on the Mount? How is the biblical concept of happiness different from happiness as most people understand it today? (CCC 1716-29)

5. What are some of the paradoxical qualities of the beatitudes? How do they contrast with a worldly desire for power, honor, pleasure, and wealth? (CCC 1719, 1722, 1723)

QUESTIONS FOR APPLICATION — Part 1:

1. What are some of the different opinions about Jesus that you have heard or read about? Why are they attractive to many people?

2. In light of the Sermon on the Mount, how should I understand the Law and view the Old Testament?

3. What does it mean to say that the one thing every person desires is joy? What are some of my experiences of joy? Did they, in some way, point toward an eternal, supernatural joy?

4. How do the Beatitudes challenge my priorities? Which of the Beatitudes is most difficult for me to understand or accept? Why?

THE TEACHINGS OF JESUS
Episode 2, Part 2

OUTLINE *(Tracks 4-6 on DVD)*

I. The Path of Non-violence

    1. Love is "willing the good of the other as other"

    2. "Love your enemies": the rhetorical climax of the Sermon on the Mount

    3. Not passivity, but provocative form of resistance

    4. Examples of this form of resistance

II. The Parable of the Prodigal Son (Lk. 15:11-32)

    A. A parable about divine mercy (John Paul II)

    B. We are children of God, yet man chooses autonomy from God

    C. By rejecting grace, man exiles himself from familial love and communion

    D. Desperation leads to awareness; better to be a slave than to feed pigs

    E. The father is faithful to his fatherhood and to his son

    F. The ring given by the father is marital, re-establishes right relationship

    G. The older son is no different, in the end, than his brother

    H. The heavenly Father waits for man to respond to his fatherly call

III. Matthew 25

    A. Peter Maurin, Dorothy Day and the Catholic Worker Movement

        1. Go-getters to go-givers: the transformation of society in Christ

    B. Mother Teresa

        1. "You did it to me"

    C. *Metanoiate*: changing the manner in which we see the world.

    D. "The Law of the Gift"

The Path of Non-violence

"YOU HAVE HEARD THAT IT WAS SAID, 'YOU SHALL LOVE YOUR NEIGHBOR AND HATE YOUR ENEMY.' BUT I SAY TO YOU, LOVE YOUR ENEMIES AND PRAY FOR THOSE WHO PERSECUTE YOU, SO THAT YOU MAY BE SONS OF YOUR FATHER WHO IS IN HEAVEN; FOR HE MAKES HIS SUN RISE ON THE EVIL AND ON THE GOOD, AND SENDS RAIN ON THE JUST AND ON THE UNJUST" (MT. 5: 43-45).

This call to love your enemies is the rhetorical climax of the Sermon on the Mount. Why? Because loving an enemy—especially those who seek to destroy you—is the greatest test of love; it is the willing of the good for the one who will not respond in kind. This difficult and challenging teaching is made even more pointedly, more concretely, in this statement: "You have heard that it was said, 'An eye for an eye and a tooth for a tooth.' But I say to you, do not resist one who is evil. But if any one strikes you on the right cheek, turn to him the other also..." (Mt. 5:38-39).

Is this an encouragement to passivity in the face of violence? No, it is something else—a new and provocative form of resistance. It rejects the two normal responses to unjust aggression, which are to either fight or flee, neither of which is ultimately effective. Slapping someone on the right cheek was a blatant gesture of contempt, requiring the back of one's hand. To fight back would make the situation worse; to run away would encourage and confirm the attacker in his violence. A perfect example of rejecting either response is seen in how Jesus reacted in the garden when he was being arrested. He did not attempt to escape, nor did he allow Peter to defend him with the sword: "Put your sword back into its place; for all who take the sword will perish by the sword" (Mt. 26:52).

Standing one's ground does something quite different: it forces the persecutor to consider another way of being, of acting, of seeing others. This is not a passive response. Instead, it suggests to him that he is connected to you more deeply than he realized, and that what separates you and him is far more superficial than he might think. "Passivity in the face of hatred amounts, once again, to the acceptance of an illusion," observes Bishop Barron, "Rather, in calling for us to turn the other cheek and hand over our shirts and go the extra mile, Jesus is, in fact, advocating a provocative, 'in-your-face' challenge to evil" (*And Now I See...*, p. 190). If someone is actually audacious enough to sue for the clothing you are wearing—an act of legal violence—offer him your coat as well. Again, in not fleeing or fighting, you signal to him the injustice and violence of his actions.

The past century was witness to many bold examples of this approach to violence, bigotry, and hatred: Archbishop Desmond Tutu resisting racism and apartheid in South Africa, Ghandi working for justice and freedom in India, Mother Teresa standing up for the poor and forgotten, and John Paul II assisting and supporting the Solidarity movement in Poland. Those who walk in peaceful, prayerful silence advocationg the rights of the unborn are also standing their ground against the aggression of the culture of death against those who are most vulnerable and innocent, the unborn. Those who are slandered, demeaned, and mocked for their public witness to truth and goodness have an opportunity to turn the other cheek, to bless the persecutor with their witness to Christ. "Bless those who persecute you," St. Paul told the beleaguered Christians in Rome, "bless and do not curse them" (Rom. 12:14).

†

The Prodigal Son

The Parable of the Prodigal Son (Lk. 15:11-32) is the best known of Jesus' parables, a powerful and rich story of God's love and mercy. In *Dives in Misericordia*, his encyclical on the mercy of God, Pope John Paul II noted that although the word "mercy" does not appear in the parable, "it nevertheless expresses the essence of the divine mercy in a particularly clear way" (sec. 5). Read carefully and prayerfully, the parable reveals a wealth of truths about our relationship with our heavenly Father.

The first sentence reveals that we are children of God: "A man had two sons. The younger of them said to his father, 'Father, give me the share of the estate that is coming to me.'" (Lk. 15:11-12) As children of God, filled with divine life, we have everything we need or could ever desire. All that we are has meaning and purpose because of the Father's life and love. And yet sin, the desire to be autonomous from God, can rupture this relationship and destroy the life of grace. Demands can be made that sever us from communion with God: "Give me my share that is coming to me." The choice, put simply, is between gratitude and greed, between humility and pride. Those who live properly in God do so with a receptive and grateful heart, receiving God's gifts and then willingly giving those gifts to others. The younger son, however, is not grateful toward his father, nor giving towards others; he seeks only his own satisfaction. In essence, he says, "You're in my way. I would be better off if you were dead."

Amazingly, God respects our freedom—which is, of course, his gift to us—even when we use it to rebel against him. In the parable, "the father divided up the property." Grace has been divided, cut off, dried up. The familial bond is broken, and the son takes his money into the "far country." The Greek word, the *chora makra*, refers to a place of great emptiness. "What is farther away," asked St. Ambrose, "then to depart from oneself, and not from a place? ... Surely whoever separates himself from Christ is an exile from his country, a citizen of the world" (*Exposition on the Gospel of Luke* 7.213-14). The physical distance is not as painful as the loss of familial love and communion; the son's inner life vanished as quickly as did his inheritance.

Desperate, he becomes the feeder of pigs, which is about as low as a Jewish worker could go. Having selfishly sought to satisfy only himself, he learns what it is like to be on the other side of the economic and emotional equation: "No one made a move to give him anything." "The younger son," wrote John Paul II, "measures himself by the standard of the goods that he has lost, that he no longer 'possesses,' while the hired servants of his father's house 'possess' them. These words express above all his attitude toward material goods; nevertheless under their surface is concealed the tragedy of lost dignity, the awareness of squandered sonship" (sec. 5).

Broken, the son decides to return to his father's house and ask to be a hired hand, knowing that even his father's slaves—who are with their master for life—have it better than he does. The longsuffering father, seeing him from a distance (a sign he had been looking for him to return), runs to meet him. The parable is not, in fact, about the son as much as it is about the father and his passionate, relentless quest. It is about the unrelenting, self-sacrificial love of God for man. "The father of the prodigal son is faithful to his fatherhood," wrote John Paul II, "faithful to the love that he had always lavished on his son. This fidelity is expressed in the parable not only by his immediate readiness to welcome him home when he returns after having squandered his inheritance; it is expressed even more fully by that joy, that merrymaking for the squanderer after his return, merrymaking which is so generous that it provokes the opposition and hatred of the elder brother, who had never gone far away from his father and had never abandoned the home" (sec. 6).

The ring given by the father to the prodigal son is marital; it symbolizes the re-establishment of right relationship, the restoration of honor undeserved but freely given. "This son of mine was dead," exclaims the father with joy, "and has come back to life…" Having walked away in petulant selfishness, the son had embraced death. Having been embraced by his waiting father, he is restored to life and grace. "He falls on your neck," wrote St. Ambrose, "to raise one prostrate and burdened with sins and bring back one turned aside to the earthly toward heaven."

It is understandable that readers are often sympathetic toward the older brother. After all, he was faithful to his father; he stayed at home and never made selfish demands. His anger seems justified. "For years I have slaved for you. I never disobeyed any of your orders, yet you never gave me so much as a kid goat to celebrate with my friends." Yet, beneath the superficial details, he is actually not so different from his brother, especially since he understands his relationship with their father in practical, economic terms. He obeys, but as a slave, not as a son. He thinks he must somehow earn his father's love; he has failed to comprehend his father's real nature and the relationship he should have had with him. His small and skewed perspective is revealed in his angry, resentful protest, "Then when this son of yours returns after having gone through your property with loose women, you kill the fatted calf for him." When we fall out of love with God, we fall into hatred of one another.

The father's answer is patient and gracious: "My son, you are with me always, and everything I have is yours." This is the key: everything that God has is given to us. His entire being is "for-giving." Yet we are tempted, in our fear and selfishness, to take, grab, cling, and possess. Yet all is gift. God is not just Creator, John Paul II explained, but "He is also Father: He is linked to man, whom He called to existence in the visible world, by a bond still more intimate than that of creation. It is love which not only creates the good but also grants participation in the very life of God: Father, Son and Holy Spirit. For he who loves desires to give himself" (sec. 7). He waits for us, if only we respond to his Fatherly call.

✝

Matthew 25

In Matthew 22:34-40, a lawyer inquired of Jesus which of the many laws which governed Jewish life (over 600) was the most important. Jesus responded: "You shall love the Lord your God with all your heart, and with all your soul, and with all your mind. This is the great and first commandment. And a second is like it, You shall love your neighbor as yourself. On these two commandments depend all the law and the prophets" (Mt. 22:37-40). Love of God and love of neighbor are not in competition but they imply each other since God is the ground of the existence of the finite world.

The parable in Matthew 25:31-46 is meant to stir us out of our complacency and see that our love of God is shown in how we love our neighbor. A tendency exists to separate God entirely from the world. While it is correct that God is not reducible to the world, God's very being grounds the world's being. The world co-inheres in God. Thus, to fail to love the least in the world is to fail to love God. Christ's judgment is meant to expand our minds and hearts so we can see and love God where our small souls refuse to find him.

Peter Maurin, one of the founders of the Catholic Worker Movement, understood the radical call to love in Matthew 25. He did not treat this call in the abstract, but took action in devoting his life to the spiritual and corporal works of mercy. He wanted the ideals of the Gospel to be the foundation of the social and political order of society so as to build a good society. Finding the Papal Encyclicals of the late nineteenth and early twentieth century illuminating on the social problem, he wanted to take those principles, grounded in the Gospels, and embed them in the surrounding culture. In 1932, Peter Maurin came to New York and met the recently converted Dorothy Day, and the two of them unleashed and lived out Catholic Social Teaching through the founding of the Catholic Worker.

FOR FURTHER STUDY: *The Good Samaritan*

Jesus often taught in parables, Pope John Paul II noted in *Dives in Misericordia*, because parables "express better the very essence of things" (sec. 3). The *Catechism* explains that Jesus used parables as an invitation to enter the kingdom of God:

> *Through his parables he invites people to the feast of the kingdom, but he also asks for a radical choice: to gain the kingdom, one must give everything. Words are not enough, deeds are required. The parables are like mirrors for man: will he be hard soil or good earth for the word? What use has he made of the talents he has received? Jesus and the presence of the kingdom in this world are secretly at the heart of the parables. One must enter the kingdom, that is, become a disciple of Christ, in order*

to "know the secrets of the kingdom of heaven." For those who stay "out-side," everything remains enigmatic. (par. 546)

The Parable of the Good Samaritan (Luke 10:25-37) has captured the imagination of Christians and non-Christians alike. Why? It is compellingly simple and is a beautiful illustration of Jesus' teaching about love. But there is another, deeper reason the story attracts so many: it is a portrait, when all is said and done, of Christ himself.

The first clue is found in the opening line: "A man was going down from Jerusalem to Jericho." Jerusalem, Origen wrote, "is paradise, and Jericho is the world" (*Exposition on the Gospel of Luke*, 7.74). Jerusalem, as a symbol of heaven, indicates a state of communion and friendship with God. Jericho, the final city to be conquered before the Israelites could enter the promised land by knocking down its famous walls, is an image of this world; it is the city of sin.

So the seventeen-mile journey from Jerusalem to Jericho symbolizes the fall of man from right relationship with God into sin: "...he fell among robbers..." Sin robs us of divine life, of friendship with God. When we fall into sin, we are alienated from God, our passions are focused on the wrong things, and our desires are disordered. We are then robbed of our dignity. In the parable, the robbers stripped the traveler "and beat him, and departed, leaving him half dead." This is what sin does: it attacks our life and leaves us beaten, battered, and in pain.

What happened next? "Now by chance a priest was going down that road; and when he saw him he passed by on the other side. So likewise a Levite, when he came to the place and saw him, passed by on the other side." On one hand, this is surely a lesson in morality. But an allegorical reading, so often used by the Church Fathers, takes us deeper. "The priest," wrote Origen, "is the law, the Levite is the prophets..." The law and pious practice, to be sure, are good things when rightly ordered. Yet here, they are going from Jerusalem to Jericho, that is, from grace to sin. When religion is emptied of a transcendent center and when piety is a means of self-justification, then the works of the law are not about serving and loving God, but about boosting our ego. They cannot save us; in fact, they place us in the most desperate of situations.

Which is why we need Jesus. "But a Samaritan, as he journeyed, came to where he was; and when he saw him, he had compassion..." It would be difficult to overstate how deeply the Jews despised the Samaritans. The Samaritans were a mixture of Jewish and pagan blood, and they claimed to be descendants of the tribes of Ephraim and Manasseh who had preserved the authentic, original Mosaic religion. They were the epitome of the despised outsider. Yet Jesus also was despised by his own people and rejected, crucified on a cross.

And what did the Samaritan do? He "went to him and bound up his wounds, pouring on oil and wine..." The metaphor here is quite obvious: Jesus approaches us in our sinful, mortally wounded state, and heals us. He does not recoil in disgust, nor does he reject us because of our weakness, but he meets us where we are; he touches us despite our condition, and he pours oil and wine on our wounds. These are symbols of the sacraments, especially of confirmation and the Eucharist. "Wine and oil," wrote St. Augustine, "have been poured on you. You have received the sacrament of the only-begotten Son. You have been lifted onto his mule. You have been brought to the inn, and you are being cured in the church" (*Sermon* 179A.7). The Church is a place of shelter and comfort as it is the household of God, "the pillar and bulwark of the truth" (1 Tim. 3:15). There we meet and have communion with others who are also recovering from sin, who are being restored to life by God's grace.

"And the next day he took out two denarii and gave them to the innkeeper..." St. Ambrose interpreted these two coins to represent the two Testaments "that contain revealed within them the image of the eternal King, at the price of whose wounds we are healed..." (*Exposition on the Gospel of Luke* 7.80). The Old Testament pointed toward the redemptive work of Christ on the cross; the New Testament recorded and revealed it. The word "redemption" comes from the Latin word *redemptio*, meaning to "buy back" or "pay for" the one who is unable to pay for their own freedom. "You were bought with a price," St. Paul told the Corinthians, "do not become slaves of men" (1 Cor. 7:23). And now that our liberation from sin and death has been purchased for us, what are we to do?

> WHICH OF THESE THREE, DO YOU THINK, PROVED NEIGHBOR TO THE MAN WHO FELL AMONG THE ROBBERS?" HE SAID, "THE ONE WHO SHOWED MERCY ON HIM." AND JESUS SAID TO HIM, "GO AND DO LIKEWISE."

We are to follow the example of Christ; we are called to be other Christs. "I have been crucified with Christ; it is no longer I who live, but Christ who lives in me; and the life I now live in the flesh I live by faith in the Son of God, who loved me and gave himself for me" (Gal. 2:20). We are to search out those who are wounded, stranded by the wayside on the road of sin. We do not ignore them, even if they are our enemies (or we think they are our enemies), but we do as Jesus did, pouring out love and compassion, communicating the power of Christ's cross and the healing touch of his Church.

QUESTIONS FOR UNDERSTANDING — Part 2:

1. What is the relationship between the Sermon on the Mount and Christ's death on the Mount of Calvary?

2. What does it mean to "love your enemy"? How is this a radical teaching? (Matt. 5:38-39, 44-45; Matt 26:52)

3. What does the Parable of the Prodigal Son teach about the mercy of God the Father and the divine communion in which each of us is called to share? (1 Tim. 2:4; 2 Peter 1:4)

QUESTIONS FOR APPLICATION — Part 2:

1. How difficult is it for me to love my enemies? What can I do to grow in my love for my "enemies" or for those I dislike?

2. Have I ever acted in ways similar to the prodigal son? Or like his older brother? How do I sometimes fail to appreciate the mercy, love, and grace of the Father?

TERMS & NAMES

Barth, Karl (1886-1968). A Swiss pastor widely considered one of the most influential Protestant theologians of the twentieth century. His commentary on Romans and his multi-volume *Church Dogmatics* are among his most important works.

***Chora Makra*:** A Greek phrase referring to the region of unlikeness to God. It is the spiritual state of resisting the gift of the divine life.

Concupiscence: the *Catechism* defines it as "the movement of the sensitive appetite contrary to the operation of the human reason" (CCC 2515). The severing of desire from the governance of reason leaves one in a state of inclination to sin.

Grünewald, Matthias (c.1470-1528). A German architect, engineer, and painter whose real name was probably Mathis Gothardt Neithardt. His most famous work is his *Crucifixion*, one of nine images on the twelve panels of the Isenheim Altarpiece, painted between 1512 and 1516.

Kierkegaard, Søren (1813-55). A Danish philosopher, theologian, and social critic who was one of the first modern existentialists. His many writings—often pseudonymous and very sarcastic—addressed ethics and morality, attacked Hegelianism and the national church, and defended the autonomy and free will of individuals.

Lwanga, Charles (1860-1886). A Ugandan Catholic martyr who served as a page and later major-domo in the court of King Mwanga II. After refusing to renounce the Faith, Charles and his companions were martyred.

Origen (c. 185-c.254). A prolific and influential third-century theologian, biblical scholar, and Church Father. He was born in Alexandria, Egypt, where he taught and lived most of his life.

Pantheism: The belief that God and the world are one, making no distinction between God's being and creation. Forms of pantheism can be found in various Eastern religions, Hegelianism, and various "New Age" belief systems.

Parable: A short story, often allegorical in nature but usually drawing upon everyday life and activities, expressing a central moral or theological point. In the Gospels, parables are usually meant to reveal the kingdom of God to disciples of Jesus; fittingly they usually require authoritative interpretation by Jesus.

Polytheism: The belief in multiple deities or gods, often arranged in a hierarchical manner with a primary god over lesser gods. Polytheistic religions were common in the ancient world (Greece, Rome, etc.) and exist today in parts of Asia and Africa.

Puritanism: A belief system that tends to overemphasize the depravity of human beings and the world. The opposition between worldly goods and spiritual goods is stark. Catholics have a different view. Hilaire Belloc summarizes it well: "Wherever the Catholic sun doth shine, there's always laughter and good red wine."

Tillich, Paul (1886-1965) A German-American theologian who is famous for his " method of correlation" - that is, an approach of exploring the symbols of Christian revelation as answers to the problems of contemporary human existence. He is best known for his three-volume work *Systematic Theology*, *The Courage to Be* and *Dynamics of Faith*.

Tolkein, J.R.R. (1892-1973). An English Catholic writer, poet, philologist, and university professor who is best known for his books *The Hobbit* and *The Lord of the Rings Trilogy*. He was a close friend of C.S. Lewis and played a vital role in the latter's conversion.

Tutu, Bishop Desmond (1931-). Anglican Archbishop Emeritus of Cape Town, South Africa. He has been active in the defense of human rights and helped bring an end to apartheid in South Africa.

Recommended Reading:

- *The Priority of Christ* by Robert Barron
- *And Now I See...: A Theology of Transformation* by Robert Barron
- *Life of Christ* by Fulton Sheen
- *The Lord* by Romano Guardini
- *Dominus Iesus* by the Congregation for the Doctrine of the Faith
- *Dives in Misericordia* by Pope John Paul II
- *The Moment of Christian Witness* by Hans Urs von Balthasar

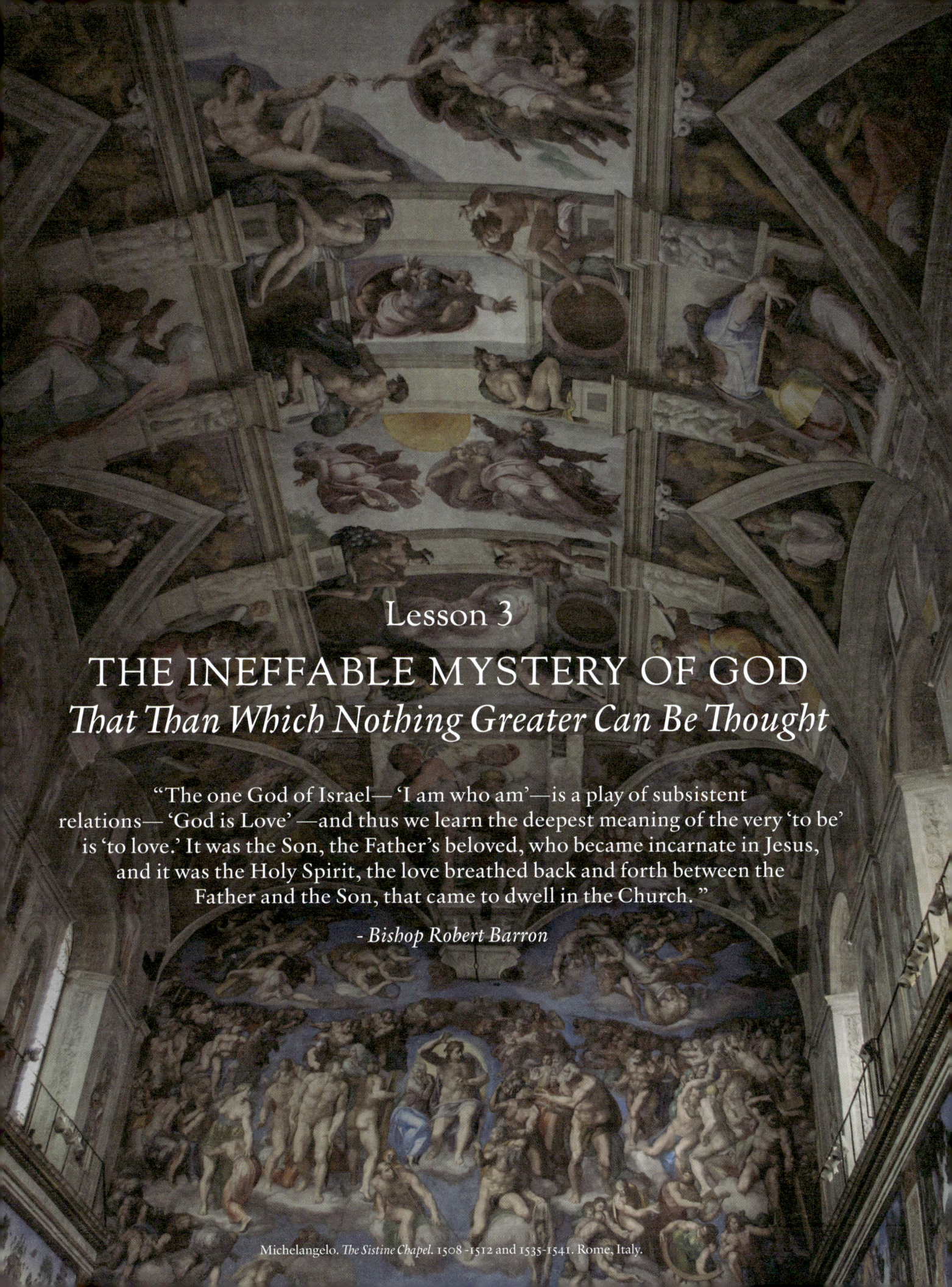

Lesson 3

THE INEFFABLE MYSTERY OF GOD
That Than Which Nothing Greater Can Be Thought

"The one God of Israel— 'I am who am'—is a play of subsistent
relations— 'God is Love' —and thus we learn the deepest meaning of the very 'to be'
is 'to love.' It was the Son, the Father's beloved, who became incarnate in Jesus,
and it was the Holy Spirit, the love breathed back and forth between the
Father and the Son, that came to dwell in the Church. "

- Bishop Robert Barron

Michelangelo. *The Sistine Chapel.* 1508 -1512 and 1535-1541. Rome, Italy.

THE INEFFABLE MYSTERY OF GOD
Episode 3, Part 1

OUTLINE *(Tracks 1-4 on DVD)*

I. The Mystery of God

 A. Moses

   1. Moses was living a "second life"

 2. Moses had been saved before from death

 3. God spoke to Moses from the bush

   i. "I Am Who I Am" (Ex. 3:14)

   ii. "This divine name is mysterious just as God is mystery" (CCC 206)

     iii. Tetragrammaton: YHWH, rendered as "Lord"

   4. God is not *a being*, but *being itself* (*ipsum esse*)

   5. God is a mystery

 B. Anselm's "Ontological Argument"

 1. God as "that than which nothing greater can be thought"

 2. God cannot be limited by the categories of human understanding

II. The Five "Ways" and the Argument from Contingency

 A. The Five "Ways" of St. Thomas Aquinas

   1. Argument from motion

   2. Argument from efficient causes

 3. Argument from contingency (only argument featured in Episode Three)

 4. Argument from gradation of being

 5. Argument from design

 B. *Contingency*: all things come and go; everything is changing

   1. It is not possible for all things to always exist

   2. They must, then, depend for their existence on some necessary reality

III. Ratzinger's Argument from Intelligibility

    A. The possibility of an intelligible Universe is conditioned by there being a *Divine Intelligence*, the *Logos*

    B. All science is conditioned by this assumption

    C. All knowledge is re-*cognizing* the forms

    D. The universe is marked by intelligence

IV. Naming God

    A. God is transcendent and radically other

    B. God is intensely immanent and present to us (Psalm 139)

        1. Omnipotence

        2. Omniscience

        3. Omnipresence

    C. The only proper response to God is love

The Mystery of God

"Our profession of faith begins with God, for God is the First and the Last, the beginning and the end of everything. The Credo begins with God the Father, for the Father is the first divine person of the Most Holy Trinity; our Creed begins with the creation of heaven and earth, for creation is the beginning and the foundation of all God's works."

– *Catechism of the Catholic Church*, par. 198.

"The bush which was unsuitable even as an image of dead gods was able to depict within itself the mystery of the living God. Moses, this is a sign to you: as you saw God dwelling in the midst of fire, by fire must you serve the God who dwells in the fire."

– St. Ephrem the Syrian, *Commentary on Exodus* (3.2).

The story of Moses and the burning bush is simply and directly told. But it is one of the most powerful and mysterious encounters between God and man recorded in the Old Testament:

> NOW MOSES WAS KEEPING THE FLOCK OF HIS FATHER-IN-LAW, JETHRO, THE PRIEST OF MID'IAN; AND HE LED HIS FLOCK TO THE WEST SIDE OF THE WILDERNESS, AND CAME TO HOREB, THE MOUNTAIN OF GOD. AND THE ANGEL OF THE LORD APPEARED TO HIM IN A FLAME OF FIRE OUT OF THE MIDST OF A BUSH; AND HE LOOKED, AND LO, THE BUSH WAS BURNING, YET IT WAS NOT CONSUMED. (EX. 3:1-2)

Moses had already lived a lifetime when he encountered the mysterious burning bush on Mount Horeb (i.e. Mount Sinai). A few hundred years prior to his birth, the patriarch Joseph—who had miraculously made his way from slavery to second-in-command of Egypt—had saved his family and people from famine. The "descendants of Israel," states the opening chapter of Exodus, "were fruitful and increased greatly; they multiplied and grew exceedingly strong; so that the land was filled with them" (Ex. 1:7). Time passed, circumstances changed, and a new king came into power in Egypt, a ruler without knowledge of Joseph. His concern was with power and politics: "And he said to his people, 'Behold, the people of Israel are too many and too mighty for us. Come, let us deal shrewdly with them, lest they multiply, and, if war befall us, they join our enemies and fight against us and escape from the land.'" (Ex. 1:9-10).

Seeking to control the Hebrews, Pharaoh made them work all the harder; then he enslaved them "and made their lives bitter with hard service, in mortar and brick, and in all kinds of work in the field; in all their work they made them serve with rigor" (Ex. 1:14). And when such physical oppression did not slow the growth of the foreigners, he ordered the midwives to kill the male offspring of the Hebrews. When the midwives thwarted this murderous plan, Pharaoh ordered his people to cast the sons of the Hebrews into the Nile (Ex. 1:22).

The baby Moses was born, then, with a death warrant on his head. He was hidden, ironically, on the very waters he was supposed to be drowned in: "And when she could hide him no longer she took for him a basket made of bulrushes, and daubed it with bitumen and pitch; and she put the child in it and placed it among the reeds at the river's brink" (Ex. 2:3). This was a sort of precursor to the parting of the Red Sea, itself a foreshadowing of baptism, which reveals water to be both an instrument of death and of life, of destruction and liberation. Moses himself would eventually be, despite his reticence and weaknesses, a divider, a liberator, an instrument of life for God's people.

But first he had to encounter the living God. Having been raised in the court of the Pharaoh, he had finally sided with his people, killing an Egyptian who was beating a Hebrew slave (Ex. 2:11-12). Fleeing to Midian, Moses married the daughter of a priest, had a son, and settled down. The course for a quiet life was set; he was happily settled. Yet God had other plans for Moses, plans providential and covenantal, which would further reveal the nature of the deity who heard the anguished cries of his people, saw the oppression they lived under, and knew their condition (Ex. 2:24-25). And so God, appearing in the burning bush to Moses, spoke to the prince-turned-shepherd, "Do not come near; put off your shoes from your feet, for the place on which you are standing is holy ground." God then identified himself as "the God of your father, the God of Abraham, the God of Isaac, and the God of Jacob." (Ex. 3:5-6)

Moses, rightly afraid, hid his face. He certainly must have wondered, "Why is God talking to *me*?" The deity then explained to Moses that he had seen the oppression of his people and heard their cries—and he had chosen Moses to go to Pharaoh and to "bring forth my people, the sons of Israel, out of Egypt" (Ex. 3:10). Here is an essential truth revealed again and again in Scripture and in history: it is always God who initiates; it is always God who calls. It is Man who responds. Moses' response, a natural and reasonable one, was to ask for a name. He knew very well that there were many gods: gods of the mountain, river, trees, land, and so forth. The answer he received was revolutionary, for this God was implying that he was not one God among many, not a being who could be delimited or defined. His name was simply "to be." The one who *is*:

> God said to Moses, "I AM WHO I AM." And he said, "Say this to the people of Israel, 'I AM has sent me to you.'" (Ex. 3:14)

Linguists and Scripture scholars have sought to adequately translate these words: "Ehyeh-Asher-Ehyeh." They are often rendered, "I am that I am," although some scholars prefer "I will be what I will be" or "I will be because I will be." It reveals a deity whose personality is known to the extent he wishes to reveal himself. His name is, simply put, "to be." He is the One who is.
The *Catechism* states:

> *In revealing his mysterious name,* YHWH *("I AM HE WHO IS," "I AM WHO AM" or "I AM WHO I AM"), God says who he is and by what name he is to be*

called. This divine name is mysterious just as God is mystery. It is at once a name revealed and something like the refusal of a name, and hence it better expresses God as what he is - infinitely above everything that we can understand or say: he is the "hidden God," his name is ineffable, and he is the God who makes himself close to men. ... The revelation of the ineffable name "I AM WHO AM" contains then the truth that God alone IS. (pars. 206, 213)

The ancient Israelites honored this essential mysteriousness and hidden nature of God by using the unpronounceable name, what is called the Tetragrammaton: YHWH. "And God said to Moses, 'I am the LORD. I appeared to Abraham, to Isaac, and to Jacob, as God Almighty, but by my name the LORD I did not make myself known to them'" (Ex. 6:2-3; cf. 3:15). This name, "Yahweh," translated as "Lord," appears over 5,400 times in the Old Testament according to the *Jewish Encyclopedia*.

The Catholic theological tradition, in keeping with this revelation to Moses on Mount Horeb, refuses to refer to God as a being, for he is not one thing among many other things. Instead, it recognizes God as *ipsum esse*—"being itself." "However," notes Nahum Sarna in *Exploring Exodus* (New York, NY, 1996), "it is not Being as opposed to nonbeing, not Being as an abstract, philosophical notion, but Being in the sense of the reality of God's active, dynamic Presence" (p. 52). The great French Thomist Étienne Gilson, in *The Spirit of Medieval Philosophy* (University of Notre Dame Press, 1991; orig. 1936), wrote that "Exodus lays down the principle from which henceforth the whole of Christian philosophy will be suspended. From this moment it is understood once and for all that the proper name of God is Being and ... this name denotes His very essence. ... There is but one God and this God is Being, that is the cornerstone of all Christian philosophy, and it was not Plato, it was not even Aristotle, it was Moses who put it in position" (p. 51).

St. Thomas Aquinas stated that God is not in any genus—that is, class or kind—not even the genus of being, and so it follows hat he cannot be defined. In fact, in all of his *Summa Theologiae*, St. Thomas never defines or explains what God *is*, only what God *is not*. Saint Anselm of Canterbury (1033-1109), in one of his theistic proofs, famously described God as "that than which nothing greater can be thought." This is simple enough at first, but further thought reveals just how strange it is. For example, if God were a being—even a supreme being—then we could say that God plus the world would be greater than God alone. Which would mean the supreme being is not "that than which nothing greater can be thought." So it must be that God plus the world is not greater than God alone. The *Catechism* offers these words of explanation and caution:

God transcends all creatures. We must therefore continually purify our language of everything in it that is limited, image-bound or imperfect, if we are not to confuse our image of God- "the inexpressible, the incomprehensible, the invisible, the ungraspable"-with our human representations. Our human words always fall short of the mystery of God. (par. 42)

God, then, is a mystery. And as we shall see, the "mystery of the Most Holy Trinity is the central mystery of Christian faith and life. It is the mystery of God in himself" (CCC 234). But first we will consider one of the five "ways" given by St. Thomas for proving the existence of God.

Arguments for God's Existence

In Question Two of Part One of the *Summa Theologiae*, St. Thomas considers the existence of God: Is God's existence self-evident? Can it be demonstrated that God exists? Does God exist? After explaining the arguments against the existence of God, the Angelic Doctor writes, "On the contrary: In Exodus 3:14 God is shown saying, 'I am who am.'" He then states, "The existence of God can be proved in five ways" (I, q. 2, a. 3).

Much has been written about these "ways," or proofs, and there have been, at times, misunderstandings about what they are intended to prove, or how they fit into the larger scope of the *Summa*. "For some," Bishop Barron writes in *Thomas Aquinas: Spiritual Master* (Crossroad: New York, 1996, 2008), "they provide a rational foundation for religious belief, and for others they represent the pathetic and arrogant human attempt to capture God in a net of concepts and logical necessities" (p. 62). But neither of these perceptions, Bishop Barron argues, is correct. "These various ways in which philosophers have proven the existence of God are utilized by our spiritual master as *manuductiones*, leadings by the hand, methods by which the fallen mind is led to an appreciation of the God of revelation" (p. 63). These are paths pointed out by the spiritual master who has already walked upon them.

The first "way" is the *argument from motion*, which states there must be a first and unmoved "mover" since motion cannot go on to infinity. The second is the *argument from efficient causes*, which states that there is a hierarchy of efficient causes, which means there must ultimately be "a first efficient cause, to which everyone gives the name of God." The third is the *argument from contingency*, which we will examine in more detail in a moment.

The fourth is the *argument from the gradation of being*, considered by many to be the most difficult to grasp of the five "ways." It rests on the observation that there are degrees of perfections in things and that different finite things have different perfections to different degrees. "Among beings," Aquinas posits, "there are some more and some less good, true, noble, and the like." This means there "is something which is truest, something best, something noblest, and, consequently, something is most being..." This leads to the conclusion that "there must also be something which is to all beings the cause of their being, goodness, and every other perfection; and this we call God."

The fifth "way" is an *argument from design*. Things "achieve their end, not fortuitously, but designedly." Yet things without knowledge cannot move to their end unless directed by someone with intelligence, "as the arrow is directed by the archer." There must, therefore, be an intelligent being who directs all natural things to their end.

Now back to the third "way," the proof from possibility and necessity, or the **argument from contingency.** Although contingency is not a word we hear in everyday conversation, it describes something we all observe and experience: the fact that things come and things go; things come into existence and then they pass out of being. Things are not static, but constantly in a state of motion, movement, growing, perishing, and so forth. We see it in how flowers bloom in the spring, fruit grows in the summer, and leaves fall in the autumn months. Our pets grow and thrive and then eventually die; the same is true for human beings, no matter how we try to avoid or deny it. Even those things that seem most permanent—the great mountains of the world, for example—are slowly but surely changing, developing, rising, and falling.

This fact of contingency is the starting point of Thomas's argument. "We find in nature," he writes, "things that are possible to be and not to be," since they are found to be generated, and to be corrupted, and consequently, it is possible for them to be and not to be. But, he notes, it is not possible for these things to always exist, for these contingent things do not possess in themselves the reason for their own existence. If they did, they would exist permanently, as well as necessarily. Such things, put another way, are *possible* but not *necessary*. They all tend, inevitably, toward nonexistence. An explanation for their existence must be found outside of them, for they must depend on something else.

There must be, therefore, a foundational explanation for their existence, some reality that grounds and explains both their existence and its own. This necessary reality, which exists through itself and which in turn explains the existence of all contingent things, is what all people call God. This means there are two levels of reality: the ordinary, day-to-day level, which is changing and fleeting in nature, and a stable, permanent level of reality that does not change. Man has an awareness of this difference, and this knowledge of contingency—even if only instinctively grasped—is the cause of an existential anxiety, the fear of our finitude and mortality. This is one reason man grasps after the supposed stability of power, money, fame, and glory, only to find it slipping through his fingers like sand on a windy day at the beach.

God only "is my rock and my salvation, my fortress," wrote the Psalmist, "I shall not be shaken" (Psa. 62:6). God is a mighty rock, a refuge, in a world of contingency and change. He alone provides lasting peace and security. This is why St. Augustine, after years of pursuing fame and meaning apart from God, finally confessed that "our hearts are restless until they rest in you" (*Confessions*, Bk. 1.1).

†

The Argument from Intelligibility

In 1968, a young theology professor teaching at Tübingen, in southern Germany, wrote a modestly-titled book, *Introduction to Christianity* (Ignatius Press, 2004, 2nd edition). However modest the title, Joseph Ratzinger's book is a profound and often startling meditation on the meaning of the Apostles' Creed. In the chapter titled, "Faith in God Today," Ratzinger outlines an argument for God's existence based on intelligibility that is very relevant in an age when science and religion are often pitted against one another. Ratzinger begins by noting that the statement, "I believe in God," is based on the presupposition that truth can actually be known, considered, and stated.

"Christian faith in God means first the decision in favor of the primacy of the logos as against mere matter," he wrote. "In other words, faith means deciding for the view that thought and meaning do not just form a chance by-product of being; that, on the contrary, all being is a product of thought and, indeed, in its innermost structure is itself thought" (pp. 151, 152). In other words, finite being as we experience it is marked by intelligibility, by a formal structure that makes it capable of being understood by the seeking, thinking mind. This recognition of the intelligible, knowable nature of things leads logically to the belief in creation. It is also the basis for scientific research and thought, for scientists rely—implicitly or otherwise—on the belief that the material realm is intelligible and open to logical study, systematic observation, and ordered experimentation.

Ratzinger quotes Albert Einstein, who said that in the laws of nature "an intelligence so superior is revealed that in comparison all the significance of human thinking and human arrangements is a completely worthless reflection" (p. 153). But he also notes that Einstein was dismissive of belief in a personal God, which the great theoretical physicist dismissed as "anthropomorphic." This reveals, Ratzinger notes, the difficulty many have in believing that the "God of the philosophers" is also the "God of faith," one and the same. But Ratzinger insists that Einstein's view is too limited, too mathematically focused, and misses the fact that "we also find equally present in the world unparalleled and unexplained wonders of beauty, or, to be more accurate, there are events that appear to the apprehending mind of man in the form of beauty, so that he is bound to say that the mathematician responsible for these events has displayed an unparalleled degree of creative imagination" (p. 155).

Thus, Ratzinger argues that universal objective intelligibility leads to the conclusion of the existence of a great Intelligence, which has thought the world into being. The Prologue to the Gospel of John says "In the beginning was the Word, and the Word was with God and the Word was God." It then states that everything that came into being did so through this creative Word. Ratzinger's argument is built upon this scriptural, theological basis. And in his 2011 Easter Vigil Homily, Pope Benedict XVI again made similar observations, stating:

> The central message of the creation account can be defined more precisely still. In the opening words of his Gospel, Saint John sums up the essential meaning of that account in this single statement: "In the beginning was the Word." In effect, the creation account that we listened to earlier is characterized by the regularly recurring phrase: "And God said …" The world is a product of the Word, of the Logos, as Saint John expresses it, using a key term from the Greek language. "Logos" means "reason," "sense," "word." It is not reason pure and simple, but creative Reason, that speaks and communicates itself. It is Reason that both is and creates sense. The creation account tells us, then, that the world is a product of creative Reason. Hence it tells us that, far from there being an absence of reason and freedom at the origin of all things, the source of everything is creative Reason, love, and freedom. Here we are faced with the ultimate alternative that is at stake in the dispute between faith and unbelief: are irrationality, lack of freedom and pure chance the origin of everything, or are reason, freedom and love at the origin of being? Does the primacy belong to unreason or to reason? This is what everything hinges upon in the final analysis. As believers we answer, with the creation account and with Saint John, that in the beginning is reason. (April 23, 2011)

The believer insists, then, that creation declares that there is an intelligible reason for all that is, and that this reason is both outside of creation and also intimately and personally concerned with creation.

Naming God

The opening chapters of Genesis reveal a fundamental spiritual dynamic: sinful man desires to either grasp at God or to flee from him. It reveals that neither approach works. It also reveals that God, while transcendent and completely other, is intensely immanent; that is, he is present to us and our situation far beyond what we can ever imagine. He is both beyond us and intimately present to us.

The tree of the knowledge of good and evil represented the truth that God is the very ground of morality. Adam and Eve, in taking fruit from the tree and eating of it, sought to grasp and make their own what belongs only to God. They attempted vainly to manipulate and control God, to somehow possess him. This ancient temptation is constantly with us, deeply imbedded in the fallen nature of man.

God's complete otherness and man's inability to grasp and control him is designated in the Catholic tradition by a number of descriptives. God is eternal, infinite, unbounded, omniscient, transcendent, and Other. "The LORD is high above all nations, and his glory above the heavens!" wrote the Psalmist, "Who is like the LORD our God, who is seated on high, who looks far down upon the heavens and the earth?" (Psa 113:4-6). The prophet Isaiah, in one of his most beautiful passages, wrote, "To whom then will you compare me, that I should be like him? says the Holy One. ... Have you not known? Have you not heard? The LORD is the everlasting God, the Creator of the ends of the earth. He does not faint or grow weary, his understanding is unsearchable" (Isa. 40:25, 28).

God is infinite, which means he cannot be measured; he is eternal, meaning he isn't bound by time; he is immutable, and so he isn't like any finite thing or creature of this world. "We call God the One, the Good, the Mind, the absolute Being, the Father, God, the Creator and Lord," wrote St. Clement of Alexandria, "We are not giving him names, but because we have no alternative, we use these words as points of reference so as not to go astray. None of these words by itself expresses God fully, but taken together they are all indicative of the power of the Almighty" (*Stromateis*, 5.12). God is, in other words, beyond our grasp, for being itself is not in or of the realm of beings.

That is one side of things, and it is a very important side. But we must not focus exclusively on God's transcendence, or we may fall into a trap. We may be tempted to think, as did Adam and Eve, that we can somehow hide from God; we can be lulled into thinking that we are so small and meaningless compared to God that he won't miss us, or know who we are, or care about what we do. But Adam and Eve, upon fleeing from God in their shame and guilt, were immediately found out (Gen. 3:6-10). God is both radically transcendent and radically immanent, or present everywhere; he not only upholds all of creation, but knows every speck within it. This immanence, the *Catechism* explains, is deeply intimate in nature:

> By calling God "Father", the language of faith indicates two main things: that God
> is the first origin of everything and transcendent authority; and that he is at the

same time goodness and loving care for all his children. God's parental tenderness can also be expressed by the image of motherhood, which emphasizes God's immanence, the intimacy between Creator and creature. (par. 239; see also Psa. 139)

King David, a man after God's own heart, reflected deeply on this radical and intimate presence. "Thou knowest when I sit down and when I rise up; thou discernest my thoughts from afar. Thou searchest out my path and my lying down, and art acquainted with all my ways" (Psa. 139:2-3). This captures a bit of God's omnipotence, which is God's unconditioned power, which is universal, loving, merciful, and mysterious (CCC, 268-271). David's Psalm also describes, as much as possible, God's omnipresence—his being inescapably present to all of reality because he stands under it. God stands under and upholds all of reality and is completely and always present to it. "O Heavenly King, Comforter, Spirit of Truth!" declares a great Byzantine hymn, "You are everywhere present and fill all things."

Sistine Chapel:

The Sistine Chapel is the principal chapel of the Vatican Palace, originally built for Pope Sixtus IV in the late fifteenth century. Well-known for being used by the cardinals for the election of new popes, it is probably most famous for the incredible frescoes rendered on the walls and ceiling by Michelangelo. He was commissioned by Pope Julius II (1503-1513) to paint the ceiling and was later commissioned by Pope Paul III (1534-1549) to paint the wall behind the altar.

The finished frescoes are extraordinary, especially considering the physical challenges faced by Michelangelo. In order to paint on the chapel's ceiling, he had to design his own scaffolding. This structure was supported by brackets in the walls, since a scaffold resting on the floor would have been a logistical nightmare and would have kept the chapel from being used. Michelangelo did not paint lying down, as is commonly believed, but the task was still formidable (he wrote a humorous poem about the work, describing the chapel as "this den").

Michelangelo's finished masterpiece depicts over 300 different figures and numerous biblical events, notably Creation, the Fall, the promise of salvation through the prophets, and the genealogy of Christ. Key figures and events include God creating Adam, Adam and Eve, Noah, Abraham, King David, the destruction of Baal, numerous prophets, and Elijah being taken up to heaven, as well as the ancestors of Jesus Christ. The *Last Judgment* is a particularly powerful work, a chilling depiction of "writhing pyramids of bodies ascending the wall into Heaven or tumbling down it to Hell," remarked historian Paul Johnson in *Art: A New History* (HarperCollins, 2003). "The impact is frightening, as it should be, and therefore edifying. The colour is gruesome, as is also right" (p. 280).

QUESTIONS FOR UNDERSTANDING — Part 1:

1. Why do you think God spoke to Moses from a burning bush? In what two ways did God identify himself to Moses? (Ex. 3:1-14)

2. God said to Moses, "I Am Who I Am." What does the name suggest or indicate about God? (CCC 206, 207, 213)

3. Explain the difference between God as *a being* and God as *being itself*. (CCC 213)

4. What are the five ways Aquinas stated that the existence of God can be demonstrated? Which, for you, is the most understandable of the "five ways"? The most difficult? Why? (CCC 31)

QUESTIONS FOR APPLICATION — Part 1:

1. If you had been Moses, standing before the burning bush, how might you have responded?

2. In what ways have you responded to the call of God? What are some things you can do to "listen" to God more closely and be more attentive to his presence?

NOTES

THE INEFFABLE MYSTERY OF GOD
Episode 3, Part 2

OUTLINE *(Tracks 5-8 on DVD)*

I. The Provident Creator

    A. God is "maker of heaven and earth" (cf. Gen. 1:1)

    B. God created *ex nihilo*, from nothing

    C. God sustains all creation (CCC 301)

    D. God is involved and immanent

    E. God and freedom (*Veritatis Spendor*)

II. The Problem of Evil

    A. Why does evil exist? (CCC, 309)

    B. Evil is the deprivation of what ought to be

  C. The example and witness of Job

    D. Georges Seurat: God the Artist with a canvas of all space and time

    E. William James and the limited capacity of minds to understand

    F. The need to consider the Cross of Christ

III. The Trinity

    A. The central mystery of the Christian faith (CCC 261)

    B. A mystery of faith, revealed by God

    C. Revealed through Jesus Christ, at his baptism and through his teachings

    D. God is a family of Love

    E. St. Augustine's analogies (*De trinitate*)

        1. Lover, loved one, love in human experience

        2. Mind, self-knowledge, self-love

IV. The Meaning of It All

    A. The question after Being

    B. Christian answer is love

    C. God is Love

THE INEFFABLE MYSTERY OF GOD: Lesson 3, Part 2

The Provident Creator

"I believe in One God, the Maker of heaven and earth." This statement from the Creed about God the Creator is a foundational belief for Christians. It is absolutely basic to Scripture, as the first verse of the Bible attests: "In the beginning God created the heavens and the earth" (Gen. 1:1). Because God is the sheer act of being itself, whatever exists apart from God must have come entirely from God.

Other ancient religions and philosophies depicted God, or the gods, fashioning the world from pre-existing matter. Or they bring order to the universe by vanquishing a rival. Scripture presents a completely different perspective. Christian theology states that God made everything—the universe and all that it encompasses—*ex nihilo*, that is, from nothing. "To say that the world is created," remarks theologian Michael Schmaus in *Dogma 2: God and Creation* (Sheed & Ward, 1976; 1969), "means that all non-divine reality comes into being without any non-divine preconditions: God is the author of everything other than himself" (p. 85).

The Christian understanding of creation has a number of significant implications. One of these is that since God is Being, he upholds and sustains all of creation and all creatures in being, "enables them to act and brings them to their final end" (CCC 301). Creation is not just an event in the past, but is, in a real sense, an ongoing reality. "Creation has its own goodness and proper perfection," explains the *Catechism*, "but it did not spring forth complete from the hands of the Creator. The universe was created "in a state of journeying" (*in statu viae*) toward an ultimate perfection yet to be attained, to which God has destined it" (CCC 302). This means that things don't really *have* a relationship to God, but *are* a relationship with God.

This view of creation also implies a deep interconnectedness of all things. We can speak of all people as being our ontological siblings, because we have all been created by the same God and are being upheld in our existence by God. We can also use the language of St. Francis and speak of Brother Sun and Sister Moon, recognizing we share this essential quality: we are all *created* and are part of creation.

God, intimately involved in the universe and present to all things, is provident. He is not the deity of deism, who simply wound up the clock of the universe and then retired to some distant corner of creation. On the contrary, God is active; in the Scriptures, God's wisdom reaches mightily from one end of the earth to the other, and orders all things well (Wis. 8:1). "Divine providence," the *Catechism* states, "consists of the dispositions by which God guides all his creatures with wisdom and love to their ultimate end" (CCC 321). So God is working, shaping, guiding, and drawing his universe according to his purposes, like an artist molding clay according to his design. The universe is still unfinished; it is a masterwork in progress.

But if God is providential and so intimately involved in his creation, doesn't this effectively do away with human freedom, making it, at best, a cosmic charade? It is a common question, and it is a good one. A key part of the answer is that we need to have a correct understanding of the word "freedom." Most modern men and women think of freedom as the ability to do as they choose, according to their needs, desires, and self-determining decisions. In many cases, this freedom is based in a relativistic view of moral choices: I decide what is best for me, choosing between two equally valid options. Pope John Paul II notes how often man, "giving himself over to relativism and skepticism (cf. *Jn.* 18:38), … goes off in search of an illusory freedom apart from truth itself" (*Veritatis Splendor*, 1).

But the traditional, or classical, sense of freedom is different. Freedom is not focused on self-determination, but on disciplining our desires in order to achieve a good, which could be the ability to play the piano, or to sacrifice for the good of one's family. The key, John Paul II states, is that "there can be no freedom apart from or in opposition to the truth" (*Veritatis Splendor*, 96). This freedom is in no way opposed to God's active providence, for all goods flow from and are oriented toward God, the supreme good, who desires to shape and guide our wills.

✝

The Problem of Evil

Yet many people who admit the logic and truthfulness of these various arguments and statements will balk when it comes to the problem of evil. If God exists, why is there so much evil in the world? If God is good, holy, omnipotent, and omniscient, it seems there should be no evil. Yet there is. And so some conclude there is no such God. For example, the influential nineteenth-century British philosopher John Stuart Mill arrived at that conclusion in his *Three Essays on Religion* (1874), stating, "Not even on the most distorted and contracted theory of good, which ever was framed by religious or philosophical fanaticism, can the government of Nature be made to resemble the work of a being at once good and omnipotent" (John Stuart Mill, *Three Essays on Religion* [New York: Henry Holt and Company, 1874], 38).

Aquinas, as is so often the case, summarized these objections very well: If one of two contraries be infinite, the other would be destroyed. But God is called the infinite good. Therefore, if God exists, there would be no evil. But evil exists; therefore, there is no God. It is a powerful argument, and its power is felt all the more when we reflect on evils and atrocities such as the Holocaust, the purges of Stalin, the forced abortions in China, and the freely chosen abortions all over the world. How can human beings so deliberately, coldly, and continually kill one another? Murder women and children? Destroy the unborn?

There is no way around it: this is the hardest, most vexing and puzzling theological question of all. Any answer will be inadequate, but we can still move toward an answer. To the question, "Why does evil exist?", the *Catechism* responds:

*To this question, as pressing as it is unavoidable and as painful as it is mysterious, no quick answer will suffice. Only Christian faith as a whole constitutes the answer to this question: the goodness of creation, the drama of sin and the patient love of God who comes to meet man by his covenants, the redemptive Incarnation of his Son, his gift of the Spirit, his gathering of the Church, the power of the sacraments and his call to a blessed life to which free creatures are invited to consent in advance, but from which, by a terrible mystery, they can also turn away in advance. **There is not a single aspect of the Christian message that is not in part an answer to the question of evil.** (par. 309; emphasis in original)*

The first point to be made is that evil is not the existence of something, but the deprivation, or lack, of what ought to be. The good is being, Jacques Maritain explained in his essay, "The Innocence of God" (*A Maritain Reader* [Image, 1966], 128), while evil, "on the contrary, of itself or insofar as evil, is absence of being, *privation* of being or of good. It is a nothingness which corrodes being. ... [E]vil is only a vacuum or a lack of being, a nothingness and a privation." It is the absence or destruction of the good, like a cavity in a tooth, or cancer attacking the lungs, or a despot stealing from the poor. Evil is therefore not a positive force opposing God, so we should never think of God creating evil.

But if God does not create evil, why does he *allow* it? One answer, with deep roots in the tradition—and articulated by Augustine, Aquinas, and their followers—is that God allows evil so as to bring about a greater good (CCC 311-312). Most of us have experienced this in some way, when an illness, failure, or calamity has eventually brought about, in a unexpected way, something good. To borrow a cliché: "No pain, no gain."

Emotional and spiritual growth often comes by coping with trials, difficulties, and the results of evil.

However, does this really explain evil so profound and horrible that it seems apparent no good could ever come of it? The story of Job gives great insight into this mystery. Job was "was blameless and upright, one who feared God, and turned away from evil" (Job 1:1), but he lost everything without warning: his money, his livelihood, his family, and his health.

His wife urged him to curse God, but he refused (Job 2:9-10). His three friends came and "sat with him on the ground seven days and seven nights, and no one spoke a word to him, for they saw that his suffering was very great" (Job 2:13). Finally, they elucidate, in very poetic and powerful ways, their conclusion: Job must be suffering because he has sinned, for God rewards the holy and chastises the sinner. Job protests, for he knows he is righteous. Eventually, he sends his friends away and he enters into a direct conversation with God, and he demands an explanation for what has happened to him. He articulates the pain and anger and bewilderment that so many have felt.

Then, in chapter 38, God begins his magnificent response:

> THEN THE LORD ANSWERED JOB OUT OF THE WHIRLWIND: "WHO IS THIS THAT DARKENS COUNSEL BY WORDS WITHOUT KNOWLEDGE? GIRD UP YOUR LOINS LIKE A MAN, I WILL QUESTION YOU, AND YOU SHALL DECLARE TO ME. WHERE WERE YOU WHEN I LAID THE FOUNDATION OF THE EARTH? TELL ME, IF YOU HAVE UNDERSTANDING. WHO DETERMINED ITS MEASUREMENTS-- SURELY YOU KNOW! OR WHO STRETCHED THE LINE UPON IT?" (JOB 38:1-5)

God takes Job on a breathtaking tour of creation and the cosmos, taking him deep into the unfathomable mystery of reality, with all of its puzzles, pains, and seeming contradictions. There are no easy answers, no Hallmark slogans, no sweet platitudes. "Job offers us no clear solution," writes Peter Kreeft, "no philosophical formula, no bright little concept, but an infinite mystery. God Himself, rather than any idea God teaches, is Job's answer. He is the God Rabbi Abraham Heschel describes as 'not an uncle, but an earthquake.'" (*You Can Understand the Bible* [Ignatius Press, 2005], 79).

The implication in the book of Job is that God is an artist who uses the entirety of space and time as his canvas, composing a work of art of astounding complexity. Within it, the myriad shades of colors, from dark to light, interact to produce incredible patterns that we, as mere mortals with limited vision, cannot see. It is as though we are standing with our noses pressed against the French impressionist George Seurat's "pointillist" masterpiece, *A Sunday Afternoon on the Island of La Grande Jatte* (1884-86), seeing only a bunch of precise dots of meticulously applied paint. But if we move back from the large painting, we would begin to see forms and shapes, then figures, and then the entire composition. But we are much like the animals mentioned by the American philosopher Williams James (1842-1910) in his book, *A Pluralistic Universe* (1909), who may walk among the bookcases in our master's library, but fail to comprehend what words and ideas are contained within the volumes there: "We may be in the universe as dogs and cats are in our libraries, seeing the books and hearing the conversation, but having no inkling of the meaning of it all." Man is tempted to think highly of what he knows, but he is better served to ponder how little he actually comprehends about the mystery of creation, life, and existence. But he can also take solace in the words of St. Thomas Aquinas: "A scrap of knowledge about sublime things is worth more than any amount about trivialities" (*Summa Theologiae*, I, 1, 5).

Finally, in contemplating the problem of evil, we must squarely consider the greatest act of evil ever committed: the crucifixion of the righteous, blameless Son of God. The Cross, considered in all of its bloody horror and injustice, reveals the heart of God, who desires to save man from sin, suffering, and death. "If suffering is present in the history of humanity," responded John Paul II in *Crossing the Threshold of Hope* (Albert A. Knopf, 1995), "one understands why His omnipotence was manifested in the omnipotence of humiliation on the Cross. The scandal of the Cross remains the key to the interpretation of the great mystery of suffering, which is so much a part of the history of mankind" (p. 63).

†

The Trinity: The Central Mystery of the Christian Faith

God is one, holy, creator, omnipotent, and omniscient: all of this is held and affirmed by observant Jews and Muslims. So, what is distinctive about the Christian doctrine of God?

The answer is found in making the Sign of the Cross: belief that the one God is three Persons—Father, Son, and Holy Spirit. God, in his unity, is communion, a perfect and eternal exchange of love. The mystery of the Trinity is, the *Catechism* emphasizes, "the central mystery of the Christian faith and of Christian life. God alone can make it known to us by revealing himself as Father, Son and Holy Spirit" (par. 261).

The *Catechism* further notes that this great mystery is the most fundamental, essential teaching in the "hierarchy of the truths of faith" (par. 234) and that it is a mystery of faith "in the strict sense"— it cannot be known unless it has been revealed by God (par. 237). In *Theology and Sanity* (Ignatius Press, 1993; orig. 1946), Frank Sheed discussed the limitations of man's imagination and intellect in relation to "what we call Mysteries in religion" (p 37). A religious or theological Mystery is not a puzzle or sheer darkness, he pointed out, nor is it "something that we can know nothing about: it is only something that the mind cannot *wholly* know" (p 37-38). He used the analogy of an art gallery into which the visitor walks deeper and deeper—never reaching the end but finding the visit to be completely satisfying. "A Mystery, in short, is an invitation to the mind" (p 38).

The well of Truth has no bottom and we can drink from it endlessly, our minds never going away thirsty. A Mystery is revealed by God—it cannot be known by human reason, nor fully explained by logic or argument. "Thus in the Mystery of the Blessed Trinity, we cannot see how God can be Three if He is infinitely One" (p 38). The human mind balks at such a statement, seeing an apparent contradiction. Or, by faith, man can simply accept the Mystery of the Trinity. But while this might make for a quiet life, Sheed dryly observed, it does not make "for any growth in the knowledge of God" (p 39).

How did God specifically reveal this mystery? Through Jesus Christ, whose unique life, teachings, and actions set him apart from the great figures of the Old Testament such as Abraham, Moses, or Isaiah. While those men talked with God, Jesus spoke and acted in the very person of God. He spoke of God, but also spoke of his own divinity. The Old Testament, read in light of the revelation of the Trinity, contains hints and suggestions of this essential dogma (see CCC 237). But the Triune nature of Yahweh, the great "I Am," was revealed with the Incarnation, first at Jesus' baptism in the Jordan River, and then in his teachings. Jesus spoke of the intimate communion between the Father, Son, and Holy Spirit. "All that the Father has is mine," Jesus told the Apostles, "therefore I said that he"—that is, the Holy Spirit—"will take what is mine and declare it to you" (Jn. 16:15). At the conclusion of St. Matthew's Gospel, Jesus commissions the apostles, saying, "Go therefore and make disciples of all nations, baptizing them in the name of the Father and of the Son and of the Holy Spirit" (Matt. 28:19). There is one "name," but three Persons. The sending of the Holy Spirit after the glorification of the Son, "reveals in its fullness the mystery of the Holy Trinity" (CCC 244; see Jn. 7:39; Acts 2:1-4).

St. Augustine spent nearly twenty years writing *De trinitate* (*On The Trinity*). One of his key points of reflection was Genesis 1:26: "Let us make man to our image and likeness." He saw this as a suggestion of a certain relationship and plurality within the Godhead. He wrote, "'Let us make' and 'our' are in the plural, and must be understood in terms of relationships. For he did not mean that gods should do the making, or do it to the image and likeness of gods, but that the Father and the Son and the Holy Spirit should do it; do it therefore to the image of Father and Son and Holy Spirit, so that man might subsist as the image of God; and God is the three."
(*De trinitate*, VII.12) His consideration of this verse eventually led to his famous analogy of "I myself, what I love, and love itself" (IX.2), a Trinitarian image of lover, loved one, and love found within the human experience.

He also used the analogy of the human mind: *Mens, Notitia sui, Amor sui* (Mind, Self-Knowledge, Self-Love). The mind is not divided into three minds, but the one mind subsists in three modalities or relations. So the Father is the *Mens* of God, the primordial ground of the divine mind. The Son is the *Notitia Sui* of God, the self-possession of the Father, and the Spirit is the *Amor Sui* of God, the love breathed out between the Father and the Son. Augustine summed up the heart of the Church's belief in the mystery of the Father, Son, and Holy Spirit by simply stating, "If you see charity, you see the Trinity" (Quoted in *Deus Caritas Est*, sec. 19; accessed at *http://w2.vatican.va/content/benedict-xvi/en/encyclicals/documents/hf_ben-xvi_enc_20051225_deus-caritas-est.html*). God is One *and* three Persons; He offers His divine life and love to those who believe in Him (CCC 257).

The Trinity is not just a mystery to us, but also *for* us.

QUESTIONS FOR UNDERSTANDING — Part 2:

1.   What does it mean to call God "Father"? (Matt. 28:19; CCC 238-239)

2.   If God is provident and all-knowing, why is there suffering and evil? (CCC 309-314)

3. How has the Trinity been revealed to us? (CCC 261, 237, 244, Mt. 3:16-17, Mt. 28:19)

QUESTIONS FOR APPLICATION — Part 2:

1. What about God do you wish to understand or contemplate more deeply?

2. Have you ever struggled with your belief in God in the midst of suffering or facing evil? How did you address your doubts and questions? Any new insight from this lesson?

3. What obstacles—intellectual, emotional, spiritual—do you face in seeking to grow in your love for God and your knowledge of him? What can you do to address those obstacles?

TERMS & NAMES

Anselm, Saint (c. 1033-1109). Archbishop of Canterbury and a Doctor of the Church. A great theologian and a great philosopher, Anselm is especially known for his defense of the existence and being of God on rational, philosophical grounds and for his writings on the atonement of Christ.

Aquinas, Saint Thomas (c. 1225-1274). Dominican philosopher and theologian, and Doctor of the Church. He is widely considered, with St. Augustine, to be the greatest theologian in the West. Aquinas drew deeply on the thought of Aristotle and Augustine, addressed the objections of pagans and Muslims, and was a profound commentator on Scripture. His *Summa Theologiae* is arguably the greatest work of theology ever composed.

Book of Job. One of the Wisdom Books of the Old Testament. It describes an innocent man's experience of inexplicable suffering and delves into the question of why there is unmerited suffering if God is just.

Deism: The disenchanted theology that asserts God is akin to an impersonal clockmaker who solely designed the cosmos without having any personal interaction with it. This belief is contrary to the Biblical faith in the Personal God who is the providential creator and sustainer of the cosmos.

Eckhart, Meister (c. 1260-c. 1328). A German Dominican theologian, philosopher, and mystic whose writings have had a profound impact on Christian mysticism.

Francis of Assisi, Saint (c. 1181-1226). An Italian friar, preacher, and founder of the Franciscan Order. He lived a life of radical poverty and preached the coinherence of all things in Christ. His life has had a profound affect on Christian living.

Gilson, Étienne (1884-1978). A highly regarded French Thomistic philosopher and historian of philosophy who was one of the leading Thomists of the twentieth century. He taught at the University of Paris and at Harvard, and set up the Pontifical Institute of Medieval Studies in Toronto, where he taught until his retirement.

Manichaeism: A Gnostic religion founded by the Persian Mani in the third century A.D. Its central teaching is that reality is reducible to two opposing principles, spirit and matter. Viewing matter with disdain, the goal of the spiritual life is to liberate the soul from its embodied existence.

Maritain, Jacques (1882-1973). A very prolific and influential French philosopher. Originally an atheist, he converted and soon began studying the work of St. Thomas Aquinas. His books addressed a wide range of topics, including metaphysics, education, art, politics, and theology.

Mill, John Stuart (1806-1873). British philosopher, economist, moral and political theorist who is famous for his contributions to Utilitarianism, the moral philosophy that has "the greatest happiness for the greatest number" as its guiding principle. His influence is primarily found in modern liberal democracies.

Patriarch: The head of a tribe, family, or clan in biblical history (e.g. Abraham, Isaac, Jacob). While being the genealogical fathers of Israel, they are also Israel's spiritual fathers.

Plato (429-347 B.C.). He is one of the most influential thinkers in the history of Western thought. A disciple of Socrates, he wrote many philosophical dialogues featuring Socrates conversing with friends about the good life and the nature of reality. Alfred North Whitehead, a twentieth-century English philosopher/mathematician, said, "the safest general characterization of the European philosophical tradition is that it consists of a series of footnotes to Plato."

Pointillism: a technique in painting in which small, distinct dots of color are applied to a given surface to form images. Georges Seurat developed this style, branching off of impressionism.

Pseudo-Dionysius the Areopagite. A Christian theologian of the late fifth to sixth centuries whose mystical writings were influenced by Neoplatonism. His most famous works are *On the Divine Names, Mystical Theology*.

Ratzinger, Joseph /Benedict XVI (1927-). A German theologian who reigned as pope from 2005-2013. As an academic and the former Prefect of the Congregation for the Doctrine of Faith, Benedict XVI has written eloquently on many doctrinal issues. He stresses that Christianity is fundamentally a personal encounter with Jesus Christ in the Church, and he warns of the dangers of today's increasing secularism and relativism.

Secularism: While it has many forms, secularism is the belief that religion (or some notion of ultimate reality) should be relegated to a "private" sphere. Hence, religion should be absent from the public sphere. It is an ethos that asks for tolerance and/or indifference to faith.

Seurat, Georges (1859-1891). A French post-impressionist painter who developed the artistic technique Pointillism. His most famous work is A Sunday Afternoon on the Island of La Grande Jatte (1884-1886), which is exhibited today at the Art Institute of Chicago.

Shema: The Jewish affirmation and proclamation of faith in one God. The first line of the Shema is, "Hear, O Israel, the Lord is our God, the Lord is One" (see Deut. 6:4).

Lesson 4

OUR TAINTED NATURE'S SOLITARY BOAST
Mary, the Mother of God

"Mary's utter willingness to magnify the Lord made of her a matrix of life.
The spring itself, in all its wild fecundity, is but a hint of the vitality
that she unleashes."

- Bishop Robert Barron

La Virgen Blanca. Fourteenth Century. Cathedral of Saint Mary of Toledo. Spain.

MARY, THE MOTHER OF GOD
Episode 4, Part 1

OUTLINE *(Tracks 1-4 on DVD)*

I. The Annunciation

    A. The angel Gabriel: "Hail, O favored one, the Lord is with you!" (Lk. 1:28)

    B. Mary called to be the new Ark of the Covenant

    C. Mary's response is her *fiat*, her humble and holy "Yes" (Lk. 1:38)

    D. Mary is the New Eve; she was conceived without sin, filled with divine life

    E. The Ave reverses Eva: the attitude of *fiat* ("let it be")

II. Mary and Zion

    A. The Bridge between Old & New Covenant

    B. Chartres Cathedral: Body of Mary

    C. Mary is a daughter of Israel, a true Jew

    D. Mary personifies Israel, the bridal people of God, faithful to the covenant

    E. Mary responded to God's call, promptly, quickly, and obediently

    F. The model disciple

III. The Mother of God

    A. The Council of Ephesus (A.D. 431)

        1. Convened to combat Nestorius, the Patriarch of Constantinople

        2. *Christotokos* (Christ-bearer) vs. *Theotokos* (God-bearer)

        3. Twelve anathemas proposed by St. Cyril of Alexandria

    B. Jesus Christ is one Person with two natures, human and divine

    C. Mary is not the mother of a human nature, but a person: Jesus Christ

    D. Calling Mary the Mother of God defends the Incarnation

MARY, THE MOTHER OF GOD: Lesson 4, Part 1

The Annunciation

"Mary's role in the Church is inseparable from her union with Christ and flows directly from it."
– *Catechism of the Catholic Church*, par. 964

"Hail, from us, Mary, Mother of God, majestic common-treasure of the whole world, the lamp unquenchable, the crown of virginity, the staff of orthodoxy, the indissoluble temple, the dwelling of the Illimitable, Mother and Virgin, through whom He in the holy Gospels is called the Blessed Who cometh in the name of the Lord."
— St. Cyril of Alexandria (*Homilies*, 4)

Two thousand years ago, Nazareth was a modest, even obscure, little town located in central Galilee. Its population was probably just a few hundred people. But it was there, in a simple hovel, that the angel Gabriel appeared to a teenage Jewish girl:

> IN THE SIXTH MONTH THE ANGEL GABRIEL WAS SENT FROM GOD TO A CITY OF GALILEE NAMED NAZARETH, TO A VIRGIN BETROTHED TO A MAN WHOSE NAME WAS JOSEPH, OF THE HOUSE OF DAVID; AND THE VIRGIN'S NAME WAS MARY. AND HE CAME TO HER AND SAID, "HAIL, FULL OF GRACE, THE LORD IS WITH YOU!" (LK. 1:26-28)

Mary, who was perhaps fourteen or fifteen years old, was understandably taken aback. St. Luke recounts that she "considered in her mind what sort of greeting this might be." It was undoubtedly a puzzling way to address the young girl, for it identified her as unique and set apart. But why? And for what purpose?

> AND THE ANGEL SAID TO HER, "DO NOT BE AFRAID, MARY, FOR YOU HAVE FOUND FAVOR WITH GOD. AND BEHOLD, YOU WILL CONCEIVE IN YOUR WOMB AND BEAR A SON, AND YOU SHALL CALL HIS NAME JESUS. HE WILL BE GREAT, AND WILL BE CALLED THE SON OF THE MOST HIGH; AND THE LORD GOD WILL GIVE TO HIM THE THRONE OF HIS FATHER DAVID, AND HE WILL REIGN OVER THE HOUSE OF JACOB FOR EVER; AND OF HIS KINGDOM THERE WILL BE NO END." (LK. 1:31-33)

This was beyond puzzling—it was unthinkable. Yet Mary's response was direct and to the point: "How shall this be, since I have no husband?" God's stunning and silent entrance into human history, the angel told her, would come about by her cooperation with the Holy Spirit. "The Holy Spirit will come upon you," he said, "and the power of the Most High will overshadow you; therefore the child to be born will be called holy, the Son of God" (Lk. 1:35). Like the Ark of the Covenant that contained the Law, Mary would be the new Ark of the Covenant, "the place where the glory of the Lord dwells" (CCC 2676).

Mary, in response to this heavenly news, offered her *fiat*—her humble and holy "Yes!"—saying, "Behold, I am the handmaid of the Lord; let it be to me according to your word" (Lk. 1:38). Already, in that moment, Mary was cooperating and collaborating with the work of her Son. In this way she became the New Eve, a fact contemplated by St. Irenaeus, writing in the late second century:

> *For just as the former [Eve] was led astray by the word of an angel, so that she fled from God when she had transgressed His word; so did the latter [Mary], by an angelic communication, receive the glad tidings that she should sustain God, being obedient to His word. And if the former did disobey God, yet the latter was persuaded to be obedient to God, in order that the Virgin Mary might become the patroness of the virgin Eve. And thus, as the human race fell into bondage to death by means of a virgin, so is it rescued by a virgin; virginal disobedience having been balanced in the opposite scale by virginal obedience.* (Against Heresies, Bk. 5, 19.1)

Just as God had invited the first Eve to freely trust him, he also invited Mary to freely place herself into his all-powerful and gracious hands. Unlike the gods of the Greeks, Romans, and other ancient pagans, the God of Israel was not violent or forceful. He extended an invitation that respected Mary's dignity and free will.

God desires man to flourish, to become who he is meant to be by sharing in the divine life. Yet this requires humility and a receptive spirit on the part of man. Eve, along with Adam, succumbed to the temptation to grasp after godliness—or, god-likeness—without God's blessing or empowering. Mary, courted by God, is filled with godliness—with God himself! "Eve sought the fruit," wrote St. Thomas Aquinas, "but did not find there what she wished for. In her fruit the blessed Virgin found all that Eve wanted" (*Exposition on the Hail Mary*).

God's command not to eat of the fruit of the tree of the knowledge of good and evil (Gen. 2:8-9, 15-17) has sometimes been misunderstood or misrepresented as an indication of divine jealousy or pettiness. But those notions are in keeping with the words of the serpent, not with the nature of God. "You will not die," the serpent told Eve, "For God knows that when you eat of it your eyes will be opened, and you will be like God, knowing good and evil" (Gen. 3:4-5). God's prohibition came from his love for the man and the woman, and his desire for them to fall in love with him. True love cannot be forced or coerced; it grows in the soil of freedom, honesty, and trust. It involves surrendering oneself to the other. Such love consists in allowing God to fulfill and complete us, not by overwhelming us or annihilating our personalities, but by infusing us with his own divine life.

Mary was filled with God's divine life. "The Holy Spirit *prepared* Mary by his grace," the *Catechism* states. "It was fitting that the mother of him in whom 'the whole fullness of deity dwells bodily' (Col 2:9) should herself be 'full of grace.' She was, by sheer grace, conceived without sin as the most humble of creatures, the most capable of welcoming the inexpressible gift of the Almighty" (par. 722). Her holy meekness and unwavering obedience reversed the disobedience of Eve. "And thus also it was that the knot of Eve's disobedience was loosed by the obedience of Mary", wrote St. Irenaeus, "For what the virgin Eve had bound fast through unbelief, this did the virgin Mary set free through faith" (*Against Heresies*, Bk. 3, 22.4).

To be blessed is to have found favor with God, to be filled with the grace—the supernatural life—of God. It is to possess the kingdom by belonging to the King (cf. Mt. 5:3, 10). As mother of the King of kings, Mary bore the Kingdom within her. As mother of the Messiah, she is also the mother of the Church. Pope John Paul II, in *Redemptoris Mater* (1987), wrote that "in her new motherhood in the Spirit, Mary embraces each and every one in the Church, and embraces each and every one through the Church" (sec. 4)

†

Mary and Zion

The Cathedral of Chartres, or *Cathédrale Notre-Dame de Chartres,* is one of the most majestic and beautiful covered spaces in the world. This magnificent church is, like most of the Gothic cathedrals in France, dedicated to the Virgin Mary. Bishop Barron, in *Heaven in Stone and Glass: Experiencing the Spirituality of the Great Cathedrals* (Crossroad, 2000), writes:

> *Suffice it to say, the great cavernous cathedrals of the Middle Ages were seen, in an almost literal sense, as the body of Mary, places of safety and birth. I can testify that, standing in the midst of Chartres, Amiens, or Notre-Dame de Paris, one feels an overwhelming sense of security, a peacefulness and serenity of spirit. The dark, all-enveloping space is evocative of the womb in which Christ himself was nurtured and in which all members of the Church come to birth.* (p. 15)

The idea of Mary as the womb in which the Christ-child came to birth takes us more deeply into the mystery of Mary. And this mystery cannot, and must not, be separated from the fact that she is a daughter of Israel, a true Jew, belonging to the holy people whom God prepared to receive his Son.

She is the daughter of Abraham, the great man of faith who left his homeland and sought out a new land—a holy land—promised by God (see Gen. 12:1-9). Like the great prophets Isaiah, Jeremiah, and Ezekiel, Mary longed for the coming of the Messiah and the Kingdom of God. (This can be seen, for example, at the wedding feast at Cana when she notices that the wedding party has run out of wine and she prompts Jesus to act. Mary is not simply addressing the immediate need of an embarrassed family; symbolically speaking, she addresses what the great prophets of Israel had been addressing for centuries: the wine of the divine life has run out.) She is the new Ark of the Covenant, for she becomes the bearer of the Divine Word—both physically and spiritually. Like the author of the Psalms and the books of Wisdom and Proverbs, she contemplates the mysteries of God and his ways, for she "kept all these things, pondering them in her heart" (Lk. 2:19).

Joseph Cardinal Ratzinger, in *Daughter Zion* (Ignatius Press, 1983), his study of Mary, observed that "the image of Mary in the New Testament is woven entirely of Old Testament threads." The major threads include that of the New Eve, the perfect woman who undoes the damage of mankind's first mother. Another is the portrait of Mary in "the likeness of the great mothers of the Old Testament: Sarah and especially Hannah, the mother of Samuel." Ratzinger further stated that "into that portrait is woven the whole theology of daughter Zion, in which, above all, the prophets announced the mystery of election and covenant, the mystery of God's love for Israel" (p. 12).

Mary personifies Israel, the bridal people of God, at its best: faithful to the covenant, attentive to the word of God, desiring to respond in love to God's will. In another essay on Mary, Ratzinger wrote, "Her life is such that she is a place for God. Her life sinks her into the common measure of sacred history, so that what appears in her is, not the narrow and constricted ego of an isolated individual, but the whole, true Israel" (*Mary: The Church at the Source* [Ignatius Press, 2005], by Hans Urs von Balthasar and Joseph Cardinal Ratzinger, p. 66). Whereas Israel was often slow to respond to God's call, Mary acted promptly, quickly, and obediently: "In those days Mary arose and went with haste into the hill country, to a city of Judah…" (Lk. 1:39).

†

The Mother of God

According to some traditions and legends, the city of Ephesus, located on the west coast of Asia Minor (present-day Turkey), was the home of the Blessed Virgin Mary in the final years of her earthly life. She was, according to these accounts, taken there by the Apostle John, to whom she had been entrusted by Christ while he was on the Cross (Jn. 19:26-27).

A few centuries later, in 431, the Council of Ephesus was held in the Church of Mary in Ephesus. The many theological issues addressed at that ecumenical council were complex, but came down to a precise and proper articulation of the nature and person of Jesus Christ. At a key moment in his public ministry, Jesus had asked his disciples, "Who do people say the Son of Man is?" (Matt. 16:13). That question was constantly on the mind of the early Christians, who grappled long and hard with the many implications of their belief that Jesus was both God and man, divine and human, sent from above and born of the virgin Mary.

The Councils of Nicaea (325) and Constantinople (381) had made important progress in defining, defending, and clarifying pressing issues and questions related to the nature, will, and person of Christ. However, in the 420's, the patriarch of Constantinople, named Nestorius, began to teach that the two natures of Christ are bound by a moral union only, not by a hypostatic union. This logically led to belief that the Son was somehow two persons, which Nestorius further emphasized by calling Mary *Christotokos* (Christ-bearer) instead of *Theotokos* (God-bearer). That implied Christ has two distinct identities: Jesus the man and Jesus the divine Word.

St. Cyril, the bishop of Alexandria, thought this teaching of Nestorius was heretical, and he called for an ecumenical council to resolve the matter. Among the twelve anathemas proposed by Cyril and accepted by the Council of Ephesus were the following:

> 1. IF ANYONE DOES NOT CONFESS THAT EMMANUEL IS GOD IN TRUTH, AND THEREFORE THAT THE HOLY VIRGIN IS THE MOTHER OF GOD (FOR SHE

BORE IN A FLESHLY WAY THE WORD OF GOD BECOME FLESH), LET HIM BE ANATHEMA.

2. IF ANYONE DOES NOT CONFESS THAT THE WORD FROM GOD THE FATHER HAS BEEN UNITED BY HYPOSTASIS WITH THE FLESH AND IS ONE CHRIST WITH HIS OWN FLESH, AND IS THEREFORE GOD AND MAN TOGETHER, LET HIM BE ANATHEMA.

Jesus Christ, in other words, does not have two identities, nor is he two persons, but is one Person with two natures, human and divine. And Mary is not just the mother of Jesus' human nature, but is the Mother of God, for Jesus is fully God, fully man—the Incarnate Son of God.

The Church, at the Council of Ephesus, did not say Mary somehow created or was responsible for the divine nature of Christ; rather "Mary's virginity manifests God's absolute initiative in the Incarnation. Jesus has only God as Father. 'He was never estranged from the Father because of the human nature which he assumed. . . He is naturally Son of the Father as to his divinity and naturally son of his mother as to his humanity, but properly Son of the Father in both natures'" (CCC 503). Scripture clearly depicts Mary as Mother of God. When the expecting Mary visited her pregnant cousin, John the Baptist leapt in Elizabeth's womb (Lk. 1:41). Elizabeth exclaimed that Mary was "blessed" and that she was the "mother of my Lord" (Lk. 1:43).

Some mistakenly conclude that the title of *Theotokos* gives undue glory to Mary and undermines the uniqueness of Jesus. But everything about Mary—and everything about authentic Marian doctrine—is Christocentric; it is meant to point to her Son and give him glory. Calling Mary the Mother of God is a defense and a declaration of the belief that Jesus is truly God, truly human. Archbishop Fulton Sheen, in *The World's First Love* (Ignatius Press, p. 76-77) used the following analogy:

> *God, Who made the sun, also made the moon. The moon does not take away from the brilliance of the sun. The moon would only be a burnt-out cinder floating in the immensity of space were it not for the sun. All its light is reflected from the sun. The Blessed Mother reflects her Divine Son; without Him, she is nothing. With Him, she is the Mother of Men. On dark nights we are grateful for the moon; when we see it shining, we know there must be a sun. So in this dark night of the world when men turn their backs on Him Who is the Light of the World, we look to Mary to guide their feet while we await the sunrise.*

Mary, put simply, is all about her Son, her Lord, her God. Her undivided discipleship is both a challenge and an encouragement to all of us, her spiritual children.

Cathedral of Chartres:

This magnificent church is, like almost all of the other Gothic cathedrals in France, dedicated to the Virgin Mary. *Cathédrale Notre-Dame de Chartres*, according to tradition, has been the home of the tunic of the Virgin Mary—the Sancta Camisia—since 876, a gift from Charlemagne. Since that time, the Cathedral has been an important pilgrimage center.

The Cathedral is located about fifty miles southwest of Paris. There have been at least five cathedrals built at Chartres, each one bigger and more impressive than the last. The first cathedral dates back at least to the eighth century, while much of the current cathedral dates back to the twelfth century. Little construction has been done since the thirteenth century, although there has been much repair of the existing cathedral over the centuries.

The cathedral, like most Gothic cathedrals, has a cruciform shape; it is 430 feet long and 105 feet wide, with a 92-foot-long, singled-aisled nave that is about 120 feet in height. The northwest tower, the tallest, is 371 feet in height. Especially stunning are the three large rose windows depicting the Last Judgment, the Glorification of the Virgin, and the Glorification of Christ. The cathedral has nearly 200 stained glass windows, the majority of which are, amazingly, original and date back to the medieval era. During World War II, the windows were removed and stored throughout the countryside; they were then put back in place after France was freed from Nazi occupation.

QUESTIONS FOR UNDERSTANDING — Part 1:

1. What was the Annunciation? What was revealed to Mary about herself? About God's plan of salvation? And what was revealed to us about Mary? (CCC 484, 2676; Luke 1:31-33)

2. What are some of the reasons Mary is called a "new Eve"? (CCC 411, 501, 511, 726, 2618)

3. If you were asked, "Why do you believe Mary was sinless?", how might you respond? What misconceptions might you have to address when giving your answer? (CCC 490-93, 722)

4. In calling Mary the "Mother of God," what are we saying about Jesus? What is the difference between a "nature" and a "person"? Why is this important to understand? (CCC 466, 481)

QUESTIONS FOR APPLICATION — Part 1:

1. What does God's calling of a young Jewish girl suggest and reveal about his nature and about his plan of salvation?

2. What are some of the qualities exhibited by Mary that you admire the most, or wish to emulate? How can Mary's example guide and inspire you to grow in your relationship with her Son?

3. If you were asked to explain why Mary is called the "Mother of God," how would you approach the topic?

NOTES

MARY, THE MOTHER OF GOD
Episode 4, Part 2

OUTLINE *(Tracks 5-8 on DVD)*

I. The Immaculate Conception

A. Declared a dogma of the Catholic Church in 1854, but has ancient roots

B. Pius IX (*Ineffabilis Deus*): Mary born "free from all stain of original sin"

    1. This is why Gabriel says, "Hail, Full of Grace"

    2. Mary gifted with "sublime grace" *(Lumen Gentium*, 53)

    3. Mary is a perfect and holy vessel for reception of the Word

    4. Mary's salvation a matter of *how*, not *if* or *what*

C. St. Bernadette and Lourdes

II. The Assumption

A. Declared a dogma of the Catholic Church in 1950, but has ancient roots

B. Pius XII (*Munificentissimus Deus*): Mary's body did not corrupt

    1. Mary did not have to wait "for the redemption of her body"

    2. Mary perfectly shared in her Son's life, death, Resurrection

    3. The Assumption is a "singular participation in her Son's Resurrection" (CCC, 966)

III. The Mother of the Church

A. Mary continues to be active today

B. Dec. 9, 1531: Mary appeared to Juan Diego in Mexico

C. The sign given: *tilma* filled with roses, imprinted with miraculous image

D. The image of the Virgin echoes Revelation 12

IV. Mother of the New Covenant

A. Human Sacrifice

    1. Rene Girard: The Scapegoat

       i.   The Scapegoat is at the foundation of society; provides communal cohesion

       ii.   Satan is the Accuser

       iii. Christ rejects Satan; thus he rejects a world ordered by violence

       iv. Christ becomes scapegoat to show us our violence

       v.   Christ orders society through love and non-violence

VIII. Hopkins' *The May Magnificat*
   A. Mary magnifies the Lord
   B. Mary, the Matrix of Life

MARY, THE MOTHER OF GOD: Lesson 4, Part 2

The Immaculate Conception and the Assumption

The two Marian doctrines that were formally declared in the past two centuries—the dogmas of the Immaculate Conception in 1854 and the Assumption of the Blessed Virgin in 1950—have ancient roots. For example, the great Greek theologian St. Gregory Nazianzen (d. 390) wrote that Jesus "was conceived by the Virgin, who had first been purified by the Spirit in soul and body; for, as it was fitting that childbearing should receive its share of honor, so it was necessary that virginity should receive even greater honor" (Sermon 38, 13; quoted in *Mary and the Fathers of the Church: The Blessed Virgin in Patristic Thought* [Ignatius Press, 1999], by Luigi Gambero, pp. 162-3). St. Gregory of Tours (d. 594), wrote this about the Assumption:

> *The Apostles took up her body on a bier and placed it in a tomb; and they guarded it, expecting the Lord to come. And behold, again the Lord stood by them; and the holy body having been received, He commanded that it be taken in a cloud into paradise: where now, rejoined to the soul, she rejoices with the Lord's chosen ones. (*Book of Miracles*, 1:4)*

These dogmas have puzzled some and upset others. Since they take the material world and physical nature so seriously, they compel us to consider more deeply the activity of God in regard to the lowly human body. As with every Marian belief and dogma, they bring us back to the Incarnation; they are ultimately Christological in nature, for whatever is said about Mary says something about her Son. On December 8, 1854, Pope Pius IX issued *Ineffabilis Deus*, his Apostolic Constitution on the Immaculate Conception. After reviewing pertinent sections of Scripture and pointing to the testimonies of Tradition, Pius IX wrote:

> *We declare, pronounce, and define that the doctrine which holds that the most Blessed Virgin Mary, in the first instance of her conception, by a singular grace and privilege granted by Almighty God, in view of the merits of Jesus Christ, the Savior of the human race, was preserved free from all stain of original sin, is a doctrine revealed by God and therefore to be believed firmly and constantly by all the faithful.*

This supernatural preservation of freedom was the reason Gabriel could exclaim, at the Annunciation, "Hail, Full of Grace." Redeemed from the moment of conception, she was filled with the divine life of God. *Lumen Gentium*, the Second Vatican Council's Dogmatic Constitution on the Church, states:

Redeemed by reason of the merits of her Son and united to Him by a close and indissoluble tie, she is endowed with the high office and dignity of being the Mother of the Son of God, by which account she is also the beloved daughter of the Father and the temple of the Holy Spirit. Because of this gift of sublime grace she far surpasses all creatures, both in heaven and on earth. At the same time, however, because she belongs to the offspring of Adam she is one with all those who are to be saved. (sec. 53)

Why, then, did God preserve Mary in this way from original sin? Was it necessary that she be filled with grace from the very beginning of her conception? Doesn't this suggest that Mary did not need to be saved?

First, we must note that God desired to prepare a holy and perfect vessel for the reception of his Word. If the Holy of Holies in the Temple had to be kept pure and undefiled, it makes sense that the Incarnate Word would reside in a perfect, unblemished Ark of the Covenant. And Mary's role in salvation was not to end with giving birth and raising Jesus, but continues for all time. Once a mother, always a mother! Her cooperation with the divine initiative was essential; her role in salvation is decisive. St. Thomas Aquinas argued that the closeness of Mary to Jesus—the intimacy of a mother and son—meant there would have to be a profound and singular effect on Mary.

> *Now Christ is the principle of grace, authoritatively as to His Godhead, instrumentally as to His humanity: whence (John 1:17) it is written: "Grace and truth came by Jesus Christ." But the Blessed Virgin Mary was nearest to Christ in His humanity: because He received His human nature from her. Therefore it was due to her to receive a greater fullness of grace than others.* (Summa Theologiae, IIIa q. 27, a. 5.)

Secondly, Mary is fully human and so needed redemption just like every man and woman. What is distinctive is not the *if* or *what* of her salvation (she did *need* to be saved and her salvation could *only* come from God), but the *how*. Grace, the life of God, is not bound or limited by time; it exists outside of time and can be applied as God wills and directs. By a sort of pre-emptive, redemptive strike, Christ's grace removed sin from the Virgin Mary even before the Word became flesh and dwelt among men.

While the dogmas of the Immaculate Conception and the Assumption were formally defined by papal authority, they have long been recognized by the faithful. A wonderful and miraculous example of how the most lowly and simple of God's faithful have given witness to these truths can be found in the story of St. Bernadette (1844-1879).

"On a cold winter day in 1858 in Lourdes, France," writes Patricia A. McEachern, in *A Holy Life: St. Bernadette of Lourdes* (Ignatius Press, 2005), "Bernadette Soubirous, a tiny, asthmatic shepherdess went in search of wood along the Gave River. The visions this humble young girl experienced that day has since deepened the faith of millions" (p. 11). The fourteen-year-old Bernadette, who lived with her family in a converted one-room prison, was looking for the wood along the Gave River, where garbage from the town was often dumped. She later described her experience as she started to wade across the river in search of fuel:

> *Scarcely had I removed my first stocking when I heard a noise like a sudden gust of wind. When I turned my head toward the prairie, I saw that the trees were not swaying at all, so I began removing my stockings again. I heard the same noise again.*

When I raised my head and looked at the Grotto, I saw a Lady in white. She was wearing a white gown with a blue sash, a white veil and a golden rose on each foot, the same color as the chain of her Rosary, which had white beads. She was surrounded with white light, but it was not a blinding light. (Ibid., p.11).

The Lady took up her rosary, made the sign of the cross, and began to pray. Bernadette joined her and found that her initial fear had left her. When they had finished the prayer, the glorious woman smiled and disappeared. Over the course of many weeks, Bernadette returned every day to the same spot. At first her story was met with disbelief; the parish priest rebuked her when she brought him a message from the Lady. She continued, however, to visit the Grotto, despite opposition. During one visit, the Lady told her to dig into the ground and find a spring. When she did so, people thought that she had lost her mind. But in time, water indeed flowed from the spot and eventually a severely crippled young boy and others were cured after bathing in it.

On March 24, 1858, the eve of the feast of the Annunciation, Bernadette felt an inner impulse to go to the grotto. The Lady was there to meet her, and Bernadette felt the urge to ask her name. Three times she petitioned, and finally, when she dared to ask a fourth time, the Lady "folded her hands together at her breast, and, raising her eyes to heaven, she said, 'I am the Immaculate Conception.'" (Ibid, p. 25-26). Bernadette, who at the time was uneducated and almost illiterate, had no idea what the strange name meant. How wonderful that Mary, herself once a teen girl of very modest means, would appear to this simple, sickly child (Bernadette later entered the religious life as a Sister of Charity, and died at the age of 35). Bernadette, who was something of a cave-girl, was visited by the Queen of Heaven who had so many centuries before received the message of an angel in a lowly dwelling and had given birth to the son of God in a cave.

Nearly a century after Pius IX had defined the dogma of the Immaculate Conception, Pope Pius XII declared as dogma the Assumption of the Blessed Virgin. In the Apostolic Constitution, *Munificentissimus Deus,* issued on November 1, 1950, Pius XII pointed out the important connection between the two dogmas, saying the two "are most closely bound to one another"
(sec. 4). It is not normal, he wrote, that God would "grant to the just the full effect of the victory over death until the end of time has come," but that is what God did in the Immaculate Conception, "and as a result she was not subject to the law of remaining in the corruption of the grave, and she did not have to wait until the end of time for the redemption of her body"
(pars. 4-5). Just as Mary was kept from original sin by God's grace, she was also kept from decay by that same grace.

After tracing the ancient heritage of the belief in the Assumption, Pius XII wrote:

We must remember especially that, since the second century, the Virgin Mary has been designated by the holy Fathers as the new Eve, who, although subject to the new Adam, is most intimately associated with him in that struggle against the infernal foe which, as foretold in the protoevangelium, would finally result in that most complete victory over the sin and death which are always mentioned together in the writings of the Apostle of the Gentiles. Consequently, just as the glorious resurrection of Christ was an essential part and the final sign of this victory, so that struggle which was common to the Blessed Virgin and her divine Son should be brought to a close by the glorification of her virginal body, for the same Apostle says: "When this mortal thing hath put on immortality, then shall come to pass the saying that is written: Death is swallowed up in victory." (par. 39).

The old Eve had failed the test in the Garden, and so returned to dust. But the new Eve had humbly accepted the Word of the Lord, embraced the will of the Father, and reciprocated the love of the Holy Spirit. She perfectly shared in the conception, life, and death of her Son, and so also perfectly shared in his Resurrection.

"The Assumption of the Blessed Virgin is a singular participation in her Son's Resurrection," explains the *Catechism*, "and an anticipation of the resurrection of other Christians: 'In giving birth you kept your virginity; in your Dormition you did not leave the world, O Mother of God, but were joined to the source of Life. You conceived the living God and, by your prayers, will deliver our souls from death.'" (par. 966)

✝

Mother of the Church

That Immaculate Mary, *Theotokos,* was assumed body and soul into heaven is not a matter of mere curiosity or historical trivia, nor is Mary simply an admirable spiritual model. As Queen of all the saints, she is alive and active in the Church, working to draw mankind into living communion with her Son. Two thousand years ago, she said, "Yes!" to God, and she has never ceased to say "Yes!" to him ever since.

There have been tens of thousands of Marian apparitions reported in recent centuries. One of the most extraordinary and captivating encounters between the Blessed Mother and a simple soul took place in Mexico nearly five hundred years ago. On December 9, 1531 (just a few years after Cortez and his men had arrived in Vera Cruz, Mexico, in February of 1519), a recent Aztec convert to Catholicism came to the hill of Tepeyac. Juan Diego was a fifty-seven-year-old landowner and mat weaver, mild-mannered and a recent convert (and an even more recent widower). Hearing a beautiful birdsong, he turned to see the bird but instead saw a young lady, about fourteen years of age, clothed in the sun, with a burst of light around her. She said to the startled man:

> *Know for certain, least of my sons, that I am the perfect and perpetual Virgin Mary, Mother of Jesus, the true God, through whom everything lives, the Lord of all things near and far, the Master of Heaven and earth. It is my earnest wish that a temple be built here to my honor. Here I will demonstrate, I will manifest, I will give all my love, my compassion, my help and my protection to the people. I am your merciful mother, the merciful mother of all of you who live united in this land, and of all mankind, of all those who love me, of those who cry to me, of those who seek me, and of those who have confidence in me. Here I will hear their weeping, their sorrow, and will remedy and alleviate all their multiple sufferings, necessities, and misfortunes.* ("Saint Juan Diego and Our Lady", Accessed at https://www.catholiceducation.org/en/culture/catholic-contributions/saint-juan-diego-and-our-lady.html)

The lady told him she wished for the bishop to build a temple there in her honor. Juan Diego conveyed the message to the bishop, a Franciscan named Juan de Zumárraga, who received his visitor kindly, listened to his story, and then asked for a sign. The sign was given to him 3 days later when the lady invited Juan Diego to take off his *tilma*, a cloak woven from cactus fibers.In it she arranged the roses that he had collected upon her instruction, which were blooming despite being out of season. When he took the cloak to the bishop and opened it, the roses spilled out and revealed a miraculous image of the Virgin Mary mysteriously imprinted on the inside of the garment. The bishop fell to his knees and promised to build the church.

Just a charming story for the faithful? Merely an enjoyable myth? Some say so, but there is one problem with this theory: the *tilma* itself. Studies have shown that the cloth is indeed from the sixteenth century and is composed of flimsy cactus fibers, which under normal circumstances would fade away in a few decades, if not sooner. But it still exists five hundred years later. Then, there is the captivating and strange image. There is no discernable under-drawing, and careful tests have shown that no known pigmentation was involved in its creation.

The symbolism in the image is stunning. The lady depicted is not a Spaniard or a Mexican, but a mestizo girl, a blend of the two. She is known as *la Morena*, the brown-skinned girl. The cincture that she wears was an Aztec sign of pregnancy. She stands in front of the sun and on the moon, and her cloak is bedecked with stars, all gods for the ancient Aztecs. It is evocative of the great vision depicted in Revelation 12: "And a great portent appeared in heaven, a woman clothed with the sun, with the moon under her feet, and on her head a crown of twelve stars; she was with child and she cried out in her pangs of birth, in anguish for delivery" (Rev. 12:1-2).

The Virgin stands with her eyes turned down, and her hands folded in prayer; her posture demonstrates her humility before One who is greater than she. Her name, Guadalupe, is probably a Spanish deformation of *coatlaxopeuh*, pronounced "cuatlasupe." It means "the one who crushes the serpent." The serpent was an important Aztec divinity, and the crusher of the serpent is the one predicted in the book of Genesis (see Gen. 3:14-15). Within ten years of this Marian apparition, almost the entire nation of Mexico had converted to Christianity, some nine million souls. That works out to about 3,000 people per day for ten years, extraordinary by any standard. And still they come: the Basilica of Our Lady of Guadalupe is the most visited religious site in the Christian world, attracting more visitors than even St. Peter's Basilica in Rome.

FOR FURTHER STUDY: *Mother of the New Covenant*

Pope John Paul II, in his 1987 encyclical *Redemptoris Mater*, wrote of how the Christian, following the example of the Apostle John, should welcome the Mother of Christ in his home, embracing her maternal charity and care. He wrote:

This filial relationship, this self-entrusting of a child to its mother, not only has its beginning in Christ but can also be said to be definitively directed towards him. Mary can be said to continue to say to each individual the words which she spoke at Cana in Galilee: "Do whatever he tells you." For he, Christ, is the one Mediator between God and mankind; he is "the way, and the truth, and the life" (Jn. 14:6); it is he whom the Father has given to the world, so that man "should not perish but have eternal life" (Jn. 3:16). The Virgin of Nazareth became the first "witness" of this saving love of the Father, and she also wishes to remain its humble handmaid always and everywhere. For every Christian, for every human being, Mary is the one who first "believed," and precisely with her faith as Spouse and Mother she wishes to act upon all those who entrust themselves to her as her children. And it is well known that the more her children persevere and progress in this attitude, the nearer Mary leads them to the "unsearchable riches of Christ" (Eph. 3:8). And to the same degree they recognize more and more clearly the dignity of man in all its fullness and the definitive meaning of his vocation, for "Christ...fully reveals man to man himself." (sec. 46)

Holy Mary, Mother of God, pray for us sinners, now and the hour of our death. Amen.

René Girard and the Scapegoat:

"There is nothing secret about the justifications espoused by myths; the stereotypical accusations of mob violence are always available when the search for scapegoats is on. In the Gospels, however, the scapegoating machinery is fully visible because it encounters opposition and no longer operates efficiently...What the myths systematically hide, the Bible reveals." -René Girard (as quoted in *First Things*, April 1996)

René Girard was born on Christmas Day, 1923, in Avignon, France. The author of many books, he had an illustrious academic career, the culmination of which was his membership in one of the most exclusive and prestigious organizations in the world— the *Académie française*.

Girard advocated an elegant theory of culture that, if true, has provocative consequences for all human endeavors. This theory postulates that a peculiar dynamic exists in all cultural environments from the nation state even to our interpersonal relationships. This dynamic serves to assure the restoration of order in the face of violence and social disintegration. Girard calls this dynamic "the scapegoat mechanism." Basically, this means that in the face of conflict, resolution will often be accomplished by assigning a particular victim responsibility for the disorder. The convergence of a divided and rancorous group on this victim will restore what is lacking in the society— unity, cohesion, and a common understanding of the circumstances.

The victim is then killed or exiled, and its death or expulsion is viewed as the means by which chaos is avoided and order is restored.

Many of the forms of ritual and myth present the reality of "the scapegoat mechanism" and serve as a means of obscuring the truth that the victims of this dynamic are innocent of the crimes that they are purported to have committed. The masking of the truth about the victims of scapegoat mechanism is essential to its effectiveness. Thus, over time, rituals and myths have developed that have the purpose of protecting and perpetuating the scapegoat mechanism. This serves a constructive purpose for culture— that there is available to a given society a means by which order can be restored if that order is threatened by conflict or crisis. Further, these rituals and myths lend an aura of the sacred to the scapegoat mechanism giving the impression that the death or expulsion of the victim has the sanction of God or the gods, and as such, those who perpetrate the violence are not responsible for their actions.

The main features of this theory were in place when Girard turned for the first time in a serious way to the Christian Scriptures. What he found astonished him and changed his life. He discovered that the Bible knew all about mimetic desire and scapegoating violence but it also contained something altogether new, namely, the de-sacralizing of the process that is revered in all of the myths and religions of the world. The crucifixion of Jesus is a classic instance of the old pattern. It is utterly consistent with the Girardian theory that Caiaphas, the leading religious figure of the time, could say to his colleagues, "Is it not better for you that one man should die for the people than for the whole nation to perish?" In any other religious context, this sort of rationalization would be valorized. But in the resurrection of Jesus from the dead, this stunning truth is revealed: God is not on the side of the scapegoaters but rather on the side of the scapegoated victim. The true God in fact does not sanction a community created through violence; rather, he sanctions what Jesus called the Kingdom of God, a society grounded in forgiveness, love, and identification with the victim.

May Magnificat

- Gerard Manley Hopkins

May is Mary's month, and I
Muse at that and wonder why:
Her feasts follow reason,
Dated due to season—

Candlemas, Lady Day;
But the Lady Month, May,
Why fasten that upon her,
With a feasting in her honour?

Is it only its being brighter
Than the most are must delight her?
Is it opportunest
And flowers finds soonest?

Ask of her, the mighty mother:
Her reply puts this other
Question: What is Spring?—
Growth in every thing—

Flesh and fleece, fur and feather,
Grass and greenworld all together;
Star-eyed strawberry-breasted
Throstle above her nested

Cluster of bugle blue eggs thin
Forms and warms the life within;
And bird and blossom swell
In sod or sheath or shell.

All things rising, all things sizing
Mary sees, sympathising
With that world of good,
Nature's motherhood.

Their magnifying of each its kind
With delight calls to mind
How she did in her stored
Magnify the Lord.

Well but there was more than this:
Spring's universal bliss
Much, had much to say
To offering Mary May.

When drop-of-blood-and-foam-dapple
Bloom lights the orchard-apple
And thicket and thorp are merry
With silver-surfèd cherry

And azuring-over greybell makes
Wood banks and brakes wash wet like lakes
And magic cuckoocall
Caps, clears, and clinches all—

This ecstasy all through mothering earth
Tells Mary her mirth till Christ's birth
To remember and exultation
In God who was her salvation.

QUESTIONS FOR UNDERSTANDING — Part 2:

1. Does the dogma of the Immaculate Conception indicate that Mary did not need a Savior? Why or why not? How is this dogma often misunderstood or misrepresented?

2. What are some theological reasons for the dogma of the Assumption of Mary? (CCC 964-66)

QUESTIONS FOR APPLICATION — Part 2:

1. Do you practice a Marian devotion, such as the Rosary? If so, what has that devotion meant to you and your spiritual life? If not, is there a Marian devotion you might want to practice?

2. What does Mary's Assumption indicate to us about her life and about our calling as disciples of Jesus?

3. Have you ever visited Lourdes or another Marian shrine? If so, what was your experience?

TERMS & NAMES

Adams, Henry (1838-1918). An American journalist, historian, academic, and novelist born into one of America's most prominent families (his grandfather and great grandfather were John Quincy Adams and John Adams, respectively), Henry is known for his autobiography *The Education of Henry Adams* and his book *Mont Saint-Michel and Chartres* which depicts the values of medieval society embodied in two of France's greatest religious sites.

Angelico, Bl. Fra (c. 1395-1455). An Italian Dominican friar and painter who is known for the mysticism in which he portrays religious subjects. Georgio Vasari, a sixteenth-century Florentine painter and writer, said that Fra Angelico believed that in order to properly paint Christ, one must be Christ-like. Accordingly, he always prayed before painting. He is a model for all artists.

The Annunciation: The announcement of the Incarnation by the angel Gabriel to the young Mary (Lk. 1:26-38). The feast commemorating the Annunciation dates back to the sixth or seventh century.

Ark of the Covenant: A chest that contained the two tablets of the Ten Commandments. It was evocative of God's presence among the Israelites and it was placed in the holy of holies. The Church calls Mary the "Ark of the Covenant" since she was the vessel through whom Christ came to dwell among his people.

The Assumption: The belief that the Blessed Virgin Mary, at the end of her earthly life, was taken up body and soul to heaven, her body never being corrupted by the grave. Declared a dogma of the Catholic Church by Pope Pius XII in 1950.

Bernadette, Saint (1844-1879). The witness of the Lourdes apparitions. She reported seeing "a small young lady" at the town's garbage dump. The lady directed her to a hidden spring in which a young boy and many were cured of their maladies.

Chartres Cathedral: Medieval cathedral of the French High Gothic Style in Chartres, France.

Council of Ephesus: Convened in 431, it was the third ecumenical Council (after Nicaea in 325 and Constantinople in 381). The Council condemned Nestorianism and formally approved the Marian title, *Theotokos*.

Cyril of Alexandria (c. 376-444 A.D.). The Patriarch of Alexandria who is one of the Church Fathers and Doctors of the Church and who was a prominent figure in the Christological debates of the 5th century.

Girard, Rene (1923-2015). A French historian, literary critic and philosopher who made significant contributions to anthropological philosophy. His theories of mimetic desire and the scapegoat mechanism were developed from his reading of novels and the Bible.

Gregory of Nazianzus, Saint (329/30-389/90). Also called "Gregory the Theologian," he was one of the Cappadocian Fathers (along with St. Basil the Great and St. Gregory of Nyssa) and is a Doctor of the Church. He was a key figure at the Council of Constantinople and wrote many influential works of theology.

Gregory of Tours, Saint (538/9-594). Bishop of Tours and a historian of early France.

Homoousios: a theological term to denote that Christ, the Second Person of the Trinity, is of the same substance as the Father, the First Person of the Trinity. Christ is one in being with the Father.

Hopkins, Gerard Manley, S.J. (1844-1889). An English poet, convert to Catholicism, and Jesuit priest known for his Victorian poetry.

Irenaeus, Saint (c. 130-c. 200). Bishop of Lyons, an early Church Father, and the first great theologian of the post-apostolic age. His major work, *Adversus Haereses* ("Against heresies"), is a detailed attack on Gnosticism and defense of the Catholic Faith.

Juan Diego, Saint (1474-1548). An indigenous Mexican who received from the Mother of God herself the image of Our Lady of Guadalupe.

Labyrinth: a maze-like passage through which it is very difficult to find one's way without guidance. Many churches and cathedrals have labyrinths on the floor where penitents walk on their knees as a sort of spiritual pilgrimage.

Nestorius (d. c. 451). Patriarch of Constantinople and heresiarch. He upheld and defended the belief that there were two separate Persons—divine and human—in the Incarnate Word. This belief was condemned by the Council of Ephesus in 431.

Theotokos: Literally, in Greek, "the one who gave birth to God," a title of the Blessed Virgin Mary formally approved by the Council of Ephesus in 431.

Lesson 5

THE INDISPENSABLE MEN
Peter, Paul, and the Missionary Adventure

"Due to their centrality, Peter and Paul are not merely of historical interest;
they live on as determining archetypes in the community of Jesus to the
present day."

- Bishop Robert Barron

Guido Reni. *Sts. Peter and Paul.* 1605. Pinacoteca di Brera. Milan, Italy.

THE INDISPENSABLE MEN
Episode 5, Part 1

OUTLINE *(Tracks 1-4 on DVD)*

I. **Unique and United**

    A. Principal archetypes for disciples of Christ

B. Peter = kingly, leadership, governing

C. Paul = prophetic, missionary, teacher

D. United in apostleship and devotion to the Lord

II. **Peter of Capharnaum**

    A. A fisherman and businessman; married; middle-class

    B. Blustery, direct, strong-willed, but loyal

    C. Name appears 191 times in the New Testament

        1. Named first on lists of apostles   (Mt. 10:2-4; Mk. 3:14-18; Lk. 6:13-16)

        2. Only apostle to be given a new name by Christ (Mt. 16:18; Jn. 1:42)

        3. Exhorted by Jesus to strengthen his brethren (Lk. 22:32)

D. Transfiguration and Transformation

    1. The prophecy and promise of the Cross

    2. Transfiguration: fullness of divine presence, action, glory

    3. Peter's three-fold denial: from light to darkness

        4. Christ's three-fold affirmation of love and duty

        5. Acts of the Apostles: Pentecost, preaching, Cornelius the centurion

E. The Call and the Confession

    1. "Follow me and I will make you become fishers of men." (Mt. 4:19)

    2. Caesarea Philippi

        i. Old Testament background (1 Kings. 4; Isa. 22)

        ii. Physical setting: site of pagan worship

        iii. Two questions (Matt. 16:13, 15)

        iv. Simon is renamed Petros/Kepha ("Rock")

        v. Appointed prime minister; given keys to the kingdom

F. Peter: Apostle and Witness
    1. Witness to the Resurrection of Christ
      2. Witness to the Gospel
      3. Martyred in Rome (c. A.D. 65)

THE INDISPENSABLE MEN: Lesson 5, Part 1

Matthew. James. Mark. John. Luke. Mary Magdalene. Silas. Barnabas.

Those are just some of the names of men and women in the early Church who played essential roles in establishing, proclaiming, and handing on the Faith. But there are two who stand out from the illustrious crowd, who were indispensable in countless ways: Peter and Paul.

As historical figures, they are fascinating enough. But they are not merely of historical interest, for they live on as Saints whose tireless work, inspired writings, and holy witness—including their death as martyrs—are vital, dynamic realities within the family of Jesus Christ. They are principle archetypes for disciples of Jesus. Peter represents the kingly, leadership element in the Church's life; Paul represents the prophetic, missionary, teaching element.

The great Swiss theologian, Hans Urs von Balthasar, in *The Office of Peter and the Structure of the Church* (Ignatius Press, 1986), reflected at length about what united and what distinguished the two men. "Despite their closeness in the Jewish-Gentile conflict," he wrote, referring to debates touched on in Acts of the Apostles and several of Paul's letters, "there is that very distance between Peter and Paul which we find between ecclesial office and the gifted theological writer" (p. 161). Peter, given a unique position of governing authority by Christ, readily acknowledged "the wisdom given" to "our beloved brother Paul" (2 Pet. 3:15-16), while the intellectually gifted Paul, following his dramatic conversion, spent time learning from the head apostle (Gal. 1:18).

United in their apostleship and devotion to the Lord, Peter and Paul had much in common. They were both first-century Jews with strong, stubborn personalities, each endowed with natural charisma and leadership qualities. But they were also, in many significant ways, a study in contrast.

✝

Peter of Capharnaum

We begin with the impetuous fisherman named Simon. Shimeon bar Johannon, his original name, was a fisherman from the town of Capharnaum along the northern shore of the Sea of Galilee. He was probably not well educated, nor very sophisticated, but likely could read and write some Hebrew and Greek. He was a businessman, neither wealthy nor poor, but likely in contact often with both classes. Historical evidence indicates that Galilean fishermen had business dealings with merchants around the eastern part of the Roman Empire. And we know he was married because Jesus healed his mother-in-law (Mt. 8:14; Mk. 1:30-31).

Peter was blustery, tempestuous, direct, honest, often strong-willed and contrary, but also deeply loyal. He loved Jesus deeply, even if he sometimes openly questioned his Master's teachings and directives. We know a great deal about Peter because his name, after that of Jesus, appears most in the four Gospels. Peter's name is first in all the lists of apostles in the New Testament (see Mt. 10:2; Mk. 3:16; Lk. 6:14; Acts 1:13), and he is described as "first" in the Gospel of Matthew (Mt. 10:2). Peter stands first or alone in many ways among the apostles and other disciples. He was the first to profess the divinity of Jesus (Mt. 16:16), and he alone received a new name, *Petros*, or "Rock," from Jesus (Mt. 16:18; Jn. 1:42). He was appointed by Jesus to be the chief shepherd (Jn. 21:15-17), and he alone is mentioned by name as having been prayed for by Jesus so that his faith wouldn't fail in the face of persecution (Lk. 22:32). He is the only apostle exhorted by Jesus to strengthen his brethren, that is, his fellow disciples (Lk. 22:32).

He gave the great sermon on Pentecost following the coming of the Holy Spirit upon the newly revealed Church (Acts 2:14-42), took the lead in appointing a replacement for Judas among the Twelve (Acts 1:15-26), and worked the first miracle of the Church (Acts 3:1-10). He was regarded as the leader and spokesman of the first Christians by the Jews (Acts 4:1-13), and was considered the leader of the Church by the common people (Acts 2:37-41; 5:15). Peter was the first person after Jesus to raise someone from the dead (Acts 9:40), and he was the first to proclaim the Gospel among the Gentiles (Acts 10), a pivotal event in the early Church.

And while numbers aren't everything, it is worth noting that Peter's name is mentioned more often in the New Testament than all of the other disciples combined: 191 times (162 as Peter or Simon Peter, 23 as Simon, and six as Cephas). In comparison, the Apostle John is next in frequency with 48 mentions. Peter's name appears at least 54 times in Acts, while James, for example, appears just four times.

†

Transfiguration and Transformation

Peter, with James and John, witnessed the Transfiguration of the Lord. In the days leading up to the Transfiguration, Jesus had directly dispelled any false notions the disciples might have had about the nature of his mission. He strongly expressed his unwavering commitment to offer himself as a sacrifice for the world. His kingdom was not of this world, and he was not a political leader or a military warrior; he was not promising comfort and wealth. On the contrary, Jesus was promising a cross: "If any man would come after me, let him deny himself and take up his cross daily and follow me" (Lk. 9:23).

This was undoubtedly disorienting to the disciples. In the midst of this confusion and anxiety, Jesus took Peter, John, and James, the inner circle of the disciples, up to the mountain to pray, ascending, as it were, toward the heavenly places. There, above the tumult of the world and facing an ominous future, Jesus revealed his glory and gave them a dazzling glimpse of their eternal calling.

But the glory witnessed by the three apostles was not just about the future. "The Transfiguration," notes Erasmo Leiva-Merikakis in *Fire of Mercy, Heart of the World: Meditations on the Gospel according to Saint Matthew* (San Francisco: Ignatius Press, 2003, 551), "is the experience of the fullness of divine Presence, action, communication, and glory now, in our very midst, in this world of passingness and disappointment." It is about the fullness of life now—not ordinary, natural life, butextraordinary, supernatural life. The Transfiguration is about the gift of divine sonship, which comes from the Father, who says of Jesus, "This is my chosen Son; listen to him" (see Mt. 17:1-13; Mk. 9:2-13; Lk. 9:28-36). Peter and the disciples had to learn that Jesus' death was necessary so his life could be fully revealed and given to the world.

"On Tabor, light pours forth from him," writes Leiva-Merikakis, "on Calvary it will be blood" (Ibid, 564). At the decisive moment, after the arrest of Christ in the Garden, as the forces of evil gathered around Jesus, Peter fell into the darkness. Facing a restless mob, he denied Jesus three times. After the cock crowed, "he broke down and wept" (Mk. 14:72).

But, of course, there is much more to the story. After the Resurrection, Jesus appeared to the disciples by the shores of the Sea of Galilee. Peter, who had urged the others to go fishing, eagerly jumped into the water to meet his Lord. What followed is deeply poignant.

The Fourth Evangelist sets the scene by specifically mentioning that Jesus had lit a charcoal fire (Jn 21:9), only the second place in the entire New Testament that a charcoal fire is mentioned. And the other place? At the site of Peter's denial, as he sat stood with the slaves and guards keeping warm outside the gate (Jn. 18:18). Jesus had already confronted Peter, in silence, immediately after that dramatic denial: "And the Lord turned and looked at Peter. And Peter remembered the word of the Lord, how he said to him, 'Before the cock crows today, you will deny me three times'" (Lk. 22:61). Following the Resurrection, Jesus confronted Peter again—not to put him down, but to build him up and, in doing so, to remind the apostle of his constant need for the Lord's power and grace. After all, Peter had brashly insisted on the evening of the Last Supper that, "Though they all fall away because of you, I will never fall away" (Mt. 26:33).

Sitting together on the beach Jesus asked Simon three times, "Do you love me?" Three times, in growing distress, Peter answered in the affirmative. And three times Jesus gave him a directive: "Feed my lambs. Tend my sheep. Feed my sheep." Jesus' words were an affirmation of his selection of Peter as head apostle (Jn. 1:42; Matt 16:16-20). They also point to how Peter was called to participate in Jesus' unique role as the Good Shepherd, a role that is emphasized at length in John's Gospel (Jn. 10:1-21; cf. Ezek. 34).

After the Ascension of the Lord, Peter continued his role as leader of the disciples and of the early Church, described in the first part of the Acts of the Apostles. He concentrated his evangelistic efforts on his fellow Jews, but was then called by God to take the Gospel to Cornelius the centurion and his household, who became the first Gentiles to embrace the Gospel (Acts 10).

The Call and the Confession

"And passing along by the Sea of Galilee," St. Mark writes, Jesus "saw Simon and Andrew the brother of Simon casting a net in the sea; for they were fishermen. And Jesus said to them, 'Follow me and I will make you become fishers of men.' And immediately they left their nets and followed him" (Mk. 1:16-18). Needless to say, this radically changed the life of Shimeon bar Johannon. In the Fourth Gospel, the significance of this radical change in his focus and priorities is shown by a change in name: "Jesus looked at him, and said, 'So you are Simon the son of John? You shall be called Cephas (which means Peter)" (Jn. 1:42). Just as God had called Abram and eventually changed his name to Abraham, God called and renamed Simon, an indication of his place and purpose in the plan of salvation.

A key part of that plan was revealed at Caesarea Philippi when Shimeon bar Johannon was given the keys to the kingdom by Jesus. The Old Testament background to the story is sometimes overlooked but is essential. King Solomon and his successors had twelve deputies or ministers who helped the king govern and rule (1 Kings. 4:7-19). The master of the palace, or prime minister, had a unique position among those twelve, as described in Isaiah 22:19-23. The prime minister wore a robe and sash befitting his office and was entrusted by the king to wield the king's authority. The symbol for that authority was "the keys of the House of David," which enabled the minister to regulate the affairs of the king's household—that is, of the kingdom. In addition, this prime minister is described by Isaiah as a "father to the inhabitants of Jerusalem and to the house of Judah" (Isa. 22:21).

Fast forward to about the year A.D. 30. Jesus and his disciples are in the region of Caesarea Philippi, a pagan area about 25 miles north of the Sea of Galilee. They likely were standing at the base of Mount Hermon in front of a well-known cliff filled with niches holding statues of pagan deities; at the top of the cliff stood a temple in honor of Caesar. Jesus first asked the disciples, "Who do men say that the Son of Man is?" (Mt. 16:13). The range of answers given—John the Baptist, Elijah, Jeremiah, one of the prophets—revealed the confusion surrounding the identity of Jesus, not unlike the confusion and controversies about Jesus in our own time.

Jesus then asked, "But who do you say that I am?" (Mt. 16:15). It was Shimeon bar Johannon—brash but correct—who responded with the great acclamation, "You are the Christ, the Son of the living God," confessing both the divinity and kingship of Jesus. He was then addressed singularly by Jesus, who renamed him *Petros*, (*Kepha* in Aramaic, the language in which they were conversing), that is, "Rock." That name was unique among the Jews, reserved in the Old Testament for God alone. Jesus, the *Catechism* notes, "entrusted a unique mission to him" by declaring he would build his Church upon the newly named Rock, granting Peter "the keys to the kingdom of heaven." In this way, Christ, "the living Stone," assures his Church "built on Peter, of victory over the powers of death. Because of the faith he confessed Peter will remain the unshakeable rock of the Church. His mission will be to keep this faith from every lapse and to strengthen his brothers in it" (CCC 552).

Jesus, heir of King David and King of kings, was appointing Peter to be his prime minister, the head of the Twelve. "The 'power of the keys,'" explains the *Catechism*, "designates authority to govern the house of God, which is the Church" (par. 553). The binding and loosing refers to prohibiting and permitting; it also includes the function of rendering authoritative teaching and making official pronouncements. All of Peter's successors have had this fundamental task: to confess that Jesus is the Son of God; everything else is commentary.

†

Martyrdom

He came to Rome sometime in the late fifties or early sixties of the first century, probably staying with Christianized Jews in the Trastevere neighborhood. Rome, the Eternal City, was the focal point of the civilization of the world, the main city of the greatest empire to have ever existed. To conquer Rome was to conquer the world; to convert Rome was to convert the world. Peter knew that Jesus, the Lord of lords, was for all the nations, and he knew the new covenant was meant for the entire world, not just for Israel and the Jewish people.

The head apostle was executed around 64 or 65, the most prominent victim of Nero's persecution of the first Christians. Tradition says he was crucified between the Janiculum and Vatican hills outside of the ancient city of Rome. Caligula had commenced the building of a circus there but had been assassinated before it was finished. Nero completed it, and many of the bloody and violent executions of Christians took place there.

Eusebius of Caesarea (c. 260–339), in his *Ecclesiastical History*, the first history of the Church, wrote: "Peter appears to have preached through Pontus, Galatia, Bithynia, Cappadocia, and Asia, to the Jews that were scattered abroad; who also, finally coming to Rome, was crucified with his head downward, having requested of himself to suffer in this way" (3:1). Peter's body was taken down from the cross by Christians and buried in the cemetery near the Circus Maximus. His tomb was guarded and revered for those first three centuries of the Church until the reign of the Emperor Constantine, who built a great basilica over the spot. That church lasted until the early sixteenth century when it was torn down by Pope Julius II and a new one was built.

In the mid-twentieth century, Pope Pius XII supervised an excavation underneath St. Peter's Basilica, resulting in the discovery of the remains of a first-century cemetery and a wall with a mysterious bit of graffiti scrawled on it: *Petros eni*, "Peter is within." When the bones were examined, it was determined that they were the remains of a sturdily built man between the ages of sixty and seventy.

Christianity is not a philosophy, a set of abstract convictions, a pleasant moral code. It is a relationship to a person, Jesus of Nazareth. Peter of Capharnaum reminds us of this truth. He was witness to the resurrection of Jesus from the dead. He was witness to the Gospel by the giving of his life. It is on that Rock that Jesus Christ built his church. "Peter, the leader of the choir," as St. John Chrysostom described him, "the mouth of all the apostles, the head of that tribe, the ruler of the whole world, the foundation of the Church, the ardent lover of Christ" (*Homily on 2 Timothy*, 3.1).

QUESTIONS FOR UNDERSTANDING — Part 1:

1. In what ways were Peter and Paul similar to one another? How were they different from each other? (Acts 22:3; 2 Pet. 3:15-16; Gal. 1:18)

2. How is Peter's unique role expressed and evidenced in the Gospels? (Mt. 10:2; Mt. 16:16-18; Jn. 1:42; Jn. 21:15-17; Lk. 22:32)

3. What was the meaning of Jesus re-naming Simon? How do the Old Testament images of kings, prime ministers, and keys help us to understand Jesus' words to Peter in Matthew 16? (Mt. 16; 1 Kgs. 4:7-19; Isa. 22:19-23; CCC 551-555)

4. What is the relationship between the Transfiguration and the Cross? (Ex. 24:9-18; 1 Kgs. 19:8-16; CCC 554, 697)

5. What connections are made in the Gospels between Peter's denial of Christ and Christ's affirmation of Peter? (Jn 18:18; Jn 21:9; Lk 22:61; Jn 1:42; Matt. 16:16-20; Jn 10:1-21)

QUESTIONS FOR APPLICATION — Part 1:

1. What do the differences in the personalities and backgrounds of Peter and Paul suggest about discipleship, leadership, and how God works in and through the Church?

2. What did Jesus mean by calling Peter and his companions to become "fishers of men"? How has God called you to be a fisher of men?

3. Who do people today say Jesus is? Why? And who do you say he is? Why?

NOTES

THE INDISPENSABLE MEN
Episode 5, Part 2

OUTLINE (*Tracks 5-8 on DVD*)

III. Paul of Tarsus

    A. Devout Jew with perfect résumé (Phil. 3:4-7)

    B. Youth and education

        1. Born in Tarsus (southeastern Turkey)

        2. A Roman citizen

        3. Comfortable with Roman, Hellenistic, Jewish cultures

        4. Classical education; foremost a student of Hebrew Scriptures

        5. Student of Rabbi Gamaliel (Acts 22:3)

        6. A brilliant, intense zealot

        7. Persecutor of the Church, first Christians (Acts 8:1-3; 9:1-3)

    C. Conversion and Mission

        1. Road to Damascus (Acts 9:3-6; 22:4-11; 26:12-18)

        2. Baptized, preaching, studying

        3. Missionary journeys

        4. Letters

        5. Martyred in Rome (c. A.D. 67)

  D. Paul's Theology of Resurrection

        1. Truth of Christ's Resurrection: A central theme in Paul's writings

      2. The Resurrection fulfilled God's plans/promises for Israel

      3. Those buried in baptism will rise again (Rom. 6:1-9)

    E. Participation in Christ

        1. "In Christ": appears often in Paul's writings

        2. The New Covenant is entrance into God's divine life

        3. The heart of the covenantal gift is the Eucharist

      4. *Koinonia* = mystical communion, fellowship

        5. Justification = made right with God by grace, through Christ

        6. Through faith we are grafted into the power of Christ

        7. Conformed and transformed by love

THE INDISPENSABLE MEN: Lesson 5, Part 2

Paul of Tarsus

Writing to the Christians in Philippi in the mid-fifties, Paul presented, in his usual brilliant and passionate style, his résumé as a devout Jew:

> THOUGH I MYSELF HAVE REASON FOR CONFIDENCE IN THE FLESH ALSO. IF ANY OTHER MAN THINKS HE HAS REASON FOR CONFIDENCE IN THE FLESH, I HAVE MORE: CIRCUMCISED ON THE EIGHTH DAY, OF THE PEOPLE OF ISRAEL, OF THE TRIBE OF BENJAMIN, A HEBREW BORN OF HEBREWS; AS TO THE LAW A PHARISEE, AS TO ZEAL A PERSECUTOR OF THE CHURCH, AS TO RIGHTEOUSNESS UNDER THE LAW BLAMELESS. BUT WHATEVER GAIN I HAD, I COUNTED AS LOSS FOR THE SAKE OF CHRIST. (PHIL. 3:4-7)

Countless articles and books have been written about Paul, but whatever else can be said, he did everything for the sake of Christ in the course of life filled with upheaval, controversy, confrontation, deep pain, and great joy.

He was born Shaul (Saul) around the year A.D. 10 in the town of Tarsus, in present-day southeastern Turkey. His parents were Jews of the Diaspora, and Shaul was born a Roman citizen. He was comfortable with all four main cultures of the first century: Mediterranean, Roman, Hellenistic, and Jewish. This made him perfectly suited to become—through miraculous and dramatic events—an evangelist, preacher, and apostle, taking the Gospel of Jesus Christ and the word of the God of Israel to the nations.

Shaul probably had a solid classical education, being schooled in Greek philosophy, literature, and rhetoric, and familiar with Homer, Plato, and Aristotle. But he was first and foremost a student of the Hebrew Scriptures, the Old Testament. He was, he stated before an angry crowd in Jerusalem, "a Jew, born at Tarsus in Cili'cia, but brought up in this city at the feet of Gamaliel, educated according to the strict manner of the law of our fathers, being zealous for God as you all are this day" (Acts 22:3). Gamaliel was arguably the greatest rabbi of the time, which means Paul studied under one of the best Scripture scholars of his day. We know that Gamaliel advocated a somewhat broad-minded, tolerant form of Judaism, but Shaul embraced a stricter, harsher form of Judaism. "I advanced in Judaism beyond many of my own age among my people," he wrote in his epistle to the Christians in Galatia, "so extremely zealous was I for the traditions of my fathers" (Gal. 1:14).

He was, then, a young, brilliant, intense religious zealot. In his twenties he became aware of a new sect based in Jerusalem, the Christian movement. It bothered him deeply; he was angered by the sect's

outrageous claim that a crucified carpenter from Nazareth was the Messiah of Israel.
He went after the followers of this crucified carpenter, Jesus of Nazareth, with deadly zeal, obtaining permission to root them out of their homes and cast them into prison. The first mention of Shaul is found in the Acts of the Apostles' account of the stoning of Stephen, the first martyr: "Then they cast him [Stephen] out of the city and stoned him; and the witnesses laid down their garments at the feet of a young man named Saul" (Acts 7:58). "And Saul," we read, "was consenting to his death" (Acts 8:1). He was going from home to home, dragging Christians off to prison. His own testimony, given before King Agrippa, is unsparing and raw: "I not only shut up many of the saints in prison, by authority from the chief priests, but when they were put to death I cast my vote against them. And I punished them often in all the synagogues and tried to make them blaspheme; and in raging fury against them, I persecuted them even to foreign cities" (Acts 26:10-11).

Shaul set out for Damascus, a great city in that day, to carry on this work of persecuting Christians. What happened on that journey was extraordinary, changing history forever:

> NOW AS HE JOURNEYED HE APPROACHED DAMASCUS, AND SUDDENLY A LIGHT FROM HEAVEN FLASHED ABOUT HIM. AND HE FELL TO THE GROUND AND HEARD A VOICE SAYING TO HIM, "SAUL, SAUL, WHY DO YOU PERSECUTE ME?" AND HE SAID, "WHO ARE YOU, LORD?" AND HE SAID, "I AM JESUS, WHOM YOU ARE PERSECUTING; BUT RISE AND ENTER THE CITY, AND YOU WILL BE TOLD WHAT YOU ARE TO DO." (ACTS 9:3-6; CF. ACTS 22:4-11; 26:12-18)

Shaul was transformed, completely, shockingly—and supernaturally. He was baptized and began to preach Jesus as the Son of God in Damascus, much to the consternation of the Christians. His own account, found in his letter to the Galatians, states that he journeyed to "Arabia and then back to Damascus" and went to Jerusalem to see the other apostles only after three years (Gal. 1:17-18).

What was he doing during that time? We don't know for certain, but he seems to have spent time in prayer, contemplating what had happened and making sense of what he had seen and heard. His whole life had to be re-thought; his understanding of Judaism and the Torah and the Prophets had been revolutionized.Everything was now centered on and around the person of Jesus Christ. This didn't involve a repudiation of Judaism, but a radical reconfiguration around the crucified and risen Messiah, Jesus of Nazareth.

Eventually, around the year 47, Shaul—now Paul—"being sent out by the Holy Spirit," embarked upon the first of at least three missionary journeys (Acts 13:3-14:26). In the course of his missionary journeys he traversed an incredible amount of the known world of the first century. He went around the eastern end of the Roman Empire, traveling through Asia Minor, Cyprus, Greece, Macedonia. He went to Antioch, Troas, Derbe, Ephesus, and crossed into Europe, visiting Philippi; he journeyed to Athens, Corinth, and Thessalonika.

His third missionary journey probably ended in 54, the same year he likely wrote his greatest epistle to the Christians in Rome. In the conclusion of that letter, he spoke of traveling even farther west, to the edges of the world: "I hope to see you in passing as I go to Spain, and to be sped on my journey there by you, once I have enjoyed your company for a little" (Rom. 15:24). He finally did make it to Rome, but as a prisoner of the Romans. It is unclear if he did ever make it to Spain. In 67, he was imprisoned again in Rome, and he was martyred not long afterwards.
Paul's letters are complex, theologically dense, often highly personal, usually very passionate,

sometimes incredibly intricate and demanding. He addressed a large range of theological and pastoral issues, including the relationship of Jewish and Gentile Christians, Christology, the Holy Spirit, justification, charity, faith, hope, the roles of men and women, morality, sacraments, Church authority, and much more. We will consider two of the central themes in his epistles: the Resurrection and participation in Christ.

✝

Resurrection

In the first century, there were several different views among Jewish religious leaders about what happened to people upon death. The Sadducees taught that the body decayed and life ended. Others believed that those who were righteous went to be with God, a belief found in the Book of Wisdom (a work that Paul alludes to more than once). Yet others, following a form of Platonism, thought the soul escaped from the dead body and ascended to a celestial realm. A common belief among Jews of the first century was that the righteous would rise with their bodies at the close of the age.

There is little in Paul's letters about Jesus' teachings, miracles, or public life. However, he speaks many times about Jesus' Resurrection from the dead—so much so that when Paul journeyed to Greece and appeared in the Areopagus, the public forum in Athens, he recited the word *anastasis* (resurrection) so often that people thought he was proclaiming a new god by that name (Acts 17:18).

Paul was acquainted with all of the various theories and beliefs about the afterlife. But his teaching about the Resurrection of Jesus was different from all of them. It was not mythological, or pantheistic. Paul did not claim that the soul had escaped from Jesus' body, or that Jesus was now with God in some hazy, vague fashion. In his first letter to the Christians at Corinth, he outlines his belief that what had transpired in the Resurrection—a real event in time and history—was meant for all of the righteous at the *eschaton*, the culmination of time and history:

> FOR I DELIVERED TO YOU AS OF FIRST IMPORTANCE WHAT I ALSO RECEIVED, THAT CHRIST DIED FOR OUR SINS IN ACCORDANCE WITH THE SCRIPTURES, THAT HE WAS BURIED, THAT HE WAS RAISED ON THE THIRD DAY IN ACCORDANCE WITH THE SCRIPTURES, AND THAT HE APPEARED TO CEPHAS, THEN TO THE TWELVE. THEN HE APPEARED TO MORE THAN FIVE HUNDRED BRETHREN AT ONE TIME, MOST OF WHOM ARE STILL ALIVE, THOUGH SOME HAVE FALLEN ASLEEP. THEN HE APPEARED TO JAMES, THEN TO ALL THE APOSTLES. LAST OF ALL, AS TO ONE UNTIMELY BORN, HE APPEARED ALSO TO ME (1 COR. 15:3-8).

The Resurrection of Christ was not the result of a mass hallucination, nor was it a cleverly devised lie or scam. There were hundreds of witnesses who had seen Jesus after he had died and was buried. And one of those, of course, was Paul himself. This belief was of "first importance," Paul further explained, because without the Resurrection, Christianity is meaningless:

> BUT IF THERE IS NO RESURRECTION OF THE DEAD, THEN CHRIST HAS NOT BEEN RAISED; IF CHRIST HAS NOT BEEN RAISED, THEN OUR PREACHING IS IN VAIN

AND YOUR FAITH IS IN VAIN. WE ARE EVEN FOUND TO BE MISREPRESENTING GOD, BECAUSE WE TESTIFIED OF GOD THAT HE RAISED CHRIST, WHOM HE DID NOT RAISE IF IT IS TRUE THAT THE DEAD ARE NOT RAISED. FOR IF THE DEAD ARE NOT RAISED, THEN CHRIST HAS NOT BEEN RAISED. IF CHRIST HAS NOT BEEN RAISED, YOUR FAITH IS FUTILE AND YOU ARE STILL IN YOUR SINS. THEN THOSE ALSO WHO HAVE FALLEN ASLEEP IN CHRIST HAVE PERISHED. (1 COR. 15:13-18).

The Resurrection, Paul contended, was the fulfillment of all of God's plans and promises for Israel. All of salvation history was concretized and established by it. All of the covenants, the Law of Moses, the writings of the many prophets, the longing of patriarchs, kings, shepherds, and so many others found fulfillment in Jesus rising from the dead. The Resurrection was the dawn of a new creation, the eighth day. "The seventh day completes the first creation," the *Catechism* explains, "The eighth day begins the new creation. Thus, the work of creation culminates in the greater work of redemption. The first creation finds its meaning and its summit in the new creation in Christ, the splendour of which surpasses that of the first creation" (par. 349). In the words of Paul: "Therefore, if any one is in Christ, he is a new creation; the old has passed away, behold, the new has come" (2 Cor. 5:17).

Those who have been buried in Christ and his death through baptism will rise again, so that "we too might walk in newness of life" (see Rom. 6:4). Through baptism, we are made sons of the Father, co-heirs with Christ, vessels of the Holy Spirit. The risen Lord had conquered death and now ruled all of creation—the very creation he brought into being that had longed for liberation from the bonds of sin, corruption, and decay. Christ is the "first fruits of those who have fallen asleep," and he opens the door for us to everlasting beatitude and communion with the Father (1 Cor. 15:20; Rom. 8:15-25).

✝

Participation in Christ

A short and simple phrase that helps us more fully appreciate and comprehend Paul's theological vision is *en Christo*: "in Christ." It appears often in Paul's writings, and it suggests mystical participation, the sharing in the being of something—or someone. Paul taught that the risen Jesus, who bears and fulfills God's promises to all who believe, possesses a *dynamis*—that is, power.

Those who had entered into the covenants of Abraham, Moses, and David had entered into communion with God in a special way. But those who enter into the new covenant in Christ enter into the very divine life of God and are made truly alive. "For as in Adam all die," wrote Paul, "so also in Christ shall all be made alive" (1 Cor. 15:22).

At the heart of this covenantal gift of supernatural life is the sacrament of the Eucharist. In 1 Corinthians 10, Paul writes, "The cup of blessing which we bless, is it not a participation in the blood of Christ? The bread which we break, is it not a participation in the body of Christ? Because there is one bread, we who are many are one body, for we all partake of the one bread" (1 Cor. 10:16-17).

The Greek word for "participation" is *koinonia*, which is mystical communion or fellowship. The primary sacramental and liturgical event in the early Church was a sharing in the life of the risen

Christ. This is a key reason for Paul's use of the image of the body in describing the intimacy and unity shared by believers with the Lord. "For just as the body is one and has many members," he told the Corinthian believers, "and all the members of the body, though many, are one body, so it is with Christ." And how does one become a member of this one body? "For by one Spirit we were all baptized into one body—Jews or Greeks, slaves or free—and all were made to drink of one Spirit. For the body does not consist of one member but of many" (1 Cor. 12:12-14).

This helps us better understand the complicated and intensely debated theme of justification, a topic at the heart of the great rending of Christendom in the sixteenth century. Paul, a student of the great Gamaliel, would have known well the Hebrew term *mispat*, which means justice or right order. *Mispat* was a quality of God—and of those humans who are in right relation to God. The best Greek translation of this term was *dikaiosyne*—righteousness or justice—a word Paul used frequently in his writings.

For Jews, the *mispat* of God was expressed in and through a myriad of laws, regulations, and covenants. Through these, man became righteous. But Paul knew that Israel, despite having the Law and the covenants, had never kept its end of the bargain; it had always failed to fulfill the requirements of the Law and the demands of the covenant. Yet that changed, thankfully, with the crucifixion and Resurrection, for Jesus was the faithful Israel meeting the faithful God of Israel. He was Law and covenant fulfilled, not only in word and deed but in flesh and blood. This is why Paul could say that we are justified—made righteous and holy—not by the works of the Law, but by the person of Jesus Christ. "But now," he told the Roman Christians, "the righteousness of God has been manifested apart from law, although the law and the prophets bear witness to it..." (Rom. 3:21). It is by mystical participation in Christ that man comes into right relationship with God.

In addition, this new covenant and new law was not limited to one nation or ethnic group, but was for all those who became one with Christ through faith and sacrament: "For as many of you as were baptized into Christ have put on Christ. There is neither Jew nor Greek, there is neither slave nor free, there is neither male nor female; for you are all one in Christ Jesus" (Gal. 3:27-28). The dream of the prophet Isaiah that all the nations would stream toward Zion, the holy city of God, had come true in Jesus risen from the dead. This is the ecstatic message Paul has for the Romans, the Galatians, the Philippians, the Corinthians, and anyone that wants to listen: "But now in Christ Jesus you who once were far off have been brought near in the blood of Christ" (Eph. 2:13).

Participation in the power of Christ comes through faith, trust, and acceptance. The word used by Paul over and over is *pistis*, which means something like trusting acceptance. Without faith, he says, we cannot be pleasing to God. Our trouble began through lack of faith; the solution will come only through a renewal of faith. But faith is not the end, for we are called to be *Christified*, fully transformed and renewed. There is no opposition between faith and good deeds, because both are gifts from God, and we are to grow in both, by God's grace.

Through faith we are grafted into the power of Jesus Christ, but then we deepen our relationship with him, we grow in his grace, we become conformed to love, we are transformed more deeply into children of God. In considering all of this, we must call to mind the famous chapter about love, which reminds us of the heart of God and the call of the Christian life: "And if I have prophetic powers, and understand all mysteries and all knowledge, and if I have all faith, so as to remove mountains, but have not love, I am nothing" (1 Cor. 13:2).

QUESTIONS FOR UNDERSTANDING — Part 2:

1. What did Paul give up in becoming a Christian and an Apostle? How did his upbringing and education prepare him for his work as Apostle, preacher, missionary, and theologian?

2. Why did Paul put so much emphasis on the Resurrection in his writings? What is the connection between the Resurrection and the new creation? (1 Cor. 15:13-20; 2 Cor. 5:17; Rom. 6:1-9; Rom. 8:15-25)

3. What is justification? What is its place in the plan of salvation? (Rom. 3:21; CCC 1987-1995, 2019-21)

QUESTIONS FOR APPLICATION — Part 2:

1. Have you ever experienced the temptation to deny or minimize Christ? To ignore him? If so, what brought about that situation? How does Christ extend his forgiveness to us?

2. What have you learned—or can you learn—from Peter and Paul that will help you in your relationship with Christ?

3. What does it mean to live "in Christ"? What are ways in which we can grow in God's divine life and experience it more deeply and fully?

TERMS & NAMES

Areopagus: A hill in Athens near the Acropolis which functioned as the Athenian court of appeals.

Ananias. A Jewish Christian of Damascus who played a role in the conversion of Paul.

Caesarea Philippi: Located about 25 miles north of the Sea of Galilee in northern Palestine, it was the site of the capital and main residence of Herod Philip. Noted for its towering cliff, beneath which was a spring and caves, the location was the site of many pagan cultic activities during the time of Christ.

Caravaggio, Michelangelo (1571-1610). An Italian, Baroque artist who contributed to the Catholic Counter-Reformation. He used a technique called chiaroscuro which places light and dark colors next to each other without intermediate colors in between.

Dawson, Christopher (1889-1970). An English scholar known for his many books in cultural history and Christendom. A Catholic convert from Anglicanism, he often wrote of the role of the Medieval Catholic Church in shaping European culture.

Diaspora: "dispersion"; the name used for the Jewish communities that settled outside of Palestine.

Eschaton: From the Greek word for "last things" or "last days," referring to the *Parousia* (Second Coming) and the final judgment. It marks the culmination of salvation history, and the complete realization of the Kingdom of God.

Eusebius of Caesarea, (c. 260-c. 340). Bishop of Caesarea, known as "the Father of Church history" for his work, *Ecclesiastical History.* A supporter of the heretic Arius, he was an opponent of St. Athanasius. Though not well-written, his works are considered invaluable sources of historical information about the early Church.

Gamaliel, (A.D., first century). A highly regarded first-century Pharisee and rabbi who was the main teacher of Paul. He was given the honorific title, "the Elder," and was considered the greatest teacher of Judaism during his lifetime.

Gentile: Any member of a non-Jewish nation.

Hellenistic Civilization: Represents the height of Greek influence in the ancient world. It spread because of the conquests of Alexander the Great (356-323 B.C.).

Justification: The act and process of being made righteous by the power and grace of God. Justification detaches man from sin, purifies his heart of sin, reconciles man with God, and conforms man to the righteousness of God (see CCC1987-1995).

Koinonia: Communion by mystical participation in the divine life.

Transfiguration: The event described in the three synoptic Gospels (Mt. 17:1-8; Mk. 9:2-8; Lk. 9:28-36) during which Jesus, while at the top of Mount Tabor with Peter, James, and John, was transformed: his garments became intensely bright, and Moses and Elijah appeared alongside him.

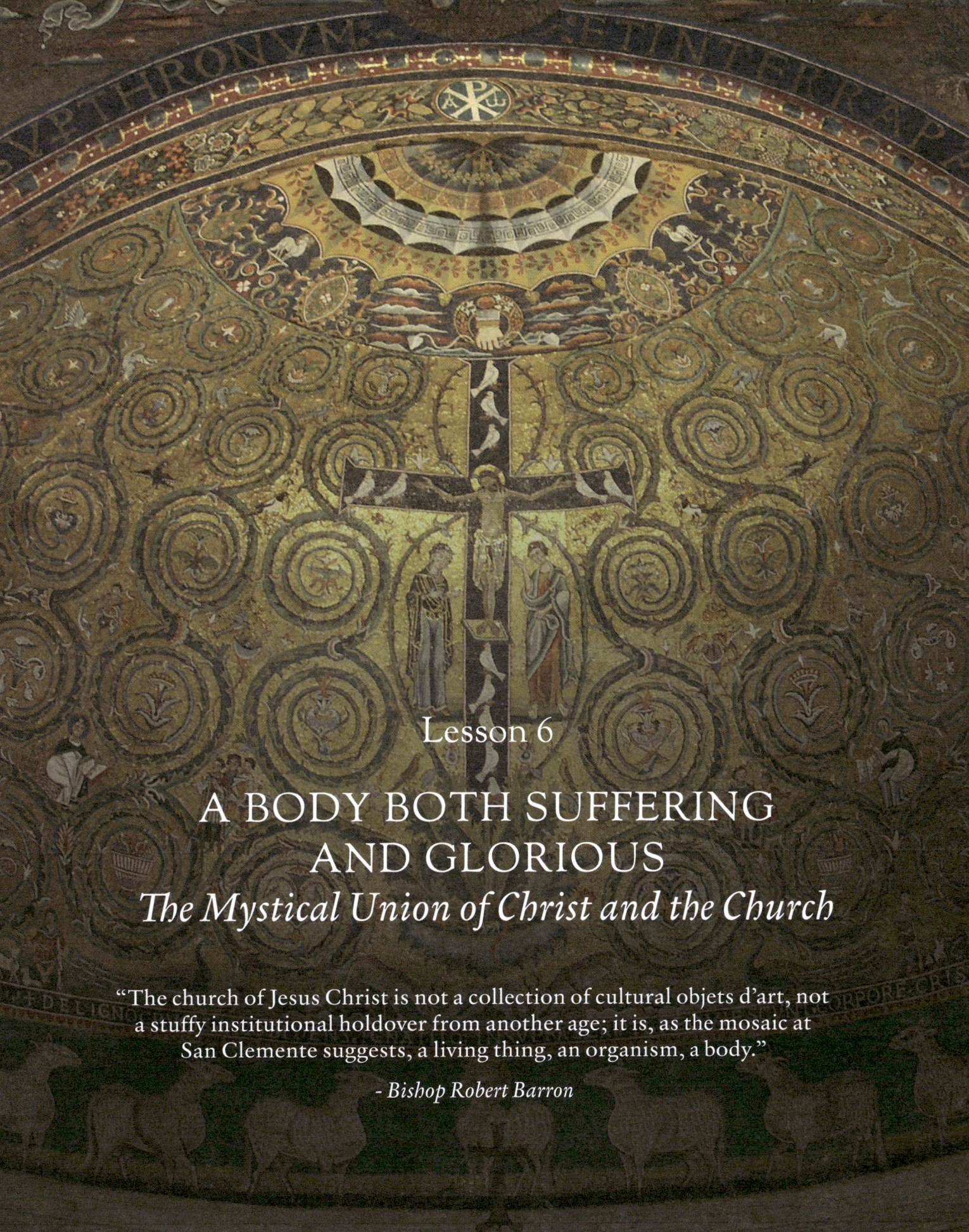

Lesson 6

A BODY BOTH SUFFERING
AND GLORIOUS
The Mystical Union of Christ and the Church

"The church of Jesus Christ is not a collection of cultural objets d'art, not
a stuffy institutional holdover from another age; it is, as the mosaic at
San Clemente suggests, a living thing, an organism, a body."

- Bishop Robert Barron

Basilica of San Clemente. Rome, Italy.

THE MYSTICAL UNION OF CHRIST & THE CHURCH
Episode 6, Part 1

OUTLINE *(Tracks 1-4 on DVD)*

I. The Mystery of the Church

    A. Can you define "Church" in a single sentence?

    B. The Church is not a human invention; in Christ, "like a sacrament"

C. The Church is a Body, a living organism

      1. "I am the vine and you are the branches" (Jn. 15)

      2. The Mystical Body of Christ (*Mystici Corporis Christi*, by Pius XII)

      3. Jesus to Saul: "Why do you persecute me?" (Acts 9:3-4)

      4. Joan of Arc: The Church and Christ are "one thing"

II. *Ekklesia*

    A. God created the world for communion with him (CCC 760)

    B. Sin scatters; God gathers

      1. God calls man into the unity of his family and household (CCC 1)

      2. God calls man out of the world

C. The Church takes Christ's life to the nations

    1. Proclamation and evangelization (*Lumen Gentium*, 33)

    2. Renewal of the temporal order (*Apostolicam Actuositatem,* 13)

III. Four Marks of the Church

A. One

    1. The Church is one because God is One

    2. The Church works to unite the world in God

      3. The Church works to heal divisions (ecumenism)

THE MYSTICAL UNION OF CHRIST & THE CHURCH

Lesson 6, Part 1

The Mystery of the Church

"Christians of the first centuries said, 'The world was created for the sake of the Church.' God created the world for the sake of communion with his divine life, a communion brought about by the 'convocation' of men in Christ, and this 'convocation' is the Church. The Church is the goal of all things, and God permitted such painful upheavals as the angels' fall and man's sin only as occasions and means for displaying all the power of his arm and the whole measure of the love he wanted to give the world: Just as God's will is creation and is called 'the world,' so his intention is the salvation of men, and it is called 'the Church.'"

– Catechism of the Catholic Church, par. 760.

"For where the Church is, there is the Spirit of God; and where the Spirit of God is, there is the Church and every form of grace, for the Spirit is truth."

– St. Irenaeus, *Against the Heresies* (3, 24, I).

What is the Church? If you had to define "the Church" in a single sentence, what would you say? Is it an institution, a structure, a gathering, a community, a people? All of the above, and more?

In saying the Nicene Creed, we profess belief in God the Father, His Son, Jesus Christ, and the Holy Spirit. We profess belief in the Trinity, the forgiveness of sins, and life everlasting. But we also profess, "I believe in one, holy, catholic, and apostolic Church." Isn't this a case of putting faith in a human institution, a deeply flawed organization? Some non-Catholic Christians might wonder, "Aren't you confusing the Creator with the creature? Isn't believing *in* the Church bordering on blasphemous?"

It would indeed be an outrageous thing to express such a belief if the Church were merely a human construct, the invention of men. But the Church is not a human invention. The Church "is in Christ like a sacrament or as a sign and instrument," states *Lumen Gentium*, the Second Vatican Council's Dogmatic Constitution on the Church, "both of a very closely knit union with God and of the unity of the whole human race..." (sec. 1). The Church participates uniquely in the life and power of

Jesus Christ. It is, St. Paul explained to the Christians at Corinth, the body of Christ: "For just as the body is one and has many members, and all the members of the body, though many, are one body, so it is with Christ. ... Now you are the body of Christ and individually members of it" (1 Cor. 12:12, 27).

So the Church is not a club, or simply an institution, or even a gathering of like-minded people. It is a body, a living organism, made up of interdependent cells, molecules, and organs. Each member of the Church is linked organically to Christ, the Head, and to each other. "But as it is," Paul explained, "God arranged the organs in the body, each one of them, as he chose. If all were a single organ, where would the body be? As it is, there are many parts, yet one body" (1 Cor. 12:18-20).

Jesus used powerful images to describe this organic, cohesive whole. Drawing on the rich imagery of the prophets, he said, "I am the vine, you are the branches. He who abides in me, and I in him, he it is that bears much fruit, for apart from me you can do nothing" (Jn. 15:5). He shocked many of his disciples when he said, "Truly, truly, I say to you, unless you eat the flesh of the Son of man and drink his blood, you have no life in you..." (Jn. 6:53). Such deliberate remarks demonstrate that Jesus did not consider himself to be a mere teacher or moral guide, but someone much greater. Someone might admire a great leader, such as Abraham Lincoln, or study and emulate a teacher such as Gandhi, but would anyone speak of eating the flesh of Lincoln or "abiding" in Ghandi?

Yet this is the language of Jesus and Scripture, and it tells us that we are members of a mystical body. Pope Pius XII, in his great encyclical, *Mystici Corporis Christi*, given in 1943, wrote:

> If we would define and describe this true Church of Jesus Christ—which is the One, Holy, Catholic, Apostolic and Roman Church—we shall find nothing more noble, more sublime, or more divine than the expression "the Mystical Body of Christ"—an expression which springs from and is, as it were, the fair flowering of the repeated teaching of the Sacred Scriptures and the Holy Fathers (sec. 13).

This mystical union is revealed in various ways in the New Testament. For example, in Matthew 25, Jesus speaks of his mystical body in exhorting his followers to a radical life of love: "Truly, I say to you, as you did it to one of the least of these my brethren, you did it to me," and "Truly, I say to you, as you did it not to one of the least of these, you did it not to me" (Mt. 25:40, 45). This goes beyond identifying certain behaviors as right or wrong, for Jesus says that helping another has something profound to do *with him*. Giving bread to the hungry and drink to the thirsty, visiting the imprisoned, counseling the doubtful, bringing peace—each is an act of service to Christ. Failure to treat others with this self-sacrificial love is to harm and turn Jesus away.

Another dramatic example is found in the account of Saul's conversion in the Acts of the Apostles. "Now as he journeyed he approached Damascus, and suddenly a light from heaven flashed about him. And he fell to the ground and heard a voice saying to him, 'Saul, Saul, why do you persecute me?'" (Acts 9:3-4). Jesus didn't ask, "Why are you persecuting my followers or my apostles or my Church?" No, he says, "Me." And when Saul asked, "Who are you, Lord?", he received this reply: "I am Jesus, whom you are persecuting" (Acts 9:5). Jesus identifies himself intimately with the Church and her sufferings.

St. Joan of Arc, while being interrogated at her trial, said, "About Jesus Christ and the Church, I simply know they're just one thing, and we shouldn't complicate the matter" (cited in CCC 795). In this, she echoed St. Augustine, who put it just as directly: "Christ and the Church are two in one flesh" (*In Ps.* 142, 3). Recognizing this unity is essential in approaching the mystery of the Church.

Ekklesia

The Church is the culmination of God's salvific actions and the means by which men are to enter into the divine life. "God created the world for the sake of communion with his divine life," states the *Catechism*, "a communion brought about by the 'convocation' of men in Christ, and this 'convocation' is the Church" (par. 760). The Church "is nothing other than 'the family of God'" (par. 1655), which is a distinctive and remarkable belief.

To appreciate this more deeply, recall that God is a great gathering force and a community of love: Father, Son, and Holy Spirit. Because all things are created by God, all things are linked to one another. So whatever is opposed to God is a source of dissolution and division. One of Satan's principle names in the New Testament is *ho diabolos*, a term derived from the Greek word *diabalein*, which means "to scatter." Sin has scattered man, tearing him away from God and introducing strife and discord within the human race. God's response to this sin and scattering was to engage in a great act of gathering. As we've already seen, this came through the call to Abraham, the establishment of covenants, and the creation of the people of Israel. They were made distinctive through the covenants and the Law, by liturgy and a particular way of life that was aimed at holiness and communion with God.

The purpose of this gathering of a people of God was not for Israel's own glory, but so the chosen people would be the first born of many sons (see Ex. 4:22; CCC 238)—that is, Israel would attract and draw together the whole world into the knowledge and worship of Yahweh. The establishment and maintaining of the distinctiveness of Israel was not *against* the world, but *for* the world. This work of gathering, of course, did not always go well; there was often disobedience, discord, idolatry, jealousy, and apathy.

"But when the time had fully come," St. Paul wrote to the Galatians, "God sent forth his Son, born of woman, born under the law, to redeem those who were under the law, so that we might receive adoption as sons" (Gal. 4:4-5). The Son, Jesus Christ, was the culmination of God's plan of salvation; he was the fulfillment of Israel, the perfection of the Law, the covenants, the prophets, and the Jewish liturgy. He was a supernatural magnet: "and I, when I am lifted up from the earth, will draw all men to myself" (Jn. 12:32). Jesus gathers; he carries out the Father's mission to call together "all men, scattered and divided by sin, into the unity of his family, the Church" (CCC 1).

Standing outside of Caesarea Philippi before the towering cliff that housed the many altars of pagan gods, Jesus told Peter, "And I tell you, you are Peter, and on this rock I will build my *ekklesia*, and the powers of death shall not prevail against it" (Matt. 16:18). This word, *ekklesia*, comes from two Greek terms—*ek* and *kaleo*—which mean "to call out," referring to a called people, an assembly. The Church is that society called out of one way of life into another way of living, set apart to be filled with another life.

This raises three key questions: Who does the calling? What are we called *from*? And what are we called *into*? In our modern culture, in Western society, we join organizations and gain memberships; we decide what groups we wish to participate in and be part of. But it is different with the Church, for we are called and summoned by someone else. "His divine power has granted to us all things that pertain to life and godliness," wrote St. Peter in his second epistle, "through the knowledge of him *who called us to his own glory and excellence*, by which he has granted to us his precious and very great promises, that through these you may escape from the corruption that is in the world because of passion, and become partakers of the divine nature" (2 Pet. 1:3-4; emphasis added). God calls, God grants, God saves. We are called to be sons and daughters who do his work and serve him as loving children. We belong to someone else. We are, by God's grace, "called and chosen and faithful" (Rev. 17:14); we are, as Paul states, "slaves of God" (Rom. 6:22) and "a slave of Christ" (1 Cor. 7:22).

We have been called out of what Scripture calls "the world," a word with specific connotations. The world stands against God; it is the realm of opposition to God. The world is filled with hatred, violence, pride, self-obsession, rivalry, jealousy, institutional corruption. As members of the *ekklesia*, we have been summoned out of this realm of spiritual death. "Now we have received not the spirit of the world, but the Spirit which is from God, that we might understand the gifts bestowed on us by God" (1 Cor. 2:12).

The Church maintains its distinctiveness, again, not because it is opposed to the world but because it was established for the sake of the world. The Church is meant to bring man into communion with God. Monsignor Romano Guardini expressed this beautifully in his book, *The Church of the Lord*:

> *The content of the Church is Christ. In preserving Him she preserves herself, for without Him she is nothing. In understanding Him and His message she understands herself, for it is He who constitutes the meaning of her existence. In handing Him on to men she herself lives, for even though she exercises the most varied cultural influences in the course of history, her essential lifework consists in bringing the reality of Christ into our existence. (*Henry Regency Co.; Chicago [1966], p. 73)

The Church has often been likened to a ship, to Noah's ark, bringing men safely through the terrors and trials of life. Just as Noah threw open the doors and windows of the ark after the waters had finally receded, the *ekklesia* is not supposed to remain hunkered down and fearful. It is called to boldly take the divine life of Christ to the nations.

The Second Vatican Council emphasized that this work of proclamation and evangelization is to be embraced wholeheartedly by the laity. By bringing the Church to the world, the laity brings the world into contact with the Church, the Body of Christ:

> *The lay apostolate, however, is a participation in the salvific mission of the Church itself. Through their baptism and confirmation all are commissioned to that apostolate by the Lord Himself. Moreover, by the sacraments, especially holy Eucharist, that charity toward God and man which is the soul of the apostolate is communicated and nourished. Now the laity are called in a special way to make the Church present and operative in those places and circumstances where only through them can it become the salt of the earth (2*). Thus every layman, in virtue of the very gifts bestowed upon him, is at the same time a witness and a living instrument of the mission of the Church itself "according to the measure of Christ's bestowal"* (Lumen Gentium, 33).

The Council, in fact, was a renewal intended to aid Catholics in rediscovering the Church's goals and focus in the modern world. The mission of the Church never changes, but our understanding of how best to live it in a specific culture does develop, deepen, and change. That mission, according to *Apostolicam Actuositatem*, the Council's Decree on the Apostolate of the Laity, is to proclaim Jesus Christ and to fill the temporal order with the light and salt of the Gospel; the laity have an essential role in this task:

> *Christ's redemptive work, while essentially concerned with the salvation of men, includes also the renewal of the whole temporal order. Hence the mission of the Church is not only to bring the message and grace of Christ to men but also to penetrate and perfect the temporal order with the spirit of the Gospel. In fulfilling this mission of the Church, the Christian laity exercise their apostolate both in the Church and in the world, in both the spiritual and the temporal orders. These orders, although distinct, are so connected in the singular plan of God that He Himself intends to raise up the whole world again in Christ and to make it a new creation, initially on earth and completely on the last day. In both orders the layman, being simultaneously a believer and a citizen, should be continuously led by the same Christian conscience (Apostolicam Actuositatem, 5).*

The Council Fathers taught that "the laity must take up the renewal of the temporal order as their own special obligation," being led by the "light of the Gospel and the mind of the Church and motivated by Christian charity." This involves a permeation of culture, of society and of all aspects of the kingdom of man with the "higher principles of the Christian life" (AA 7). This task is not the priority of priests or religious. The laity, because of their skills in the marketplace, in the institutions of society, and in the everyday activities of men, can perform this crucial activity in a much-needed and primary way. "The apostolate in the social milieu, that is, the effort to infuse a Christian spirit into the mentality, customs, laws, and structures of the community in which one lives, is so much the duty and responsibility of the laity that it can never be performed properly by others" (AA 13).

Lay people, in other words, have a specific vocation; they are called by the Father to cooperate with the Holy Spirit in gathering together mankind into the mystery of the Church, the Body of Christ.

†

The Four Marks:
One, Holy, Catholic, and Apostolic
(continued)

The Church, the Creed states, is "one, holy, catholic, and apostolic." These four characteristics, remarks the *Catechism*, "inseparably linked with each other, indicate essential features of the Church and her mission. The Church does not possess them of herself; it is Christ who, through the Holy Spirit, makes his Church one, holy, catholic, and apostolic, and it is he who calls her to realize each of these qualities" (par. 811). This lesson and the following contain reflections on these four marks in light of what we have already considered regarding the nature of the Church.

The Church is one because God is one. "Hear O Israel, the Lord your God is Lord alone" (Deut. 6:4). The *shema* from the book of Deuteronomy is the most sacred prayer in Judaism. It is echoed in the opening line of the Creed: "*Credo in unum Deum.*" St. Cyprian, writing in the third century, said, "God is one and Christ is one: there is one church and one chair founded, by the Lord's authority, on Peter" (*Letter,* 43.5).

The Church must be one, for its whole purpose is to unite the world around the one God. Jesus, in his great high priestly prayer prior to the Last Supper, prayed:

> *I do not pray for these only, but also for those who believe in me through their word, that they may all be one; even as thou, Father, art in me, and I in thee, that they also may be in us, so that the world may believe that thou hast sent me. The glory which thou hast given me I have given to them, that they may be one even as we are one, I in them and thou in me, that they may become perfectly one, so that the world may know that thou hast sent me and hast loved them even as thou hast loved me (Jn. 17:20-23).*

This emphasis on unity is bothersome to some people. Isn't it, they wonder, a bit imperialistic, exclusive, and overbearing? We live, after all, in a culture that stresses the importance of diversity, tolerance, and uniqueness. There are many different religions and philosophies; people, including Christians, disagree about nearly everything. Isn't this threatened by the Catholic teaching on the unity of the Church?

The Catholic Church has possessed, from the very beginning, a healthy and creative way of dealing with this important issue. It is rooted in the belief that Jesus Christ is not just one of many interesting religious figures, but is the *Logos,* the Second Person of the Trinity. Since this is so, whatever is good, true, and beautiful in other religions, philosophies, or cultures can find its home within the Church of Christ. Tertullian may have scoffed, "What has Athens to do with Jerusalem?" but the history of Christian thought is one of constant interaction with and consideration of other theologies and philosophies. Origen, Augustine, and Ambrose used the philosophies of Plato and Plotinus to illumine the faith. Thomas Aquinas made extensive use of Aristotle, Averroes, Avicenna, and many others. At its best, the Catholic tradition reverences philosophy. So much so that the only reason we are able today to read Plato, Aristotle, Cicero, or Julius Caesar is because Catholic monks copied and preserved their works down through the centuries.

And what about other religions? *Nostra Aetate,* the Second Vatican Council's declaration on the relationship of the Church to non-Christian religions, says:

> *The Catholic Church rejects nothing that is true and holy in these religions. She regards with sincere reverence those ways of conduct and of life, those precepts and teachings which, though differing in many aspects from the ones she holds and sets forth, nonetheless often reflect a ray of that Truth which enlightens all men. Indeed, she proclaims, and ever must proclaim Christ "the way, the truth, and the life" (John 14:6), in whom men may find the fullness of religious life, in whom God has reconciled all things to Himself.* (sec. 2)

And *Unitatis Redintegratio,* the Council's decree on ecumenism—that is, relations with non-Catholic Christians—opens with a reflection on Christ's words, "that they all may be one," and laments the "rifts" and "dissensions" that have separated Christians from one another. It frankly notes the serious disagreements that still exist, but then states:

Moreover, some and even very many of the significant elements and endowments which together go to build up and give life to the Church itself, can exist outside the visible boundaries of the Catholic Church: the written word of God; the life of grace; faith, hope and charity, with the other interior gifts of the Holy Spirit, and visible elements too. All of these, which come from Christ and lead back to Christ, belong by right to the one Church of Christ. (sec. 3)

All truth leads back to Christ, for he is, he declared, "the way, and the truth, and the life; no one comes to the Father, but by me" (Jn. 14:16). And he has only one Church, for he has but one Bride.

QUESTIONS FOR UNDERSTANDING — Part 1:

1. What does the *Catechism* mean in stating, "The world was created for the sake of the Church" (par. 760)? How is the Church "the goal of all things"? What is the relationship between the world and the Church? (CCC 760, 168-9)

THE MYSTICAL UNION OF CHRIST & THE CHURCH

2. What are some of the biblical images or names used to describe or name the Church? (CCC 753-757)

3. How is the Church "in Christ, like a sacrament"? (LG 1) What is the relationship between Jesus Christ and the Church? (CCC 774)

4. What are the four "marks" of the Church? How is the Church "one"? (CCC 811-16)

QUESTIONS FOR APPLICATION — Part 1:

1. What are some of the common misrepresentations of the nature and mission of the Church you encounter? Which are the most difficult to counter or respond to? Why?

2. Is it sometimes difficult to see the Church as a supernatural body established by Jesus Christ for the salvation of souls? If so, why? What can you do to better appreciate the supernatural character of the Church?

3. The word "ekklesia" means "to call out." Who does the calling? From what have you been called? To what are you being called? How can you better hear and respond to the call?

THE MYSTICAL UNION OF CHRIST & THE CHURCH
Episode 6, Part 2

OUTLINE *(Tracks 5-8 on DVD)*

I. Four Marks of the Church

    A. Holy

        1. The Church is holy because her Head, Christ, is holy

        2. The Church contains sinners, but is herself holy

    3. The Church is made holy by God's grace

  C. Catholic

        1. *Kata holos* = "according to the whole"

        2. The Church is the new Israel, universal

        3. The Church transcends cultures, languages, nationalism

  D. Apostolic

        1. From the lives, witness, and teachings of the apostles

        2. The Church hands on Tradition

    3. The Church is hierarchical, governed by priests

        4. Divine revelation and the development of doctrine

          i. No new divine revelation

          ii. Development of doctrine is about growth, not change

        iii. The Church is the servant of the Word of God

THE MYSTICAL UNION OF CHRIST & THE CHURCH

Lesson 6, Part 2

The Four Marks: One, Holy, Catholic, and Apostolic

The Church is holy because Jesus Christ, the head of the Church, is holy. It is holy because the Church is Christ's body. "We believe in the holy church," St. Peter Chrysologus wrote, "because the church is in Christ, and Christ is in the church" (*Sermon*, 60:14).

The Church reveals and brings the holiness of Christ to the world. This is accomplished through liturgy and sacraments, the witness of saints and martyrs, the proclamation of Scripture, adherence to Sacred Tradition, teaching and preaching, art and architecture, and much more. This is the Church's entire purpose: to make saints, to make people holy. Everything it does and everything it has is devoted to that end.

"It is difficult to conceive any proposition," wrote Ronald Knox in *The Church on Earth* about the holiness of the Church, "that would call forth more indignant protests from non-Catholics and more demands of explanation from Catholic themselves" (Sophia Institute Press, 2003 [Orig. 1929], p. 21). Issues immediately arise; questions are asked. "What about the far less than holy things that the Church has done and continues to do in the world?" One hears a litany of historical examples supposedly proving the tainted and corrupt, if not overtly evil, nature of the Church: the Crusades, the Inquisition, the persecution of Galileo, the burning of witches, the opposition to modern political reforms, the support of slavery, institutional corruption, too much wealth and worldly preoccupations, and in recent years, the abuse of children by priests and the countenancing of this by some bishops.

Given such a list of abuses, how can we possibly speak of the Church as holy? First, to say that the Church is holy is not to deny for a moment that the Church is filled with sinners. To say that the Church is holy is not to deny for a moment that sons and daughters of the Church—even those of the highest rank—have done all sorts of cruel, stupid, and sinful things. But this does not mean the Church is not the bearer of grace. St. Augustine, in battling the Donatists in the fourth century, brought this fact to the fore. The Donatists believed that only morally pure priests could validly celebrate the sacraments and be real conduits of grace. But Augustine opposed Donatism, insisting that even unrighteous priests and sinful bishops can validly administer the sacraments. It is God's holiness and grace that guarantee the sacraments, not the moral uprightness of the priest. Paul's words remind us that all we have is a gift from God:

For what we preach is not ourselves, but Jesus Christ as Lord, with ourselves as your servants for Jesus' sake. For it is the God who said, "Let light shine out of darkness," who has shone in our hearts to give the light of the knowledge of the glory of God in the face of Christ. But we have this treasure in earthen vessels, to show that the transcendent power belongs to God and not to us" (2 Cor. 4:5-7).

We are "earthen vessels," flawed, fragile, unimpressive; the real power belongs to God alone. The history of the Church bears witness to this fact. God's grace—which makes the church holy—has come through very weak, sometimes sinful, channels. The Church, Knox explained, "is a faultless society in the sense that her organization is perfectly designed to lead her members to perfection if they will" (*The Church on Earth*, 24).

The Church is catholic. The word "catholic" comes from the Greek terms *kata holos*, which means "according to the whole." The Catholic Church is a universal church, for God works to gather the whole world unto himself. St. Cyril of Jerusalem, writing in the fourth century, expressed it profoundly in his *Catechetical Discourses*:

> *[The Church] is called Catholic then because it extends over all the world, from one end of the earth to the other; and because it teaches universally and completely one and all the doctrines which ought to come to men's knowledge, concerning things both visible and invisible, heavenly and earthly; and because it brings into subjection to godliness the whole race of mankind, governors and governed, learned and unlearned; and because it universally treats and heals the whole class of sins, which are committed by soul or body, and possesses in itself every form of virtue which is named, both in deeds and words, and in every kind of spiritual gifts (Lecture 18; par. 23).*

The Catholic Church is the new Israel (Gal. 6:16), and hence is a magnet attracting Jew and Gentile, male and female, rich and poor, young and old. When Pilate put the sign, "Jesus of Nazareth, King of the Jews," over the cross of Jesus, he made sure it was stated in the three major languages of the day. Ironically, because of it, he became thereby the first evangelist of the Catholic Church. At Pentecost, the frightened but expectant disciples were filled with the Holy Spirit, and the first thing they did was to preach with power and courage in the tongues of the many nations (Acts 2). Jews from all over the world heard them in their own languages, thereby reversing the curse of the tower of Babel (Gen. 11:1-9).

The Catholic Church, at its best, has always exulted in this universality, this surprising ability to transcend cultures, languages, and national identities. So, for example, in the Middle Ages, an Italian such as Anselm could become a monk and abbot in France and then end his life as the Archbishop of Canterbury in England. Thomas Aquinas, another Italian, could be educated in Germany and become a world-renowned professor in Paris.

The apostles, Karl Adam noted in *The Spirit of Catholicism*, did not see the Church "as one particular sect, but as a society embracing the whole of redeemed humanity. The Church is not an institution to be established within humanity, which for that reason introduces new lines of division and produces a sectional organization and a sort of new synagogue. On the contrary, it is so world-wide in its nature that it breaks down all barriers and all divisions. It is as big and as wide as humanity itself" (New York, 1948 [rev. ed.], pp. 166-7).

Finally, the Church is apostolic. That is, it is from the apostles, from the confession of Peter and the teaching of the other original disciples of Jesus. The Church is not a club, philosophical society, or political movement, but a body of men and women gathered by, for, and around a very particular man, Jesus, whom the apostles knew.

This is why apostolic succession is so important; it is the claim that the bishops of the Church derive their office and authority from the Apostles themselves. They have not been elected by the people; they have been ordained by other bishops who themselves were ordained by other bishops, going all the way back to apostolic times. *Dei Verbum*, the Second Vatican Council's Dogmatic Constitution on Divine Revelation, states:

> *In His gracious goodness, God has seen to it that what He had revealed for the salvation of all nations would abide perpetually in its full integrity and be handed on to all generations. Therefore Christ the Lord in whom the full revelation of the supreme God is brought to completion (see 2 Cor. 1:20; 3:13; 4:6), commissioned the Apostles to preach to all men that Gospel which is the source of all saving truth and moral teaching, and to impart to them heavenly gifts (sec. 7).*

The Apostles then handed on, by preaching, personal example, and observances, what they had been told by Christ, what they had learned from living with him and witnessing his example. "But in order to keep the Gospel forever whole and alive within the Church, the Apostles left bishops as their successors, 'handing over' to them 'the authority to teach in their own place'" (sec. 7). In this way, apostolic preaching—which is expressed in a unique and special manner in the inspired books of the New Testament—"was to be preserved by an unending succession of preachers until the end of time. Therefore the Apostles, handing on what they themselves had received, warn the faithful to hold fast to the traditions which they have learned either by word of mouth or by letter (see 2 Thess. 2:15), and to fight in defense of the faith handed on once and for all (see Jude 1:3)" (sec. 8).

In his letters to Timothy, his "son in the faith," Paul remarks about the laying on of hands, the gesture by which the leaders of the ancient Church were chosen and empowered. "Do not neglect the gift you have," the Apostle exhorted the young leader, "which was given you by prophetic utterance when the council of elders laid their hands upon you" (1 Tim. 4:14). The bishops, in turn, ordain priests and deacons by the laying on of hands. This is why we speak of the apostolic Church as being hierarchical (*hieros* = "sacred"; *arche* = "head, first place"), that is, a Church governed by priests.

The Church would not be the Church if it were to deny the Creed and the truths contained within it. "The Church's universal mission is born from the command of Jesus Christ and is fulfilled in the course of the centuries in the proclamation of the mystery of God, Father, Son, and Holy Spirit, and the mystery of the incarnation of the Son, as saving event for all humanity" (*Dominus Iesus*, sec. 1). The history of the Church is filled, sadly, with men who have denied, skewed, and distorted Church teaching about the Trinity, the divinity of Jesus Christ, the Resurrection, and many other truths. If the validity of these doctrines was simply put up to a vote by the faithful or theologians, the Church would lose integrity.

A related and common question is "Why does the Church today look so different from the Church in ancient times? If the apostolic teaching has been passed down faithfully from generation to generation, how do we explain the wild complexity of the tradition and what appear to be novelties of all kinds?" These questions were raised by many of the Protestant leaders the sixteenth century, but the issue had been around for much longer. Writing around 434, St. Vincent of Lerins explained that an authentic development of doctrine is not a matter of creation, but of clarification:

But perhaps someone is saying, Will there then be no progress of religion in the Church of Christ? Certainly there is...but it is truly progress and not a change of faith. What is meant by progress is that something is brought to an advancement within itself; by change, that something is transformed from one thing into another (Commonitoria 23, 28).

The most famous, and arguably most influential, explanation of this progress is found in Bl. John Henry Newman's classic work, *An Eassay on the Development of Christian Doctrine*, first published in 1845. Newman began writing the book while an Anglican, but in the course of his study he discovered that his arguments against the Catholic Church were crumbling (he entered the Church and was eventually made a cardinal). Many of Newman's detailed and brilliant arguments are summarized by his statement that "I have maintained that modern Catholicism is nothing else but simply the legitimate growth and complement, that is, the natural and necessary development, of the doctrine of the early church, and that its divine authority is included in the divinity of Christianity" (New York: Longmans, Green and Co., 1949, p. 157). Along the same lines, the *Catechism* emphatically teaches that there is no new public revelation between the death of the Apostles and the return of Christ, but "even if Revelation is already complete, it has not been made completely explicit; it remains for Christian faith gradually to grasp its full significance over the course of the centuries" (par. 66).

Divine revelation, because it is supernatural and of God, cannot ever be completely grasped and understood by man, who is finite and limited. Yet the Church, in order to better understand, explain, and present the truths of divine revelation, works to clarify and focus the endless riches contained in that revelation. This process, far from being a corruption of revelation, is at the service of that revelation, for the Church is the servant of the Word of God (CCC 86). In this context we can better understand the role and authority of the bishops and the pope. Newman saw that it is precisely *because* doctrine develops that there is a need for a living voice of authority to determine the difference between legitimate developments and corruptions.

"He cannot have God for his Father," wrote St. Cyprian, "who has not the Church for his mother" (*Treatise* 1.6). Henri de Lubac, who wrote some of the greatest works on ecclesiology in the past century, put it bluntly: "the Church is our mother. We would not be Christians if we did not acknowledge in her this essential characteristic" (*The Motherhood of the Church* [Ignatius Press, 1982], p. 75). She is the spiritual mother who gives us new birth through baptism, feeds us with the Word of God, teaches us the Faith, nourishes us with the Body and Blood of her head, Jesus Christ (CCC 169, 171, 181).

QUESTIONS FOR UNDERSTANDING — Part 2:

1. How can it be said that the Church is holy when there are so many examples of sinful Catholics? (CCC 825)

2. What does "catholic" mean? In what ways is the Church "apostolic"? (CCC 830-831, 857-63, 865)

3. What is the difference between doctrine *changing* and doctrine *developing*? What is the "deposit of faith," and how does it relate to the development of doctrine? (CCC 66, 78, 84-85, 94-95)

QUESTIONS FOR APPLICATION— Part 2:

1. What does the word "evangelization" bring to mind? What are some ways in which you have evangelized, or could evangelize? What are some steps you can take to evangelize better, or more often?

2. The Second Vatican Council emphasized that the laity "must take up the renewal of the temporal order as their own special obligation" (AA 7). What can you do to take part in this renewal? What challenges will you face in that work? How can you overcome those challenges?

3. How might studying and reflecting on the four marks of the Church increase both your understanding of the Church and your love for her?

THE MYSTICAL UNION OF CHRIST & THE CHURCH

NOTES

✠

TERMS & NAMES

Apostolate: From the word "apostle," it refers to work accomplished on the behalf of Christ and the Church. The laity have a unique role in the Church's apostolate: "Since the laity, in accordance with their state of life, live in the midst of the world and its concerns, they are called by God to exercise their apostolate in the world like leaven, with the ardor of the spirit of Christ" (AA 2).

Aristotle (c. 384-c. 322 B.C.). Greek philosopher who was a student of Plato (a student of Socrates) and tutor of Alexander the Great. A key figure in Western philosophy, Aristotle wrote about metaphysics, music, logic, politics, ethics, biology, and many other subjects.

Cyril of Jerusalem, Saint (c. 315-387). Bishop of Jerusalem and Doctor of the Church. He is known for his defense against Arianism and his rich works of catechetical instruction, *Catechetical Lectures* and *Mystagogic Catecheses*.

De Lubac, Henri (1896-1991). Influential French Jesuit theologian who is noted for his translations of early Church and medieval writings and works about ecclesiology, the interpretation of Scripture, and the relationship between grace and nature. He was named a Cardinal by Pope John Paul II, with whom he had a long friendship.

Donatists: Schismatics in Africa who, in the fourth century, broke away from the Catholic Church. Donatism was separatist and rigorist in character, insisting that the valid celebration and administration of the sacraments depended upon the moral character of the priest.

Ecclesiology: The theological study of the origin, nature, and mission of the Church. From the Greek word, *ekklesia*, from which is derived the word "church" (via the Germanic languages).

Ecumenism: From the Greek word referring to "the inhabited world," this is the movement and pursuit of authentic unity between the Catholic Church and those Christian churches or groups not yet in full, visible unity with her. Ecumenism takes various forms, ranging from informal interaction to formal dialogue.

Joan of Arc, Saint (c. 1412-1431 A.D.). A peasant girl who claimed divine guidance and led the French army to important victories during the Hundred Years' War.

Logos: The source of all intelligibility. It is the sacred reality that is the source of beauty, goodness and truth. Christ is the *Logos Incarnate*, the Word made Flesh.

Newman, Blessed John Henry, (1801-90). Cardinal, theologian, and author who was the most famous convert from Angelicanism in the nineteenth century. Newman entered the Catholic Church in 1845, and wrote on subjects including Church history, faith, philosophy, ecclesiology, and the development of doctrine.

Satan: Of Hebrew origin, meaning "adversary" or someone who plots opposition to another. Satan is a fallen angel who is in complete opposition to God and who seeks to ruin his work. He is also called Beelzebul (Mk. 3:22; Matt 10:25; 12:24), the evil one (Matt. 13:19; Jn 17:15; 1 Jn. 5:18, 19), the ruler of this world (Jn. 12:31; 14:30), the great dragon (Rev. 12:9), the serpent or serpent of old (2 Cor. 11:3; Rev 12:9, 14, 20:2), and the tempter (Matt. 4:3; 1 Thess. 3:5). He is also called "the devil" (Matt. 4:1; 25:41; Lk. 4:2; Jn. 13:2; Acts 10:38), which derives from the Greek word *diabolos* (Latin, *diabolus*), which also means "to throw apart" or "to scatter".

Second Vatican Council (Vatican II; 1962-1965): The twenty-first Ecumenical Council of the Catholic Church that was meant to reinvigorate the Church's evangelical mission to the modern world.

Wojtyla, Karol / Saint John Paul II (1920-2005). The Polish pope who has been acclaimed as one of the most influential leaders of the twentieth century.

Lesson 7

WORD MADE FLESH,
TRUE BREAD OF HEAVEN
The Mystery of the Liturgy and the Eucharist

"The liturgy is the privileged communion with the Lord;
it is the source and summit of the Christian life. And therefore
those who participate in it never leave unchanged;
they never go back the same way they came."

- Bishop Robert Barron

Alexander Coosemans. *Allegory of the Eucharist.* 1641-1689. Musée de Tessé. Le Mans, France.

THE MYSTERY OF THE LITURGY & THE EUCHARIST
Episode 7, Part 1

OUTLINE *(Tracks 1-4 on DVD)*

I. **Communion with the Lord**

    A. Aristotle: the best activities are the most useless

    B. Romano Guardini: "The Playfulness of the Liturgy"

    C. Liturgy exists for its own sake; we "do liturgy" because it is good to do

    D. Mass is a microcosm of God's right order preserved

II. **The Gathering**

    A. The Mass brings about real unity amidst authentic diversity

    B. This unity is focused on the person of Jesus Christ

    C. Singing is an embodied expression of harmony

    D. We call to mind our sins, acknowledging our guilt and need for forgiveness

    E. The Gloria: we render to God due glory; we love God for his own sake

III. **The Telling of the Stories**

    A. Proclamation of the Word of God: Old Testament, Responsorial Psalm, New Testament epistle, Gospel

    B. They draw us into the biblical world and the story of salvation

    C. Scripture, inspired by God, tells the story of God

    D. Preaching is meant to bring about a transforming encounter

    E. The Creed: the great profession of faith

THE MYSTERY OF
THE LITURGY & THE EUCHARIST

Lesson 7, Part 1

Communion with the Lord

"How freely did I weep in Your hymns and canticles; how deeply was I moved by the voices of your sweet-speaking Church! The voices flowed into my ears; and the truth was poured forth into my heart, where the tide of my devotion overflowed, and my tears ran down, and I was happy in all these things."
– St. Augustine, *Confessions* (Bk. 9, ch. 6).

"The Eucharist is 'the source and summit of the Christian life.' 'The other sacraments, and indeed all ecclesiastical ministries and works of the apostolate, are bound up with the Eucharist and are oriented toward it. For in the blessed Eucharist is contained the whole spiritual good of the Church, namely Christ himself, our Pasch.'"
– *Catechism of the Catholic Church*, par. 1324.

The great twentieth-century theologian Monsignor Romano Guardini wrote several books about the liturgy, most notably *The Spirit of the Liturgy* (1935), a book that had such an impact on a young Joseph Ratzinger that the man who would be Benedict XVI eventually wrote a book of the same title in honor of it. One of the chapters in Guardini's book was titled, "The Playfulness of the Liturgy."

This might seem a bit strange, especially since Guardini was deeply orthodox and reverent. Whatever did he mean in referring to "playfulness" proper to liturgy? After reflecting on the impressive structure and necessary organization found within the life of the Church, Guardini wrote, "The Church, however, has another side. It embraces a sphere which is in a special sense free from purpose." He then stated:

> *When the liturgy is rightly regarded, it cannot be said to have a purpose, because it does not exist for the sake of humanity, but for the sake of God. In the liturgy man is no longer concerned with himself; his gaze is directed towards God. In it man is not so much intended to edify himself as to contemplate God's majesty. The liturgy means that the soul exists in God's presence, originates in Him, lives in a world of divine realities,*

truths, mysteries and symbols, and really lives its true, characteristic and fruitful life. ...
with endless care, with all the seriousness of the child and the strict conscientiousness of
the great artist, has toiled to express in a thousand forms the sacred, God-given life of the
soul to no other purpose than that the soul may therein have its existence and live its life.
The liturgy has laid down the serious rules of the sacred game which the soul plays before
God. (The Spirit of the Liturgy, New York: Sheed & Ward, 1935; translated by Ada
Lane. Accessed at http://www.ewtn.com/library/LITURGY/SPRLIT.txt)

Guardini was not implying liturgy isn't important, but rather that it is so important that attempts to turn the liturgy into a practical program or a "teaching moment" are not only bound to fail, they fail to comprehend what liturgy is.

Aristotle said that the best things in life are the most useless, because those are the things that we do for their own sake. Useful things are subordinated to some greater end. In keeping with Guardini's point, we can say that liturgy is useless; that is, it is does not have a practical purpose. It does not serve a utilitarian end. Liturgy exists for its own sake; we "do liturgy" because it is good to do. Joseph Ratzinger, in his book, *The Spirit of the Liturgy*, wrote, "Play takes us out of the world of daily goals and their pressures and into a sphere free of purpose and achievement, releasing us for a time from all the burdens of our daily world of work. Play is a kind of other world, an oasis of freedom, where for a moment we can let life flow freely." He also noted that liturgy is "a kind of anticipation, a rehearsal, a prelude for the life to come, for eternal life..."
(Ignatius Press, 2000, pp. 13,14).

The Mass is a microcosm of God's right order preserved. To participate in Mass is to participate in the eternal liturgy of heaven, to enter into the unceasing praise given to God by the angels and saints, described so beautifully in the final book of the Bible:

> AND THE FOUR LIVING CREATURES, EACH OF THEM WITH SIX WINGS, ARE FULL
> OF EYES ALL ROUND AND WITHIN, AND DAY AND NIGHT THEY NEVER CEASE
> TO SING, "HOLY, HOLY, HOLY, IS THE LORD GOD ALMIGHTY, WHO WAS AND IS
> AND IS TO COME!" AND WHENEVER THE LIVING CREATURES GIVE GLORY AND
> HONOR AND THANKS TO HIM WHO IS SEATED ON THE THRONE, WHO LIVES FOR
> EVER AND EVER, THE TWENTY-FOUR ELDERS FALL DOWN BEFORE HIM WHO IS
> SEATED ON THE THRONE AND WORSHIP HIM WHO LIVES FOR EVER AND EVER;
> THEY CAST THEIR CROWNS BEFORE THE THRONE, SINGING, "WORTHY ART
> THOU, OUR LORD AND GOD, TO RECEIVE GLORY AND HONOR AND POWER, FOR
> THOU DIDST CREATE ALL THINGS, AND BY THY WILL THEY EXISTED AND WERE
> CREATED" (REV. 4:8-11).

The philosopher Dietrich von Hildebrand, in his book *Liturgy and Personality*, said that we find harmony precisely in the act of praise (Dietrich von Hildebrand, *Liturgy and Personality* [Steubenville: Hildebrand Press, 2016]). *Sacrosanctum Concilium*, the Second Vatican Council's Constitution on the Sacred Liturgy, stated "that every liturgical celebration, because it is an action of Christ the priest and of His Body which is the Church, is a sacred action surpassing all others; no other action of the Church can equal its efficacy by the same title and to the same degree" (sec. 7). And the *Catechism*, drawing upon *Lumen Gentium*, describes the Eucharist as "the source and summit of the Christian life" (par. 1324; *Lumen Gentium*, sec. 11). It would be difficult to overstate the significance and greatness of the liturgy and the Eucharist.

In this episode/lesson, we will take a tour of sorts through the Mass, looking at how the liturgy really is a "sacred game which the soul plays before God."

†

The Gathering

Those who come together for liturgy come from all walks of life and from every sort of social, educational, and economic background. They are young and old, life-long Catholics and new converts, spiritual giants and struggling sinners. They are drawn by God and shaped into a community, rooted in baptism and gathered around the altar.

While the world is constantly fragmenting into factions and splintering into special interest groups, the Mass brings about true unity amidst authentic diversity. That unity is focused in the person of Jesus Christ; it is a gift of the Father, realized through the power of the Holy Spirit. It is a unity that reflects man's awareness of who is before God, not before other men. "On entering the church," explained Ven. Louis of Granada, "a man must leave behind any authority he has over other men, for before God no man has any authority. Again, the care and anxieties which a man has in regard to his home, family and business or work are good, but they should be left at the door of the church, except when he wants to speak to God about them" (quoted in *The Mass and the Saints* [Ignatius Press, 2009], by Thomas Crean, O.P., p 20).

Once we have gathered, we sing. Singing at the Mass is not merely filler or entertainment, but an embodied expression of harmony among the children of God. The liturgy begins with our declared belief in the greatest mystery of the Faith: "In the name of the Father, and of the Son, and of the Holy Spirit, Amen." This announces who we are: sons and daughters of the Triune God who has called, redeemed, and saved us, drawing us into "the unity of his family, the Church" (CCC 1). We have been redeemed and given new birth by God, who is love. And so we are connected to everyone and everything in a deep and profound way—because God is the source and ground of all being. This is what the British novelist Charles Williams (much admired by C. S. Lewis) called co-inherence. "This principle," explains Bishop Robert Barron in *Bridging the Great Divide* [Sheed & Ward, 2004], "is obviously on display in the one-in-the-otherness of the trinitarian persons, but it can also be glimpsed in the participation of all created things through the divine power and in the interdependence of the members of Christ's body" (p. 39). This is not radical individualism, nor pantheism, but an expression of how love and self-gift are at the heart of God's creative work.

After making the sign of the cross, we are called to bring to mind our sins. "There are saints indeed in my religion," wrote G. K. Chesterton, "but a saint only means a man who really knows he is a sinner" (*Alarms and Discursions*, London, 1924; quoted by Bishop Barron, p. 40). The saints, who are the great heroes of the Church, are those who are so perfectly ordered toward the life and light of God that they are keenly sensitive to every failure to embrace that life and turn toward that light. The path to sainthood and to growth in divine life cannot be traveled without acknowledging our sin and guilt. This has never been a popular message; it is especially repugnant to modern man. Chesterton noted that many people in the modern world think it is "morbid" to confess one's sins:

The morbid thing is not to confess them. The morbid thing is to conceal your sins and let them eat away at your soul, which is exactly the state of most people in today's highly civilized communities (Daily News, January 8, 1908; quoted in Common Sense 101: Lessons from G.K. Chesterton, *by Dale Ahlquist [Ignatius Press, 2006].*

At the beginning of the Liturgy, we pray, 'Lord have Mercy; Kyrie eleison.' This means that we are a people in need of mercy and forgiveness, called by our merciful Father to extend mercy and forgiveness to others.

The *Gloria* is one of the greatest prayers of the Church. It begins with the words from the great hymn sung by the multitude of heavenly host that appeared to the shepherds announcing the birth of Christ: "Glory to God in the highest, and on earth peace to people of good will" (see Lk. 2:13-14). Rendering God due glory is the formula for a well-ordered life, properly focused on the goodness and love of God, not on money, power, pleasure, or other wordly goods. We are, St. Augustine said, to love God for his own sake and everything else for the sake of God. "For it is the nature of love," wrote St. Catherine of Siena, "to love when it feels itself loved, and to love all things loved of its beloved. So when the soul has by degrees known the love of its Creator toward it, it loves Him, and, loving Him, loves all things whatsoever that God loves" (Vida D. Scudder, ed., *Saint Catherine of Siena as Seen in Her Letters* [New York: E.P. Dutton & Co., 1905], 195).

✝

The Telling of the Stories

The next major section of the liturgy is the proclamation of the Word of God. This usually includes a reading from the Old Testament, a Responsorial Psalm, a New Testament epistle, and then the Gospel reading, which is usually linked thematically to the first reading. Why are these texts read? So we can be drawn into the power and reality of the biblical world and the story of salvation. *Dei Verbum*, the Second Vatican Council's Dogmatic Constitution on Divine Revelation, states:

> *The Church has always venerated the divine Scriptures just as she venerates the body of the Lord, since, especially in the sacred liturgy, she unceasingly receives and offers to the faithful the bread of life from the table both of God's word and of Christ's body. She has always maintained them, and continues to do so, together with sacred tradition, as the supreme rule of faith, since, as inspired by God and committed once and for all to writing, they impart the word of God Himself without change, and make the voice of the Holy Spirit resound in the words of the prophets and Apostles.* (sec. 21)

The many stories, narratives, and events described in Scripture tell the story of God, and are inspired by God, who has gifted them to his family. They are an inscripturated expression of God's love, and in hearing them proclaimed in the midst of the Church, we encounter anew the voice of God. "For in the sacred books, the Father who is in heaven meets His children with great love and speaks with them; and the force and power in the word of God is so great that it stands as the support and energy of the Church, the strength of faith for her sons, the food of the soul, the pure and everlasting source of spiritual life." (DV 21).

Karl Barth, the great Protestant biblical theologian of the past century, said the Christian preacher or theologian has the task of pulling his readers and listeners into the strangeness and dense texture of the Biblical world. He introduces them to characters such as the patriarch Abraham, the prophet Isaiah, the king David, the virgin Mary, the apostles Peter and Paul, and, of course, Jesus himself. The homilist explains and "unpacks" the readings, showing how and why these men and women act and speak as they do. He tells of the supremely distinctive character of God himself, who is the transcendent speaker and actor in Scripture. By entering into and moving through this world, we learn how to speak, contemplate, and think in a different way. "But preaching is not speech-giving," explains Fr. Peter John Cameron, O.P.:

> No one was ever saved by a message. It would have been a waste of time for the Word to become flesh if it sufficed for the Father to send a memo instead of his Son. No one was ever saved by a mere discourse. Preaching is so much more than this. The history of civilization is rife with ingenious, mesmerizing, virtuous prophets, visionaries, and teachers. And yet, people today remain as confused, miserable, prone to malice, cynical, negative, fearful, lonely, and lost as they ever were. Something more than a good teacher is required. According to Joseph Cardinal Ratzinger (now Pope Benedict XVI), the aim of preaching "is to tell man who he is and what he must do to be himself. Its intention is to disclose to him the truth about himself, that is, what he can base his life on and what he can die for." And that disclosure is not a discourse; it is an encounter. (Why Preach: Encountering Christ in God's Word [Ignatius Press, 2009], p. 15)

This is, or should be, a transforming encounter, one that takes us out of our old world and immerses us in a new world. Whether we know it or not, the secular world shapes us constantly, teaching us how to think, feel, act, and react. The liturgy resists this by bringing us into an entirely new space, one filled with the presence of Christ.

After the readings and the homily, we recite the Creed, the great profession, or "rule," of faith that comes from the Councils of Nicaea (A.D. 325) and Constantinople (A.D. 381). It is a summation of the biblical worldview, and a statement of belief in it. The symbol of faith "is a summary of the principal truths of the faith and therefore serves as the first and fundamental point of reference for catechesis" (CCC 188). The Creed is followed by the Prayer of the Faithful, a concrete expression of the fact that we gather together as a mystical body, connected in this life by the divine life of God, sharing in the sorrows and joys of one another. We pray for the suffering, the sick, those who are afraid, those who are in power, and many others, precisely because their suffering, their sickness, their fear, and their responsibility are ours as well.

QUESTIONS FOR UNDERSTANDING — Part 1:

1. In what ways can it be said that liturgy is "play" or "a sacred game"? What is liturgy not meant to be?

2. How should worshipping and praising God bring harmony and peace? How does it help establish order in one's life? (CCC 374, 1844, 2845; Jn. 14:27; Col. 3:14)

3. What is the main point of the Scripture readings and homily? What should good preaching accomplish?

QUESTIONS FOR APPLICATION — Part 1:

1. How does approaching liturgy as "play" change how you understand or perceive worship of God? Do you think that such "playfulness" is contrary to the sacred nature of liturgy, or supportive of it?

2. Reflect on the music that you hear and sing at Mass. Would you say that it encourages harmony? Is it reflective in nature? Entertaining? Conducive to worship of God?

3. Prior to attending Mass, spend time reading and reflecting on the Scripture readings for that liturgy. What do the readings tell you about God? About his plan of salvation? What do they reveal or help you understand about your life?

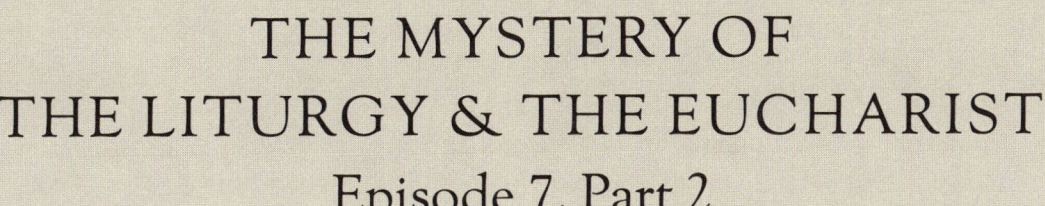

THE MYSTERY OF
THE LITURGY & THE EUCHARIST
Episode 7, Part 2

OUTLINE *(Tracks 5-8 on DVD)*

I. The Offering

    A. The Liturgy of the Eucharist

    B. The offering of sacrifices

        1. God does not need our sacrifice

        2. Sacrifice is an expression of thanksgiving, dependence

    C. Through God's goodness, bread and wine are offered

    D. The Eucharistic Prayer

II. The Real Presence

    A. John 6 contains some of the most challenging, shocking words in the Bible

    B. Miracle of the loaves and fishes (Jn. 6:11-13)

        1. Prayer, thanksgiving, distribution of bread

        2. Foreshadowing the Last Supper, institution of the Eucharist

    C. "It is I, do not be afraid" (Jn. 6:20): Similar to "I AM" (Ex. 3:14)

    D. A series of four exchanges/discourses marked by "Truly, truly"

        1. The people seek physical comfort, not truth (Jn. 6:26)

        2. God, not Moses, gave the manna from heaven (Jn. 6:32)

        3. Those who believe have eternal life (Jn. 6:47)

        4. Eat the flesh of the Son of man and drink his blood (Jn. 6:53-54)

    E. Jesus spoke literally and sacramentally

    F. Jesus emphasized the scandalous nature of his words

    G. Many of the disciples drew away from Jesus; the Eucharist is a stumbling block

    H. Peter: "Lord, to whom shall we go? You have the words of eternal life." (Jn. 6:68)

III. St. Thomas Aquinas and Transubstantiation

A. The great hymns, *Pange Lingua* and *Adoro te Devote* (Corpus Christi)

B. Transubstantiation: the total substance of bread and wine becomes the substance of the Body and Blood of Christ

C. Key terms: truly, really, substantially contained, etc.

D. The mystery of the Eucharist is closely related to the mystery of the Incarnation

E. "This is my Body" and "This is the chalice of my Blood"

F. Jesus—really, truly, and substantially present—is now offered to the Father

IV. "Our Father"

A. The fundamental Christian prayer (CCC 2759)

B. The summary of the whole Gospel (CCC 2761)

C. The center of the proclamation of the Gospel (CCC 2763)

D. Affirmation that we are children of God, reborn through baptism, desiring to partake of Jesus Christ

E. The Eucharist is the sacrament of the kingdom of God

V. Communion and Sending

A. Having received the Lord and given thanks, we are blessed and sent

B. Transformed, we are sent to proclaim God's Word and transform the temporal order

THE MYSTERY OF
THE LITURGY & THE EUCHARIST

Lesson 7, Part 2

The Offering

The first major part of the Mass, called the Liturgy of the Word, is completed. Now begins the second major section, the Liturgy of the Eucharist. The Liturgy of the Word corresponds roughly to the synagogue service in the Jewish tradition, while the second section corresponds roughly to the temple service, at the heart of which was the offering of sacrifice.

In the first episode of this series on the person of Jesus Christ, we discussed the meaning and purpose of sacrifice in the Christian Faith. We saw that God has no need of our sacrifices; rather, they are an expression of our thanksgiving and our dependence on him. In offering sacrifice, we take some aspect or part of God's creation and we return it to him as a sign. God has no need for sacrifice; it benefits us rather than God. Yet it is pleasing to God because it is beneficial to us. And our being increases in the measure that we give it back to God.

The logic of sacrifice and the law of the gift govern the Liturgy of the Eucharist. At the start of this part of the Mass, gifts of bread, wine, and water are brought forward to the priest so they might be offered to God. To say bread and wine is to say wheat and vine; to say wheat and vine is to say earth, soil, water, wind, sunshine; to say earth and soil, wind, and sunshine is to say the solar system and the cosmos. The tiny gifts that are presented are evocative of the entire universe. "The gifts, offerings and sacrifices," wrote St. Albert the Great, "are at the same time those who offer, the things that they offer, and the one who will be offered in them to the Father" (Crean, p. 109).

The priest then says the *Berakah* prayer, "Blessed are you, Lord God of all creation, for through your goodness we have received the bread we offer you: fruit of the earth and work of human hands, it will become for us the bread of life...Blessed are you, Lord God of all creation, for through your goodness we have received the wine we offer you: fruit of the vine and work of human hands, it will become our spiritual drink." Just before the Eucharistic Prayer proper, we invoke the angels, one of several times in the liturgy that we do so. "May our voices be one with theirs, as we join in their unending hymn of praise." We express our desire to join in songs of praise with those creatures who are perfectly ordered and harmonically arranged around the praise of God: all the angels and saints.

Then, "with the Eucharistic Prayer—the prayer of thanksgiving and consecration—we come to the heart and summit of the celebration" (CCC 1352). This is the central moment of Mass: the transformation of the bread and wine into the Body and Blood of Jesus Christ. We have offered our gifts to God, and since God doesn't need them, they come back elevated and perfected as the very life and existence of Jesus. "Sacrifice is so called from being 'made sacred,'" wrote St. Isidore of Seville in his *Etymologies*, "because by mystical prayer it is consecrated on our behalf in memory of the Lord's passion; whence, at His command, we call this the Body and Blood of Christ. Consisting of the fruits of the earth, it is sanctified and becomes the Sacrament, by the invisible operation of the Holy Spirit. The sacrament of the bread and chalice is called by the Greeks "the Eucharist," which means "thanksgiving" in Latin. What is better than the Blood and Body of Christ?" (*Etymologies*, 6.19).

What, indeed, is better? Nothing. And yet there have been, from the beginning, those who refuse to accept the teaching and gift of the Body and Blood of Jesus Christ. In fact, many of the first disciples left Jesus because of his teaching about the Eucharist.

✝

The Real Presence

The sixth chapter of John's Gospel contains some of the most challenging and shocking words found in all of Scripture. Those specific words are found at the end of this long chapter, but their impact is better appreciated with some context. The chapter begins with the well-known story of the miraculous multiplication of the loaves and fishes, recounted in all four of the Gospels.

> JESUS THEN TOOK THE LOAVES, AND WHEN HE HAD GIVEN THANKS, HE DISTRIBUTED THEM TO THOSE WHO WERE SEATED; SO ALSO THE FISH, AS MUCH AS THEY WANTED. AND WHEN THEY HAD EATEN THEIR FILL, HE TOLD HIS DISCIPLES, "GATHER UP THE FRAGMENTS LEFT OVER, THAT NOTHING MAY BE LOST." SO THEY GATHERED THEM UP AND FILLED TWELVE BASKETS WITH FRAGMENTS FROM THE FIVE BARLEY LOAVES, LEFT BY THOSE WHO HAD EATEN. (JN. 6:11-13)

These actions—prayer, thanksgiving, distribution of bread—were clearly meant to set the stage for the coming remarks by Jesus about the Eucharist, as well as foreshadowing the institution of the Blessed Sacrament. Having miraculously fed the people with physical food, Jesus withdrew to spend time in prayer. That night the Apostles set sail on the sea, heading across to Capernaum. A great storm arose, and suddenly Jesus appeared, walking on the wild waters toward the boat. "It is I," he said, "do not be afraid" (Jn. 6:20).

This declaration—"It is I"—was an act of self-revelation, similar to that described in Exodus 3, when Yahweh, speaking from the burning bush, told Moses, "I AM" (Ex. 3:14; see Jn. 8:24, 58; 13:19; 18:6). Walking on the water was also similar to the Israelites walking through the waters of the Red Sea in fleeing Egypt, but Jesus does it by his own power. His words, combined with the dramatic demonstration of his power over nature, showed him to be not only the new Moses, but the God of Moses.

What follows is a series of four progressively deepening exchanges and discourses (6:22-59), each transition marked by Jesus' use of the phrase, "Truly, truly." In the first, Jesus criticizes the people for seeing him as the ticket to a free meal: "Truly, truly, I say to you, you seek me, not because you saw signs, but because you ate your fill of the loaves" (Jn. 6:26). While the people should seek to understand the signs and the one who performed them, they instead seek a full belly. As Jesus does so often in the Fourth Gospel, he moves the focus of his listeners from earthly concerns to heavenly matters. The conversation turns to the miracle of manna in the desert, and Jesus says, "Truly, truly, I say to you, it was not Moses who gave you the bread from heaven; my Father gives you the true bread from heaven" (Jn. 6:32).

The manna was considered by Jews to be the greatest miracle performed by Moses, and many of them believed the coming Messiah would be able to create manna as a sign of his true identity. They also associated this new manna with the Passover, and believed that the manna symbolized divine instruction or the divine word. Jesus states, "I am the bread of life..." (Jn. 6:35), and argues that when the Scriptures refer to bread from heaven, they refer to him and his teaching—not to Moses and the manna. He then makes this startling remark: "For this is the will of my Father, that every one who sees the Son and believes in him should have eternal life; and I will raise him up at the last day" (Jn. 6:40). This is a strong invitation to faith, an invitation that will be extended even further momentarily, for faith in Jesus leads to faith in the Eucharist.

The Jews murmur and wonder why this ordinary looking man, the son of Joseph, is saying such outrageous things. This complaining is similar to the murmuring in the desert, when the people failed to trust God and his servant, Moses (Ex 16:2; 17:2-3; Num 11:1). Jesus then says, "Truly, truly, I say to you, he who believes has eternal life" (Jn. 6:47). Belief in Jesus and his words are essential; without them, man will perish from spiritual starvation. And while the manna was given in a miraculous fashion by God, Jesus is God *become* flesh, who now offers his very flesh: "I am the living bread which came down from heaven; if any one eats of this bread, he will live for ever; and the bread which I shall give for the life of the world is my flesh" (Jn. 6:51).

There is now a dispute—literally, a violent quarrel—about the meaning of these words. But Jesus, rather than alleviating the rapidly growing tension, takes matters even further: "Truly, truly, I say to you, unless you eat the flesh of the Son of man and drink his blood, you have no life in you; he who eats my flesh and drinks my blood has eternal life, and I will raise him up at the last day" (Jn. 6:53-54). The term "flesh and blood" meant, for Jews, the entire person. Jesus was speaking both literally and sacramentally. But Jesus does not alleviate the rapidly growing tension by reframing his language as a metaphor; instead, he takes matters even further.

It's impossible to imagine anything more theologically problematic and, yes, disgusting for first-century Jews. The Mosaic Law strongly condemned the drinking of blood (Gen. 9:4; Lev. 17:10-13; Dt. 12:16). Yet here was a man—a Jew!—saying, "Eat my flesh! Drink my blood!" Jesus, in fact, emphasized the scandalous nature of his words by moving from the word *phago*, which means "eat" (6:50, 51), to *trogain*, which means to gnaw or chew (6:53ff). In other words, when the Jews object to the physical realism of his language, he intensifies the physical realism! It's worth noting that the promise—they "will live forever"—appears only twice in the Bible: here and Genesis 3:22, where it refers to eating from the Tree of Life.

Many of the Jesus' disciples could not handle his words, and drew apart from him. This is the only instance in the Gospels where disciples left Jesus in such numbers; it is the only instance of such a break over a point of doctrine. "The Eucharist and the Cross are stumbling blocks," says the *Catechism*:

> It is the same mystery and it never ceases to be an occasion of division. "Will you also go away?": the Lord's question echoes through the ages, as a loving invitation to discover that only he has "the words of eternal life" and that to receive in faith the gift of his Eucharist is to receive the Lord himself. (CCC 1336)

But what did Peter say? "Lord, to whom shall we go? You have the words of eternal life; and we have believed, and have come to know, that you are the Holy One of God" (Jn. 6:68-9). Peter confesses the truth of the Real Presence, and the Catholic Church has confessed the same ever since.

†

St. Thomas and Transubstantiation

In addition to being one of the greatest philosophers and theologians in history, St. Thomas Aquinas was also a splendid writer of poems and hymns. Pope Urban IV, after inaugurating the Feast of Corpus Christi ("the Body of Christ"), had the Dominican friar compose an office—a series of prayers and hymns—for the feast. Thomas responded with one of the most beautiful poetic works of the Middle Ages. We still sing the great hymns *Pange Lingua* and *Adoro te Devote* from that office of Corpus Christi. For example:

> Down in adoration falling,
> Lo! the sacred Host we hail,
> Lo! o'er ancient forms departing
> Newer rites of grace prevail;
> Faith for all defects supplying,
> Where the feeble senses fail.
>
> To the everlasting Father,
> And the Son Who reigns on high
> With the Holy Ghost proceeding
> Forth from Each eternally,
> Be salvation, honor, blessing,
> Might and endless majesty.
> Amen.

Thomas Aquinas loved the Eucharist; every day he said Mass and then assisted at a second Mass. Whenever he struggled with his writing, he would go to the Tabernacle and rest his head against it, asking the Lord for inspiration. Near the end of his life, he wrote a treatise on the Eucharist. When he finished, he was not convinced he had done justice to the Blessed Sacrament, so he placed the text at the foot of the cross and he prayed. A voice came from the cross: "You've written well of me, Thomas. What would you have as a reward?" The brilliant scholar responded with deep humility, "I will have nothing except you."

In that great treatise, Thomas discussed the notion of transubstantiation. He said that, at the consecration, the total substance of the bread becomes the substance of the Body of Christ. The total substance of the wine becomes the substance of the Blood of Christ, even as the accidents of bread and wine remain unchanged. If those terms seem odd to us, we can rightly translate them as *reality* (substance) and *appearance* (accidents). The deepest reality of the bread and wine change into the Body and Blood of Christ, even as the appearances of bread and wine remain unchanged. Even in our everyday experience, appearance and reality are not always the same. It certainly seems, for instance, as though the sun really moves across the sky. But we know, in fact, it doesn't. In an analogous way, the elements look and taste and smell as if they are bread and wine, but in reality they are Jesus's Body and Blood.

The Catholic Church teaches that while Christ "is present in many ways to his Church," such as in the reading of the Word, in prayer, and in the midst of those who gather in His name, he is present "most especially in the Eucharistic species" (CCC 1373; SC 7). The *Catechism* summarizes the Catholic understanding of Real Presence in this way:

> *The mode of Christ's presence under the Eucharistic species is unique. It raises the Eucharist above all the sacraments as 'the perfection of the spiritual life and the end to which all the sacraments tend.' In the most blessed sacrament of the Eucharist 'the body and blood, together with the soul and divinity, of our Lord Jesus Christ and, therefore, the whole Christ is truly, really, and substantially contained.' "This presence is called 'real' - by which is not intended to exclude the other types of presence as if they could not be 'real' too, but because it is presence in the fullest sense: that is to say, it is a substantial presence by which Christ, God and man, makes himself wholly and entirely present."* (CCC 1374).

In explaining this unique presence the Catechism uses certain key words and phrases: *truly, really, substantially contained, presence in the fullest sense, substantial presence, wholly and entirely present.*

Transubstantiation refers to a change (*trans-*) of the substance—the reality—of bread and wine into the true Body, Blood, Soul, and Divinity of Christ, that is, Christ in his entirety. It is important to note that the Church never states this change is a visible one; it is a sacramental change and the Real Presence is a sacramental presence (CCC 1380). Bread and wine no longer exist, but are substantially converted into Christ. The accidents, the appearances, of bread and wine remain, but the bread and wine do not remain. It is a profound mystery, but no more so than the astounding mystery of the Incarnation, from which the Eucharist flows and in which it is rooted. The Word took on flesh in order to be man and dwell among men; he now dwells among us in another manner—sacramentally—but just as truly: "In his Eucharistic presence he remains mysteriously in our midst as the one who loved us and gave himself up for us, and he remains under signs that express and communicate this love..." (CCC 1380).

To help us understand further, consider that God creates through the power of His word. "Let there be light," he said, and there was light. "Let the earth come forth," and it came forth. God's word does not just describe, it effects what it says. "For as the rain and the snow come down from heaven," wrote the prophet Isaiah, "and return not thither but water the earth, making it bring forth and sprout, giving seed to the sower and bread to the eater, so shall my word be that goes forth from my mouth; it shall not return to me empty, but it shall accomplish that which I purpose, and prosper in the thing for which I sent it" (Isa. 55:10-11). Such is the way and the work of the divine Word.

We believe that Jesus is the Son of God, the Lord of lords and King of kings. He is the very *logos*, the Word of God made flesh. The same Word by which the entire cosmos was created became incarnate in the person of Jesus—therefore, what Jesus says, *is*. "Lazarus, come out," and the dead man came out. "Little girl, get up," and the dead girl gets up. "My son, your sins are forgiven," and those sins are forgiven. What Jesus says simply and truly is. His word never returns to him empty, but rather, completely full and fulfilled.

The night before he died, he took bread in his hands, and said, "This is my body, which will be given up for you." He took the cup and held it, and said, "This is the cup of my blood" (Luke 22:19-20). Jesus' word is the divine word that does not simply describe, but rather affects, creates, changes reality in the most radical sense. When the priest pronounces the words of consecration, he is not using his own words; he is using those divine words of Christ, which can affect and change reality.

Jesus—really, truly, and substantially present—is now offered to the Father, and the rhythm of the law of the gift becomes even more intense. The cross of Jesus was the perfect sacrifice, the summation of the whole history of Israel's offerings in the temple; it is the blood of the new and everlasting covenant. This sacrifice is, at every Mass, re-presented to the Father. But the Father has no need of this sacrifice, and so returns it to us, breaking as it were against the rock of the divine self-sufficiency, and redounding to our benefit. We will now come forward to receive this Body and Blood as our food and drink.

†

Our Father

After Christ's Body and Blood are offered to the Father, we pray in Jesus' own words, the "Our Father." This prayer, also called the Lord's Prayer, is "the fundamental Christian prayer" (CCC 2759), "the summary of the whole Gospel" (CCC 2761), and "the center of the proclamation" of the Gospel (CCC 2763). It was used in the ancient Church in the instruction of those receiving baptism and was the focus of many spiritual treatises of the Church Fathers. Why does the Our Father appear in the Liturgy of the Eucharist, between the Eucharistic Prayer and Communion. First, in the ancient Church the catechumens would leave after the Liturgy of the Word to receive instruction and so wouldn't be able to say the Lord's Prayer, which they were not prepared to utter. Secondly, it prepares us to receive the Eucharist: "[the Lord's Prayer] knocks at the door of the Banquet of the kingdom which sacramental communion anticipates" (CCC 2770).

The Lord's Prayer is our affirmation that we are children of God, reborn through baptism, and desiring to partake of Jesus Christ, who gives us his Body and Blood as spiritual nourishment in our life here on earth, anticipating the Lamb's Supper––everlasting communion with the Triune God.

We state, in saying the Lord's Prayer together, "give us this day our daily bread." The word in the Greek for "daily" is *epiousion*, or "super-substantial." This is a cry for the Eucharist. Then we do receive the living Body and the life-Blood of Jesus, becoming, more and more, members of his mystical body and conformed to eternal life, divinized, eternalized. Alexander Schmemann, the renowned twentieth-century Orthodox theologian, wrote, "If assembling as the Church is, in the most profound sense of the term, the beginning of the eucharistic celebration, [and] its first and fundamental condition, then its end and completion [of the eucharistic celebration] is the Church's entrance into heaven, her fulfillment at the table of Christ, in his kingdom." The Eucharist, he noted, is "the sacrament of the kingdom of God." (*The Eucharist* [St. Vladimir's, 1988], 27). The Eucharist, wrote John Paul II, "is truly a glimpse of heaven appearing on earth. It is a glorious ray of the heavenly Jerusalem which pierces the clouds of our history and lights up our journey" (*Ecclesia de Eucharistia*, sec. 19).

†

Communion and Sending

After we have received the Lord and have given thanks, we are blessed and sent. No one in the Bible has ever encountered God without afterwards being sent on mission. Abraham, Jacob, Joseph, Moses, Isaiah, Peter and Paul—each of them was transformed and then sent forth to proclaim God's Word. Lay people are called to transform the temporal order through their pursuit of the universal call to holiness, lived out in the home, in school, in the work place. Liturgical people are summoned to be great Catholic journalists, poets, business leaders, teachers, captains of industry, media executives, actors, physicians, politicians, and parents. Second only to the words of consecration, the most sacred words of the liturgy are, "The Mass has ended; go in peace, glorifying the Lord by your life." No one comes to Christ and goes back the same way he came!

QUESTIONS FOR UNDERSTANDING — Part 2:

1. What is sacrifice? Why and how is it so central to the liturgy? How is this centrality expressed during the liturgy? (CCC 1323, 1352)

2. What did Jesus mean when he said, "Eat my flesh" and "Drink my blood"? What are some ways in which the language of John 6 points to the liturgy and the Eucharist? (Jn. 6; Ezek. 39:17-18)

3. The Catechism says the Eucharist and the Cross are stumbling blocks and, "It is the same mystery" (par. 1336). What does this mean? (CCC 1367, 1374, 1413; 1 Cor. 1:18; 1 Cor. 1:23)

4. What did Pope John Paul II mean when he wrote that the Eucharist "is truly a glimpse of heaven appearing on earth"?

QUESTIONS FOR APPLICATION — Part 2:

1. Read John 6 and ask yourself: How did Jesus go about revealing the truth about the Eucharist? How might you have reacted if you had been present? How do Jesus' words challenge you? Encourage you?

2. Do you ever find the Eucharist, the Real Presence, or transubstantiation to be a stumbling block or cause for doubt? Why do you think many Catholics doubt or don't believe in the Real Presence?

3. If possible, spend some time before the Blessed Sacrament in prayer. Consider reading and reflecting on the words of St. Thomas Aquinas: "I will have nothing except you."

TERMS & NAMES

Constantinople, First Council of (A.D. 381). Convened by the Emperor Theodosius I to further address the Arian heresy and to deal with additional issues relating to the Church's teaching about the person of Christ and the Divinity of the Holy Spirit.

Guardini, Romano (1885–1968). A prominent priest, theologian, professor, and author who was born in Italy, but lived most of his life in Germany. He wrote several books on spirituality, prayer, the liturgy, culture, and faith, but is best known for his book, *The Lord*, which is a masterful study of the life of Christ.

Isidore of Seville, Saint (560-636). Bishop of Seville, and the first of four Spaniards to be declared Doctors of the Church (the other three being Saint John of the Cross, Saint Teresa of Ávila, and Saint John of Ávila). He was a prolific writer; one of his best known works was a comprehensive encyclopedia titled, *Etymologies*, or *Origins*.

Nicaea, Council of (A.D. 325). The first Ecumenical Council of the Church, called by the Emperor Constantine (a convert to the Church) to address the Arian controversy. The Council became known as the "synod of the 318 Fathers," although the exact number of bishops present has been long debated.

Sacrament: From the Latin word, *sacramentum*, meaning "an oath" (itself a translation of the Greek word, *mysterion*), which emphasizes "the visible sign of the hidden reality of salvation" (CCC 774). The *Catechism* states the "sacraments are efficacious signs of grace, instituted by Christ and entrusted to the Church, by which divine life is dispensed to us" (par. 1131).

Transubstantiation: The name given to the change (*trans-*) of the substance—the essence, or reality—of bread and wine into the true Body, Blood, Soul, and Divinity of Christ, that is, Christ in his entirety. The substance alone of the bread and wine are mysteriously transformed into the substance of the Body and Blood of Christ, while the accidents (color, taste, etc.) remain unchanged.

von Hildebrand, Dietrich (1889-1977). A German philosopher and theologian who Pope Pius XII called the "Twentieth Century Doctor of the Church." Pope John Paul II also said that he is "one of the greatest ethicists of the twentieth century." He studied philosophy under Edmund Husserl and other phenomenologists.

Lesson 8

A VAST COMPANY OF WITNESSES
The Communion of Saints

"The Church revels in the variety of its saints
because it needs such diversity in order to represent,
with even relative adequacy, the infinite
intensity of God's goodness."
- Bishop Robert Barron

Manfredo Ferrari. *Saint Teresa of Calcutta*. 1985.

✠

THE COMMUNION OF SAINTS
Episode 8, Part 1

OUTLINE *(Tracks 1-4 on DVD)*

I. St. Katharine Drexel

A. Birth, childhood, family: devout Catholic

B. As a teenager, developed a detailed program for growth in holiness

C. Katharine and two sisters left with large estate after the death of their parents

D. Supported Indian missions; struggled with spiritual turmoil

E. Traveled to Europe and met Pope Leo XIII

F. Decided to become a nun and found an order to reach "Indians and Colored people"

G. Established outposts, schools, a university, houses throughout the U.S.

H. Died on March 3, 1955, at the age of 96

I. Justice: heart and soul of the ethical life

    1. Justice is the virtue by which each is given his due

    2. Justice is the only cardinal virtue directed to the other

II. St. Thérèse of Lisieux

A. Thérèse: one of the strangest, most fascinating of all the saints

B. Praise from Pope John Paul II, who proclaimed her a Doctor of the Church in 1997

C. The significant influence of her autobiography

D. Difficult childhood: physical illness, psychological disturbances

E. Seeking, at fifteen, to enter the convent, she went to Rome and spoke to Pope Leo XIII

F. A month later, Thérèse was given permission to enter Carmel

G. She called her spiritual path "the little way"; she was the Little Flower

H. "My vocation is love!"

I. Intense physical and spiritual suffering in her final months

J. Thérèse viewed her struggle as a participation in the pain experienced by non-believers

K. Prudence: the queen of the virtues in the classical tradition

L. Supernatural prudence is "a moral sensibility radically in service of the love of God"

Saint Katharine Drexel

"To make a man a saint, it must indeed be by grace; and whoever doubts this does not know what a saint is, or a man."
– Blaise Pascal, *Pensées*, 24.

"Indeed, the Saints have ever been, are, and ever will be the greatest benefactors of society, and perfect models for every class and profession, for every state and condition of life, from the simple and uncultured peasant to the master of sciences and letters, from the humble artisan to the commander of armies, from the father of a family to the ruler of peoples and nations, from simple maidens and matrons of the domestic hearth to queens and empresses."
– Pope Pius XI, *Divini Illius Magistri*, sec. 99.

Prudence, according to St. Thomas Aquinas, is the "queen of the virtues," but justice is the heart and soul of the ethical life. Justice, wrote the German philosopher Josef Pieper, "is the virtue which enables man to give to each one what is his due" (*The Four Cardinal Virtues* [Notre Dame, IN: University of Notre Dame Press, 2003], p. 44). Justice, it should be noted, is the only cardinal virtue that is directed to the other. The other three virtues of temperance, prudence, and courage pertain to man's perfection in relation to himself.

"Now what happens," asks Bishop Robert Barron in *The Priority of Christ*, "to the virtue of justice when it is transfigured by the love that is the divine life? It becomes radicalized, absolutized, elevated, perfected, turning into a total gift of self, a willingness to render to the other beyond what is merely his due." He adds: "The woman whom I propose as an exemplification of elevated justice is St. Katharine Drexel, an heir to a multi-million dollar fortune who was so impressed by the needs of the excluded 'other' that she gave away the entirety of her wealth and the whole of her life on his behalf" (p. 317).

Katharine Drexel was born in Philadelphia on November 26, 1858, the same year as the apparitions at Lourdes. Her father was Francis Anthony Drexel, an internationally known banker and one of the richest men in America. Her mother, Hannah Langstroth Drexel, died five weeks after giving birth to Katharine. Despite this, Katharine's childhood was quite idyllic. Her father remarried a year and a half after Katharine's birth, and Katharine knew and loved her stepmother, Emma Bouvier, as her mother.

Katharine and her siblings were given a first-class education in languages, literature, philosophy, music, and painting. The family lived in a large mansion in Philadelphia and spent the summers at a lovely country estate outside the city. She visited Europe several times during her youth, staying in the finest hotels and taking in the sights, especially those dear to Catholic pilgrims. Her father and stepmother were both devout Catholics; they had a chapel in their home, and her father spent a half hour in prayer there every day after coming home from work. And three afternoons a week, her parents would open their magnificent home to the poor and those in need. The Drexels drilled into their children the conviction that their wealth had been entrusted to them and was meant to be used for the common good, a conviction rooted in the writings and witness of Aquinas, Ambrose, and Chrysostom.

In 1872, at age fourteen, Katharine met Fr. James O'Connor, who would exert a powerful influence on her spiritual development for many years. O'Connor was the pastor of the parish where the Drexels' summerhouse was located, and he became the young woman's spiritual mentor. Under his guidance, she laid out a rather astonishing and detailed program for growth in holiness and perfection. This included many daily prayers, giving money to the poor, regular reception of Holy Communion, and seeking to overcome vanity.

Katharine's formal education ended in 1878, when she was twenty, and in January of the following year she was officially presented to Philadelphia society. What should have been a momentous highlight of her young life was instead met with boredom and disinterest; she felt rather bored and nonplussed by it all. Her life soon changed dramatically when her beloved stepmother was diagnosed with cancer. The deeply devoted Katharine nursed her stepmother diligently, and was greatly moved by Emma's acceptance of her suffering as part of God's salvific plan. Her stepmother died in January 1883. Then, just two years later, her father was killed in an accident at work.

Francis Drexel's large estate was divided among his three daughters and more than forty charitable institutions. Each of the daughters received a substantial fortune, approximately four million dollars each, worth a hundred times more in today's currency. Not long after her father's death, Katharine met Bishop Martin Marty and Fr. Joseph Stephan, the director of the Bureau of Catholic Indian Missions. She had had an interest in Indian missions since her childhood, and she agreed to invest some of her fortune in the Church's work with the Native American community. In addition to giving a large amount of money to the Indian missions, Katharine decided she would also go to visit Indian territory in the Great Plains and see first-hand the effect of her donations in building schools, hospitals, convents, and churches. By the year 1907, the Drexel family had donated $1.5 million to the Indian missions.

Katharine's initial involvement with the work of missions to the Native Americans coincided with a period of great inner turmoil. Following the deaths of her parents, Katharine's health suffered, and she wrestled with anxiety and indecision as she struggled to find her place and purpose in life. She told her spiritual director she felt like a little girl who had ripped the face off of her beautiful porcelain doll only to discover that it was stuffed with straw.

Seeking answers and solace, she went with her sisters to Europe and visited a number of resorts and spas, as well as some major religious sites. She was contemplating the possibility of pursuing the religious life. Distraught over the death of her parents and in poor health, she concluded her sojourn to Europe with a visit to Rome, where she had an audience with Pope Leo XIII. Kneeling before the pontiff, she asked for his help in finding missionary priests and sisters for her beloved Native Americans. To her great surprise, Leo XIII responded, "Why not, my child, yourself become a missionary?" The question cut her to her soul. After the conversation, she was "sick all over, so sick that she could not get out of the Vatican soon enough." Once outside, she "sobbed and sobbed."

The Pope's question had struck a deep nerve. But it also served to focus her desire. Perhaps she should become a nun—or even more than that, a founder of a religious order dedicated to the poorest and most forgotten of Americans. She made the momentous decision to found "a missionary order for Indians and Colored people." Her spiritual director—now Bishop O'Connor, in Omaha—was initially reticent about her decision, unconvinced that an aristocrat who was accustomed to the finest things in life could accept the discipline of a religious life and the demands of a missionary's life. But, Bishop Barron explains, "Katharine's natural sense of moderation and self-control became a supernaturalized temperance, and her ordinary sense of fairness became elevated justice, a desire to render to the other even beyond what is his due. Since all here below is passing, she must give all to the demands of the eternal" (p. 322). This is all the more remarkable because this insight and decision came to her after she had inherited such a vast amount of wealth.

Bishop O'Connor finally relented, and in May 1889, Katharine entered the novitiate of the Sisters of Mercy of Pittsburgh. Her goal was to learn the ways of the religious life in preparation for the establishment of her own order. Two years later, she made her final profession as the first member of the Sisters of the Blessed Sacrament for Indians and Colored People. Devotion to the Eucharist, explains Bishop Barron, "which had been inculcated in her since she was a small child, provided the spiritual focus and energy of her order, for it is the embodiment of Jesus' love unto death, the act that reestablished justice between God and sinners" (p. 324).

Bishop O'Connor, her long-time spiritual director, died in 1889, but Archbishop Patrick John Ryan of Philadelphia stepped forward and gave her the support she needed in her ambitious endeavor. From the beginning, Katharine managed to attract a large number of young women eager to share her life. They gathered at a motherhouse outside of Philadelphia and spent three years in formation and training before they set out for missionary work.

Their first work included establishing an outpost among the Pueblo Indians of New Mexico, setting up a school for African-American children in Virginia, and working among the Navajos of Arizona. Perhaps Mother Drexel's most important foundation followed—the founding of Xavier University in New Orleans as a center for advanced studies for black young people, which was simply unheard of at the time. All of the money for this work of education, evangelization, and health care came from one source: Katharine's trust fund. In time, she set up houses and schools all across the country, until her finances had run dry. She had utterly emptied herself out for her mission. Poverty was an essential part of her work and her person.

For the next twenty-five years, Katharine ruled over her community, traveling often to visit and encourage sisters at the many outposts established by the order. She always took the cheapest route in traveling (at a time when travel was rarely easy or comfortable). Late in 1935, on a trip to St. Louis, Mother Drexel suffered a serious heart attack. Her doctors told her that she would survive only if she cut back severely on her grueling schedule. And so, at the age of seventy-seven, she began the last and extremely productive era of her life. She spent hours and hours of each day either in her small room at the motherhouse, or in front of the Blessed Sacrament, praying for the success of her order.

Katharine died on March 3, 1955, at the age of ninety-six. Her order, grounded in her spirit and her generosity, continues to this day, carrying on her work of elevated justice.

St. Thérèse of Lisieux

Josef Pieper argued that prudence, which is the queen of the virtues in the classical philosophical tradition, is extremely difficult for modern man to comprehend or appreciate. "Modern man," he wrote, "cannot conceive of a good act that might not be imprudent, nor of a bad act which might not be prudent. He will often call lies and cowardice prudent, truthfulness and courageous sacrifice imprudent" (*Four Virtues*, p. 5). Prudence is a cause of the other virtues; it is the measure of justice, fortitude, and temperance. When the natural virtue of prudence is transformed by grace, the supernatural life of God, explains Bishop Barron, it is "elevated into supernatural prudence, which is to say, a moral sensibility radically in service of the love of God. ...A feel for the expression of divine love in concrete situations is infused or supernatural prudence" (*The Priority of Christ*, p. 299). St. Thérèse of Lisieux is a model of this supernatural prudence, for although many of her actions seem imprudent from the viewpoint of the natural order, they reveal a bold and extravagant way of love.

Thérèse of Lisieux is one of the strangest and most fascinating of all of the saints. She was a cloistered nun who died at the age of twenty-four, known at the time only to her family and the handful of her fellow sisters. Yet within a few years of her death, she had a worldwide following, was declared a saint of the Church, and was eventually named a Doctor of the Church. Pope Pius X, who in 1914 signed the decree introducing her cause for canonization, called her the "greatest saint of modern times," and Pope Pius XI, who proclaimed her blessed in April of 1923 and canonized her in May of 1925, described her as the "Star" of his pontificate.

Pope John Paul II, who named Thérèse a Doctor of the Universal Church in 1997, wrote:

> *Her teaching not only conforms to Scripture and the Catholic faith, but excels ("eminet") for the depth and wise synthesis it achieved. Her doctrine is at once a confession of the Church's faith, an experience of the Christian mystery and a way to holiness. Thérèse offers a mature synthesis of Christian spirituality: she combines theology and the spiritual life; she expresses herself with strength and authority, with a great ability to persuade and communicate, as is shown by the reception and dissemination of her message among the People of God.*

> *Thérèse's teaching expresses with coherence and harmonious unity the dogmas of the Christian faith as a doctrine of truth and an experience of life. In this regard it should not be forgotten that the understanding of the deposit of faith transmitted by the Apostles, as the Second Vatican Council teaches, makes progress in the Church with the help of the Holy Spirit: "There is growth in insight into the realities and words that are passed on... through the contemplation and study of believers who ponder these things in their hearts (cf. Lk 2:19 and 51). It comes from the intimate sense of spiritual realities which they experience. And it comes from the preaching of those who have received, along with their right of succession in the episcopate, the sure charism of truth" (Dei Verbum, n. 8).*

In the writings of Thérèse of Lisieux we do not find perhaps, as in other Doctors, a scholarly presentation of the things of God, but we can discern an enlightened witness of faith which, while accepting with trusting love God's merciful condescension and salvation in Christ, reveals the mystery and holiness of the Church. (Divini Amoris Scientia, October 19, 1997, sec. 7).

The response to her defies natural explanations. When a reliquary containing her bones was brought to Ireland and the United States during the 1990s, millions came to see it. How do we explain this? It is due to the influence of her extraordinary autobiography, *The Story of a Soul*. Many readers, upon first encountering it, find it somewhat sentimental and overly emotional. Yet even a short list of the number of sophisticated intellectuals who found Thérèse compelling is impressive: Popes Pius X, Pius XI, Pius XII, and John Paul II, Thomas Merton, Hans Urs von Balthasar, Dorothy Day, and Edith Stein, to name just a few.

Thérèse's story is marked by a great sense of order. Her life, she tells us, can be divided into three periods, the first of which lasted from her birth until the death of her mother when Thérèse was four. She was born on January 2, 1873, the youngest child of Louis Martin and his wife Zélie, two very pious members of the French middle class. Thérèse enjoyed a very happy childhood. The youngest child, she was doted on by everyone, especially her father. Very early in life, she had the intuition that she would follow her sister Pauline into the Carmelite convent and become a religious, and she never wavered from this resolution.

Her idyllic childhood came to an abrupt end with the death of her mother in 1877, when Thérèse was only four. This marked the end of the first stage of her life, and the start of the second. After her mother's death, Thérèse became withdrawn, moody, "sensitive to an excessive degree." Her time at school in Lisieux was not pleasant, for she was taunted and picked on by her classmates. For the first time in her life, she felt herself "weighed and found wanting."

The full effects of her mother's death were manifested when Pauline, who was a substitute mother figure for Thérèse, entered the convent at Carmel. Thérèse experienced a strange malady, with both physical and psychological symptoms, some of them frightening. She would cry violently, suffer from severe headaches, and fall into fits of shivering. When Pauline took the veil, Thérèse had a particularly violent episode, screaming and shrieking in fear, shaken by convulsions, and having visions of monstrous, nightmarish creatures. Of this period, she later wrote, "I was absolutely terrified of everything...nails in the wall of the room took on the appearance of big charred fingers." She became convinced that this malady was the work of the devil. Yet, in time, she came to see this period as a testing and spiritual purging.

She then experienced a transforming manifestation of grace. On May 13, 1883, Thérèse found herself in bed, unable to function, when she noticed a statue of the Blessed Mother: "all of a sudden, the Blessed Virgin appeared beautiful to me..." But what especially struck her was "the ravishing smile of the Virgin." From that moment, her pain—physical and emotional—left her. Although a simple episode, it contains a deep spiritual truth: one will not be reconciled to God until one accepts God's presence as a sheer grace.

The next great step in Thérèse's spiritual journey was another private, seemingly small affair. It took place on Christmas day. Thérèse liked to perform little acts of kindness, but if the people for whom she did them were not sufficiently surprised or gratified, she would respond with frustration and tears. The Martin family had a custom that Thérèse and the other children would come home from

Midnight Mass and draw little gifts from their shoes. She loved this little tradition and delighted in her father's cooperation with it. But this year her beloved father seemed indifferent to it, and when Thérèse went upstairs and was presumably out of earshot, her father muttered, "Well, fortunately this will be the last year."

She then realized that her father—her little King—was not perfect, and that she—the little Queen—was not the center of the universe. Normally, she would have dissolved in tears and anguish. "But Thérèse was no longer the same; Jesus had changed her heart." Suppressing her tears, she went back down the stairs and, with unfeigned enthusiasm, took out each item and rejoiced over it." It was a small and simple thing, but it signaled the breakthrough of love. "When faced with the temptation to self-regard," notes Bishop Barron, "she resolved to love, to will not her own good but the good of her father" (*The Priority of Christ,* p. 308).

The desire to become a Carmelite, which had been in her since childhood, now became a burning preoccupation for Thérèse, "a divine call so strong that had I been forced to pass through flames I would have done it out of love for Jesus." The problem was that she was too young, barely fifteen years old. She was able to convince her father, and she was eventually able, through charm and stubbornness, to convince a number of bishops and ecclesiastics who opposed her. But then the bishop of Bayeux refused to let her enter Carmel early, and her family told her to give up.

Instead of giving up, she decided to take her case to Rome. Having journeyed to the Eternal City with a group of pilgrims, she was part of an audience that met with Pope Leo XIII on November 20, 1887. Though directed to say nothing to the pontiff, Thérèse blurted out, "Holy Father, in honor of your jubilee, permit me to enter Carmel at the age of fifteen." Leo smiled and told her to do what her superiors ordered. But she persisted, "O Holy Father, if you say yes, everyone will agree." The Pope responded, "Go...go...you will enter if God wills it." At that point, still begging and weeping, she was carried off by two papal guards.

Just a month later, the bishop of Bayeux relented and Thérèse was given permission to enter Carmel. For the next nine years, until her death at twenty-four, she never left the confines of the Lisieux Carmel, living the simple life of a Carmelite religious. But in those few years she cultivated a spiritual path she came to call "the little way." It was not the path of her great Carmelite forebears, Teresa of Ávila and John of the Cross; it was not the way of spiritual athletes, but a way that can be followed by any simple believer. It was rooted in humble spiritual childhood and in becoming a little child in the presence of God the Father: dependent, hopeful, waiting to receive gifts. "Jesus deigned to show me the road that leads to this Divine Furnace and this road is the surrender of the little child who sleeps without fear in its Father's arms."

It involved a ready willingness to do simple and ordinary things out of love, such as little acts of kindness, small sacrifices accepted graciously, putting up with annoying people. At the heart of the "little way" is the prudence to know—in every situation, great and small—what is the path of love, willing the good of the other. At one point, Thérèse confessed her desire to do everything that the great figures in Church history had done: to be a priest, a martyr, an evangelist, a missionary, a doctor. But she felt that she could never accomplish any of it. Then she read the magnificent passage from St. Paul's first letter to the Corinthians: "But earnestly desire the higher gifts. And I will show you a still more excellent way" (1 Cor. 12:31). She realized that love was the form of all the other virtues, the quality shared by every single saint, the dynamic supernatural power that makes possible the work of the missionary, the martyr, the doctor, and the priest.

She resolved that her vocation would be to love:

> *Swept by an ecstatic joy, I cried: "Jesus, my love! At last I have found my vocation. My vocation is love! I have found my place in the bosom of the Church and it is You, Lord, who has given it to me. In the heart of the Church, who is my Mother, I will be love. So I shall be everything and so my dreams will be fulfilled!"...*
>
> *Long ago only pure and spotless victims were accepted by Almighty God. The divine justice could be satisfied only by immaculate victims, but the law of love has replaced that of fear, and love has chosen me as victim—feeble and imperfect creature that I am. Is the choice of me worthy of love? Yes, it is, because in order for love to be fully satisfied it must descend to nothingness and transform that nothingness to living fire. I know, Lord, that "love is repaid by love alone." And so I have sought and I have found the way to ease my heart—by giving You love for love.* (Thérèse of Lisieux, trans. by John Beevers, *The Story of a Soul* [New York: Image Books, 2001, original edition 1957], 161-162.)

Those readers—even the most skeptical of them—who react negatively to the overly emotional, sentimental style of the Little Flower are usually converted by her account of her terrible struggle with unbelief at the end of her life. This intense spiritual suffering coincided almost exactly with the onset of the tuberculosis that eventually took her life. Thérèse was plagued by terrible doubts concerning the existence of heaven. This was not a matter of fleeting doubt or passing fear; rather, it lasted up to the moment of her death. "The trial was to last not a few days or a few weeks, it was not to be extinguished until the hour set by God himself and the hour has not yet come."

Thérèse interpreted this struggle as a participation in the pain experienced by many of her contemporaries who don't believe in God: "During those very joyful days of the Easter season, Jesus made me feel that there were really souls who have no faith...He permitted my soul to be invaded by the thickest darkness." How remarkably similar this sounds to Mother Teresa, who suffered through decades of doubts and spiritual dryness and darkness. Yet until the end of her earthly life, she continued to communicate her spiritual doctrine of the "little way." "She was convinced," writes Bishop Barron, "that her final illness was a gift from Jesus, a final opportunity to live, the last step on the little way of elevated prudence" (*The Priority of Christ,* p. 315).

QUESTIONS FOR UNDERSTANDING — Part 1:

1. Why is justice considered "the heart and soul of the ethical life"? How is justice in the Catholic tradition different from in the modern world?

2. What is "elevated justice"? How did St. Katharine Drexel's life give witness to the reality of elevated justice? (CCC 1803-1804, 1807, 1810)

3. What are some examples of prudence? Of "supernatural prudence"? How did Thérèse model this supernatural prudence? (CCC 1806; Mt. 10:16; 1 Cor. 12:31)

4. Why do you think Thérèse's approach to the spiritual life became so popular and widespread? Is it completely unique, or is it rooted in basic Catholic spirituality? Explain.

QUESTIONS FOR APPLICATION — Part 1:

1. What do you find most impressive or unique about Katharine Drexel's life? Do you think it was money or something else that held her back from embracing the decision to become a religious?

2. What are some of the strange or fascinating qualities of Thérèse that intrigued or interested you the most? Why?

3. What does it mean to you to be a "little flower"? What are three or four ways in which you can work to become a "little flower"?

THE COMMUNION OF SAINTS
Episode 8, Part 2

OUTLINE *(Tracks 5-7 on DVD)*

I. St. Edith Stein

    A. Stein: Born in 1891, seventh child of pious Jewish parents

    B. Possessed precocious literary gift, attracted to rituals of Judaism

    C. Becomes fascinated with philosopher Edmund Husserl, phenomenology

    D. In 1913, begins study with Husserl, works on doctorate

    E. Her conversion: gradual, interior, with much intellectual wrestling

    F. Read St. Teresa of Ávila's autobiography and said, "That is the truth"

    G. Entered the Church on January 1, 1922

    H. Entered the convent at Carmel in June of 1933; final vows in 1938

    I. Stein and her sister arrested in August of 1942 by Gestapo: "Come Rosa, we're going for our people"

    J. August 9, 1942: Arrived in Auschwitz, where they are murdered in the gas chambers

    K. John Paul II: "We bow down before the testimony of the life and death of Edith Stein…"

    L. Courage/fortitude: "constancy in the pursuit of the good" (CCC 1808)

    M. Transfigured by grace, it becomes a moral resistance of fear, informed by the love of Christ

II. St. Teresa of Calcutta

    A. Born Agnes Gonxha Bojaxhiu on August 26, 1910 in Skopje, Serbia (present-day Republic of Macedonia)

    B. Felt called to religious life at a young age

    C. Joined the Loreto Sisters

    D. Learned English in Ireland and went to India to teach

    E. This encounter with poverty stirred her compassion for the poor

    F. On the train to Darjeeling, she felt called to devote herself to serve the poor

    G. Founded the Missionaries of Charity

    H. Missionaries of Charity formed in Jesuit and Franciscan spirituality

    I. Lived a life of radical poverty, service, and prayer

    J. Noble Peace Prize in 1979

    K. Experienced aching sense of God's absence

    L. Participation in Christ's Passion

    M. Elevated Temperance: disciplining of the desires to serve the demands of love

THE COMMUNION OF SAINTS: Lesson 8, Part 2

St. Edith Stein

Courage, or fortitude, the *Catechism of the Catholic Church* explains, "is the moral virtue that ensures firmness in difficulties and constancy in the pursuit of the good. It strengthens the resolve to resist temptations and to overcome obstacles in the moral life. The virtue of fortitude enables one to conquer fear, even fear of death, and to face trials and persecutions" (par. 1808). When this natural virtue is transfigured by grace, writes Bishop Barron, "it becomes a moral resistance of fear, motivated and informed by the love of Christ which the agent has received" (*Priority of Christ*, p. 281). What does this courage look like? The life and death of St. Edith Stein, Sr. Teresa Benedicta of the Cross, provides us with "an icon of a contemporary martyr" whose death for the sake of Christ is a testimony to supernatural, extraordinary courage.

Edith Stein was born October 12, 1891 in Breslau, a town situated now within the borders of Poland but then part of the German empire. She was the seventh and youngest child of pious Jewish parents. Like Katharine Drexel and Thérèse of Lisieux, she had loving parents and was, she readily admitted, quite spoiled. She became precociously interested, at an early age, in literature and in the rituals of Judaism. As the years passed, her passion for literature grew, but her faith faded, and by the time she was a teenager she no longer believed in God.

The young and talented Edith believed she was destined for some sort of greatness within the academic world. Excelling at university, Edith became fascinated with the work of the philosopher Edmund Husserl and his new intellectual movement of phenomenology, which endeavored to heal the rift between subjectivity and objectivity introduced into Western philosophy by Immanuel Kant.

Edith wished to study with the master himself and so, in 1913, she moved to Göttingen, where Husserl taught. She was enamored of the natural beauty of the place and by its rich intellectual culture. In short order, she was introduced to Husserl and to the circle of brilliant students that had formed around him, which included Dietrich von Hildebrand and Max Scheler. She labored away at her doctoral studies, exploring the theme of empathy or fellow-feeling—the "feeling with" another mind which must be ingredient in every act of intellection. The work was stressful and she often felt overwhelmed. "This excruciating struggle," she wrote, "to attain clarity was waged unceasingly inside me, depriving me of rest day and night ... Little by little, I worked myself into a state of veritable despair" (Edith Stein, *Life in a Jewish Family* [Washington, DC: ICS Publications, 1986], 277). But she survived this period of struggle with marked success, earning her doctorate in 1915, just two years after arriving in Göttingen. Soon after she finished her work, Husserl received an appointment to the University of Frieburg in Breisgau and he asked Edith to go with him as an assistant.

Before taking up her duties with Husserl, Edith acted upon her desire to help in some way with the Great War. She became a practical nurse and for six months worked in fairly squalid conditions among the sick and the wounded. She then returned to her work with Husserl, and she found it less than satisfying as he treated her as little more than a glorified secretary.

In 1917, Edith paid a courtesy call to the widow of Adolf Reinach, an old acquaintance from her Göttingen days, who had been killed in the war. She expected to find the young widow devastated, but instead she found her sad but fundamentally at peace. The serenity, she learned, was the product of the woman's Christian faith. "It was my first encounter with the Cross and the divine power that it bestows upon those who carry it. For the first time, I was seeing with my very eyes the Church, born from her Redeemer's sufferings, triumphant over the sting of death. That was the moment my unbelief collapsed and Christ shone forth." (Quoted in Waltraud Herbstrith, *Edith Stein: A Biography* [San Francisco: Ignatius, 1992], 56.)

This was an extraordinary breakthrough for the intense, rationalistic woman who long ago had given up on religious faith. She was struck by the fact that most of her colleagues in the Husserl circle—as well as the Master himself—were devout Christians (Scheler and von Hildebrand were Catholic, and Husserl was Lutheran). This caused her to doubt her earlier rejection of religion. Also, phenomenology itself, which urged openness to any and all phenomena, encouraged her to investigate more objectively the phenomenon of religion.

Edith's conversion was not sudden and dramatic, like the Apostle Paul's, but was more like Augustine's or Newman's—gradual, interior, accompanied by a greeat deal of intellectual wrestling. One night, while staying at a friend's home, Edith searched through their library to find something to read. She took St. Teresa of Ávila's autobiography, *The Life of Saint Teresa of Ávila, Written by Herself*, and stayed up all night reading it. The next morning, she declared simply: "That is the truth." It seems as though the reading of Teresa's autobiography was the galvanizing moment, the occasion for all of the strands to come together. The next day she bought a missal and a copy of the Catholic catechism.

After several weeks of reading and praying, Edith approached the local priest and asked to be baptized. When he balked due to her recent conversion, she said, "*Prufen-Sie mich,*" that is, "Test me!" She was received into the Church on January 1, 1922, at that time the Feast of the Circumcision of the Lord, the first shedding of Jesus' blood.

She wanted to join the Carmelites, the order of her spiritual hero, St. Teresa of Ávila, but her spiritual director advised her to wait, and Edith became a teacher at St. Magdalena's, a teachers' training academy run by the Dominican sisters. While there, Edith began to live what was essentially a religious life.

Edith fell in love with the Eucharist, spending hours a day in silent adoration. The Dominicans were so impressed by her devotion that they set up a special chair for her near the Blessed Sacrament. Edith had found a new center. During these years, she deepened and broadened her scholarship, becoming a well-known lecturer throughout Germany. Her work was to reconcile the classical Catholic philosophy of Aquinas with the contemporary pheomenology of her Master, Husserl. She had been directed in this work by Fr. Erich Przywara, a Jesuit theologian, who encouraged her to translate into German certain works by John Henry Newman and Thomas Aquinas.

Her desire to enter Carmel, inspired by Teresa of Ávila, continued to grow, and in June of 1933, she was accepted at the Carmel of Cologne. Though she was far older, at the age of forty-two, than most of the postulants and novices, she took readily to Carmelite life, as though she was born for it. She moved into the rhythm of prayer and basic work, but she also, at the prompting of her superiors, took up her intellectual research, producing the lengthy philosophical treatise *Finite and Eternal Being* as well as a thorough study of St. John of the Cross, *The Science of the Cross*.

In 1938, Sister Teresa Benedicta of the Cross made her final vows. In November of the same, *Kristallnacht* (the Night of the Broken Glass) took place, and Jews all over Germany were suddenly in grave danger. Concerned for her safety, Edith's superiors transferred her to the Carmel at Echt in Holland in 1939. Facing the reality of persecution and possible death, she wrote in her will:

> *Even now I accept the death that God has prepared for me in complete submission and with joy as being his most holy will for me. I ask the Lord to accept my life and my death ... so that the Lord will be accepted by His people and that His Kingdom may come in glory, for the salvation of Germany and the peace of the world"* (June 9, 1939; from http://www.vatican.va/news_services/liturgy/saints/ns_lit_doc_19981011_edith_stein_en.html).

In 1940, the Nazis overran Holland, and the danger that had loomed over Edith in Cologne now threatened again. The Dutch bishops bravely raised their voices in protest over the ill-treatment of Jews, and the Archbishop of Utrecht ordered that Nazi policy be condemned from every pulpit in the country. The Nazis retaliated swiftly and brutally, ordering the arrest of all Jews who had converted to Catholicism.

On Sunday August 2, 1942, the Gestapo came for Edith and her sister, who had joined Edith in the convent. Amidst the confusion of the convent, Edith calmly said, "Come Rosa, we're going for our people." The sisters were held briefly in a camp and then they were packed onto what amounted to a cattle car for their trip to Auschwitz. A former student of Edith's reported an encounter with Edith when the train was briefly stopped at a platform in Germany. After exchanging pleasantries, the nun told her to convey this message to the mother superior in Echt: "We are going to the East," a word with both literal and spiritual meaning.

On August 9, 1942, Edith and Rosa arrived at Auschwitz. The exact details of what happened to them are unknown, but they were most likely taken directly from the train to the gas chamber where they were put to death. Their bodies were subsequently burned. "The elevated *fortitudo* of Edith Stein," writes Bishop Barron, "was visible in her willingness to accept the full implications of that solidarity and that union" (*Priority of Christ*, p. 297). And Pope John Paul II, in remarks made on beatifying Edith Stein in Cologne, Germany, on May 1, 1987, said:

> *We bow down before the testimony of the life and death of Edith Stein, an outstanding daughter of Israel and at the same time a daughter of the Carmelite Order, Sister Teresa Benedicta of the Cross, a personality who united within her rich life a dramatic synthesis of our century. It was the synthesis of a history full of deep wounds that are still hurting ... and also the synthesis of the full truth about man. All this came together in a single heart that remained restless and unfulfilled until it finally found rest in God.*

† Saint Teresa of Calcutta

Known throughout the world by her religious name of Teresa, Agnes Gonxha Bojaxhiu was born August 26th, 1910, in Skopje, Serbia (present-day Republic of Macedonia). Having discerned a call to religious life, Agnes applied to and was accepted by the Institute of the Blessed Virgin Mary (Sisters of Loreto) in Ireland, where she received the name "Sister Teresa of the Child Jesus." In the year 1929, she arrived in India where she worked on behalf of her religious community's apostolate, primarily in the field of education. Sister Teresa professed her solemn vows in the year 1937, and was then known, according to the rule of the Loreto community, as Mother Teresa.

On September 10th, 1946, on a train ride from Calcutta to Darjeeling, Mother Teresa received an inspiration which she believed to be from the Lord Jesus himself- to satisfy his "thirst" by dedicating her life to the service of the poor. She was beckoned by the Lord to "come, be my light"- a light that would be radiant in some of the darkest corners of misery and despair. This mission would take her from the religious life with the Loreto sisters and into a new, and seemingly "experimental," way of religious life. In April, 1948, she received permission from the Holy See to begin her mission to bring the consolation of Christ to the poorest of the poor. On October 7th, 1950, the religious community founded by Mother Teresa, known as the Missionaries of Charity, was formally established and given permission to fulfill its purpose in the Diocese of Calcutta. The number of aspirants to this community continued to grow and requests for the Missionaries of Charity to establish houses throughout India grew along with the order. In 1965 the Missionaries of Charity was established as a community of pontifical right, which basically allowed the expansion of the order globally. By the 1970s, Mother Teresa's sisters labored on six continents. By the year 1997, the year of Mother Teresa's death, there were 610 Missionaries of Charity foundations in 123 countries staffed by 4000 sisters—all of whom had dedicated their lives to fulfill Christ's invitation to Mother Teresa to "come, be my light." Mother Teresa died on September 5th, 1997. She was beatified by Pope Benedict XVI on October 19th, 2003, and canonized by Pope Francis on September 4, 2016.

Bishop Barron identifies Saint Teresa of Calcutta as an example of the elevation of the virtue of temperance. Temperance is moderation in action, thought, or feeling. It is a sense of restraint or control over excess in attachment or desire. The virtue of temperance is usually manifested in the moderation of the desires for self-preservation—desires such as hunger, thirst, and sex. Thus, the person in whom temperance is evident will have achieved significant mastery over these particular desires.

Bishop Barron explores the characteristic of the elevation of the virtue of temperance by grace in his book *The Priority of Christ*:

> *Now what happens when this moral virtue is invaded and elevated by grace? Chastity becomes radicalized in what Aquinas call "virginity," the willingness not only to order sexual desire but to eschew sexual relations altogether so as to realize a supernatural end. In Thomas' own language, 'It (virginity) is made praiseworthy only by its end and purpose, to the extent that it aims to make him who practices it free for things divine.' The love of God has so seized a person that she is willing to give up permanently and*

definitively activity that the naturally chaste person would only discipline, in order that she might be utterly available to God. And when ordinary abstinence is invaded by the divine life, it becomes the radical asceticism of the Desert Fathers, of St. Benedict, St. Francis, and Charles de Foucauld. (The Priority of Christ, p. 329-330)

Bishop Barron continues:

Obviously no one can sensibly abstain absolutely from food and drink as one might from sex, but one can press and push the natural disciplining of sensual desire into a radical form—once again, for the sake of loving and serving God more fully. In the strict sense, temperance is not in itself the realization of the good but rather the necessary prerequisite to that realization. This remains true in regards to elevated temperance. Neither celibacy nor radical asceticism is sought for its own sake. Were that the case, each would be at best a rather peculiar form of ascetical athleticism, a test of endurance. They are, in point of fact, conditiones sine qua non *for the achievement of a love that seeks to imitate, however inadequately, the unlimited love of God.*
(The Priority of Christ, p. 330)

The condition for the possibility of Saint Teresa of Calcutta's sanctity, a sanctity which bore its fruit in the manner in which the Missionaries of Charity grew and developed over time, was the moderation of her own desires, a natural virtue that was elevated through her relationship with the Lord. Foreseeing the demands of her particular mission, she cultivated, in the day-to-day experiences of her own life, a decision to have less so that others might have more. On a practical level this meant an acceptance of what the Church calls "the evangelical counsels," or a life vowed to the realization of poverty, chastity, and obedience. These radical expressions of religious life are all, in their own way, conditioned by the virtue of temperance and become the means by which a person can be liberated from the constraining impulses of one's desires for mission. For Mother Teresa, this brought about the realization of the biblical insight that she would decrease so that the Lord might increase. The mysterious effect of this rigorous spiritual commitment was not that Saint Teresa simply disappeared, but that all that was good, true, and beautiful in her was all the more evident. She became for others radiant with Christ's light because she allowed Christ's invitation in her own life to be fulfilled—she said yes to the summons to "come, be my light."

Saint Teresa of Calcutta was one of the most recognized women of her time. For many in the popular culture, she became a representation and archetype of the possibilities of altruism. And yet she was much more that this, as Saint Teresa herself insisted, "I don't want our work to become a business but to remain a work of love." That love was not an abstraction or a matter of feelings, but a work of mercy by which all of those served by the Missionaries of Charity would know that they too were brothers and sisters of the Lord Jesus and the sons and daughters of God.

The work that Saint Teresa and her Sisters sought to accomplish was not directed by idealism and was not what we might characterize as "social work," but was instead a concrete expression of their acceptance of the words of the Lord Jesus as unequivocally true: "As often as you did it to one of the least of these my brethren, you did it to me" (Mt. 25:40). Their particular way of life displays the practical implications of accepting these words as the truth.

Saint Teresa trusted in Christ that he could make of her a light that would illuminate some of humanity's darkest places and as his light she retreated into the gloominess of the slums. She did this not for merely humanitarian reasons but because the Lord in whom she had placed her trust called her to serve the poorest of the poor and had insisted that his life and presence would be found in precisely those people that so many in the world had learned to treat as invisible or unnecessary. The tenacity with which she engaged this mission was made all the more impressive by the revelation after her death that her work brought her little emotional consolation and that for many years she lacked even the feeling of closeness to God's presence that we often presume to be a given in the lives of the saints. Reliant on a faith that surpassed either consolations or feelings, Saint Teresa's temperance, elevated by grace, became a living, embodied testimony to the "The light shines in the darkness, and the darkness has not overcome it" (Jn. 1:5).

QUESTIONS FOR UNDERSTANDING — Part 2:

1. What are some of the differences between natural courage and supernatural, extraordinary fortitude? (CCC 1808, 2473)

2. How does Edith Stein's journey to the convent differ from that of Katharine and Thérèse? What similarities are to be found? Why was she so willing to accept her death at the hand of the Nazis?

3. In light of the *Catechism's* definition of temperance—"[it] is the moral virtue that moderates the attraction of pleasures and provides balance in the use of created goods"—how was Saint Teresa of Calcutta a great exemplar of this virtue? More to it, why is she an example of "elevated temperance"? (CCC 1809)

QUESTIONS FOR APPLICATION — Part 2:

1. What challenges or difficulties are you facing that require courage? Reflect on the example of Edith Stein and consider how it can help you in facing difficulties.

2. Is there anything holding you back from embracing God's call and will in your life? If so, how will you address it?

TERMS & NAMES

Cardinal Virtues: Four essential natural virtues: prudence, justice, fortitude, and temperance. These virtues, or habits, control and guide the other natural virtues and perfect and increase human love. These four are identified in the Book of Wisdom: "If anyone loves righteousness, [Wisdom's] labors are virtues; for she teaches self-control and prudence, justice and courage" (Wis. 8:7; CCC 1805).

Husserl, Edmund (1859-1938). German philosopher who was the founder of phenomenology. He influenced the thought of Edith Stein, Martin Heidegger, Jean-Paul Sartre, Emmanuel Levinas, Max Scheler, Jacques Derrida, and John Paul II.

Phenomenology: The study of human experience and of the ways things present themselves to us in and through such experience (Sokolowski, Robert. *Introduction to Phenomenology*, Cambridge Press: 2000, pg. 2). It is the attitude of preparing the mind to properly receive reality in contrast to imposing a theoretical model onto reality.

Pope Leo XIII (1810-1903). Reigned as pope from 1878-1903. Through his encyclical *Aeterni Patris,* he encouraged the study of Thomas Aquinas as a model for the dependent relationship of faith and reason. His encyclical *Rerum Novarum* was very influential in the Church's social thought.

Scheler, Max (1874-1928). One of the most influential philosophers of twentieth-century Germany. His work influenced Martin Heidegger, Dietrich von Hildebrand and John Paul II.

Theological virtues. These are faith, hope, and love (see 1 Cor. 13:13), infused by God into the human soul at baptism; they "adapt man's faculties for participation in the divine nature" (CCC 1812). "They inform all the moral virtues and give life to them" (CCC 1841).

NOTES

Lesson 9

THE FIRE OF HIS LOVE
Prayer and the Life of the Spirit

"Prayer is born of that awareness, felt more than thought, that the transcendent world impinges on our lowly realm and hence can be contacted... The mystical coming together of these two longings —our longing for God and God's longing for us—is prayer."

- Bishop Robert Barron

Gian Lorenzo Bernini. *The Ecstasy of Saint Teresa*. Cornaro Chapel of Santa Maria della Vittoria. Rome, Italy.

PRAYER & THE LIFE OF THE SPIRIT
Episode 9, Part 1

OUTLINE *(Tracks 1-4 on DVD)*

I. **The Fire of His Love: Prayer and the Life of the Spirit**

   A. What is prayer?

   B. There are many forms and expressions of prayer

   C. Prayer is the conscious communion with the Source of all that is

   D. Three basic types of prayer: adoration, petition, and contemplation

II. **Beginning with Thomas Merton**

   A. One of the best-known and most influential Catholic authors of the past century

   1. Most famous book: *The Seven Storey Mountain* (1948), the story of his conversion

   2. Dozens of other books, as well as essays and poetry

   B. Nomadic childhood: New York, Bermuda, France, England

   C. Rome in 1933: Spiritual awakening while visiting churches

   D. Columbia University (1935) and "Catholic atmosphere"

   E. Purchased Etienne Gilson's *The Spirit of Medieval Philosophy*

   1. A "big concept": the nature of God's existence

   2. God is the sheer act of being itself

   F. Began attending Mass at Church of Corpus Christi

   G. Entered the Church on November 16, 1938

   H. In December 1941, entered the monastery at the Abbey of Our Lady of Gethsemani

   I. At Gethsemani, Merton felt the power of *adoratio*, or adoration of God

III. **St. John of the Cross**

   A. Mystic, poet, and Doctor of the Church

   B. Became a Carmelite friar in 1563

   C. Met Teresa of Ávila, who convinced him to join the reform of the Carmelite order

   D. Kidnapped, imprisoned, and beaten by Carmelites that resisted his reforms

E. During imprisonment, he began composing poems and commentary in his mind

    1. *The Ascent of Mount Carmel* (1579-1585)

    2. *The Dark Night of the Soul* (1582-1585)

    3. *The Spiritual Canticle* (finished in 1591)

    4. *The Living Flame of Love* (finished in 1591)

F. Fundamental principle: God is All, the creature is nothing

G. His books describe and explain the purification of the soul and union with God

H. The "purgative way": ridding ourselves of attachments, substitutes for God

I. The "dark night of the soul": letting go of even concepts and images of the mind

J. The mystical marriage between Christ and the individual soul

PRAYER & THE LIFE OF THE SPIRIT: Lesson 9, Part 1

The Fire of His Love

"One of the paradoxes of the mystical life is this: that a man cannot enter into the deepest center of himself and pass through that center into God, unless he is able to pass entirely out of himself and empty himself and give himself to other people in the purity of selfless love."

– Thomas Merton, *New Seeds of Contemplation* (New York: New Directions Publishing Corporation, 1961), 64.

"The love of God does not consist in tears or in delight and tenderness, which for the greater part we desire and find consolation in; but it consists in serving with justice and fortitude of soul and in humility. Without such service it seems to me we would be receiving everything and giving nothing."

– St. Teresa of Ávila [from Sermon in a Sentence: *A Treasury of Quotations on the Spiritual Life, Vol. 4: St. Teresa of Ávila* (Ignatius Press, 2005), selected and arranged by John P. McClernon, p. 119].

"Prayer," wrote St. Clement of Alexandria, "is conversation with God" (*Stromateis*, 7). In a similar vein, St. Francis de Sales wrote, in his *Treatise on the Love of God*, "The chief exercise of prayer is to speak to God and to hear God speak in the bottom of your heart" (6, 1). "But as for me," wrote King David, "my prayer is to thee, O LORD" (Psa. 69:13).

People enter into this conversation of prayer all of the time. They are usually religious people, but studies show that many non-believers also pray. But what is prayer? What exactly are we doing when we pray? Despite being so common—or perhaps because it is common—trying to define and explain prayer can be elusive.

Part of the reason is that prayer is multifaceted and complex; it takes numerous forms and is expressed in countless ways. Listening, speaking, singing, dancing, processing, painting, maintaining silence, reading sacred texts, emptying the mind of absolutely everything: all of these can be forms of prayer.

But is there a common denominator among all these forms and types of prayer? Can we speak coherently and helpfully about what all types of prayer have in common?

"For me," explained St. Thérèse of Lisieux in her autobiography, "prayer is a surge of the heart; it is a simple look turned toward heaven, it is a cry of recognition and of love, embracing both trial and joy." *The Catechism of the Catholic Church* quotes the great mystic, St. John Damascene: "Prayer is the raising of one's mind and heart to God or the requesting of good things from God" (par. 2559). Prayer is conscious communion with the Source of all that is. It is born of the awareness—felt or intuited as much as consciously thought—that the transcendent realm is real and breaks into our world. Prayer is the desire to reach out, to touch, and to communicate with that unseen, but very real, realm. By means of pure prayer, stated St. Maximus the Confessor, "the soul escapes completely from the midst of creatures, carried to God, as it were, on wings" (*Centuries on Charity*, 1, 11).

There are three basic types of prayer: prayer of adoration, prayer of petition, and prayer of contemplation. We will consider and explore each of these with the help of great figures of the Catholic spiritual tradition: Thomas Merton, St. John of the Cross, and St. Teresa of Ávila.

✝

Beginning with Thomas Merton

Talk of prayer, contemplation, mysticism, and spirituality usually brings to mind images of monks chanting in choir stalls or ascetic hermits living a severe and quiet life in the desert. Those are powerful and important expressions of spiritual devotion and discipline, but the first person we will consider is someone much closer to our own time and culture. In fact, Thomas Merton (1915-1968) was one of the most well-known and influential Catholic authors of the twentieth century, an American whose sixty books—on topics ranging from the monastic life to literature to pacifism—have sold millions of copies. His autobiography, *The Seven Storey Mountain* (1948), has sold over one million copies, has been translated into numerous languages, and is considered one of the finest accounts of conversion and spiritual transformation ever written.

Merton was born in Prades, France, on January 31, 1915. His father, Owen Merton, was a New Zealander, and his mother, Ruth Jenkins, was an American. They were both artists, and had met while studying art and painting in Paris. Merton's mother died when he was six, and he and his father embarked on a semi-nomadic life, living in New York, Bermuda, France, and England. In 1930, Merton began attending Oakham School, a boarding school in Rutland, England. His father had been battling a brain tumor for many years, and in 1931 he died, leaving Merton alone in the world.

The young Merton traveled around Europe, and in 1933 he spent time in Rome, a visit that marked the start of a spiritual awakening, however faltering. He visited numerous churches in Rome and began to pray. After visiting the church at Tre Fontane, a Trappist monastery, Merton wrote that he "walked up and down in the silent afternoon, under the eucalyptus trees, and the thought grew on me: 'I should like to become a Trappist monk.'" But, he adds, "There was very little danger of my doing so, then." It was just a "daydream" (*The Seven Storey Mountain* [Harcourt, Brace and Co., Inc., 1948], p. 141).

Instead of pursuing the daydream, Merton turned back into spiritual darkness. He went to Cambridge, where he gained a reputation for drinking and womanizing. Although not mentioned in the published version of *The Seven Storey Mountain* (it was apparently removed from earlier drafts), Merton fathered a child that year, and after it was covered up with money and connections, he agreed to move to the United States. In January of 1935 he enrolled at Columbia University in Manhattan, where he studied English literature and quickly gained a more positive reputation for his literary talent and intellectual gifts.

"I was being drawn back into the Catholic atmosphere," he wrote, "and I could feel the health of it, even in the merely natural order, working already within me" (SSM, p. 207). One day, in February of 1937, Merton entered a Scribner's bookstore on Fifth Avenue in Manhattan, and bought a copy of *The Spirit of Medieval Philosophy*, written by the great French Thomist, Étienne Gilson. When he later saw the "Nihil Obstat ... Imprimatur" on the first page, a "feeling of disgust and deception struck me like a knife in the pit of the stomach. ... Such is the terror that is aroused in the enlightened modern mind by a little innocent Latin and the signature of a priest." He admitted that while he long admired Catholic culture, he "had always been afraid of the Catholic Church. That is a rather common position in the world today" (SSM, 208). Merton considered throwing the book away. He had assumed, like most of his peers and friends, that God was a "noisy mythological figure," and religion the stuff of neuroses and projections.

But, "instead of getting rid of the book, I actually read it. ... And the one big concept which I got out of its pages was something that was to revolutionize my whole life." That concept was *aseitas*, a word "which can be applied to God alone, and which expresses His most characteristic attribute..." He learned that God does not require any justification for existence, for his very nature is existence: "And to say that God exists *a se*, of and by and by reason of Himself, is merely to say that God is Being Itself. *Ego sum qui sum*" (SSM, 209). Merton realized that God is not one being among many, but *ipsum esse subsistens*—the sheer act of being itself. He had never imagined that people could speak of God in such a compelling and intellectually satisfying way.

Merton realized that his concept of God, prior to reading Gilson's book, was shallow and illogical. "There is," he reflected, "in every intellect a natural exigency for a true concept of God: we are born with the thirst to know and to see Him, and therefore it cannot be otherwise" (SSM, 211). This God began to pull and tug at Merton with a great power; his thirst for God and for truth grew immensely, and his life began to change. He tried attending Protestant services—his mother had been a Quaker—but he was unsatisfied with what he found and experienced. One Sunday morning, he awoke with the deep desire to go to Mass, and despite his fears and anxieties at not knowing precisely what to do, he attended Mass at "the little brick Church of Corpus Christi, hidden behind Teachers College on 121st Street" in Morningside Heights, not far from Columbia. (SSM, 250). He wrote of the experience:

> *What a revelation it was, to discover so many ordinary people in a place together, more conscious of God than of one another: not there to show off their hats or their clothes, but to pray, or at least to fulfill a religious obligation, not a human one. (SSM, 251)*

The sermon that day was short and rather simple, but it made a deep impression on Merton. It was on fundamental beliefs about the humanity and divinity of Jesus Christ, and the salvific work accomplished in and through him. "I wonder," he wrote with obvious regret, "what would have happened in my life if I had been given this grace [of faith] when I had almost discovered the Divinity of Christ in the ancient mosaics of the churches of Rome. What scores of self-murdering and Christ-murdering sins would have been avoided—all the filth I had plastered upon His image in my soul during those last five years that I had been scourging and crucifying God within me?" (SSM, 253).

He soon asked a priest at the parish for instruction, and on November 16, 1938, he was baptized and received Holy Communion for the first time. He realized that his vocation, the vocation of every Catholic, was to be a saint. He began exploring different religious orders, hoping they would accept him as a candidate for priesthood. He was initially accepted by the Franciscans, but when the order learned of the indiscretions in his past, he was let go.

In 1940, Merton became a professor of English at St. Bonaventure University, a small Franciscan school in Olean, New York. Further changes took place and his spiritual life deepened; he stopped drinking so much, quit smoking altogether, and no longer went to movies. These renunciations of worldly pleasures foreshadowed the decision that soon followed. In April 1941, at the urging of his good friend Daniel Walsh, a professor of philosophy at Columbia, Merton took a retreat during Holy Week at the Abbey of Our Lady of Gethsemane near Bardstown, Kentucky. Upon arriving there, Merton recounted, "I felt the deep, deep silence of the night, and of peace, and of holiness enfold me like love, like safety. The embrace of it, the silence! I had entered into a solitude that was an impregnable fortress." (SSM, 385).

Merton felt he had found the still-point around which the whole country turned without knowing it. He felt there at Gethsemani something of the power of *adoratio*—the ordering of one's life around the proper praise and adoration of God. By the following December, just days after the attack on Pearl Harbor, Merton entered the monastery, commencing twenty-five years as a monk, poet, and spiritual writer. Most fundamentally, he dedicated himself to a life of prayer. Near the end of *The Seven Storey Mountain,* Merton wrote:

> *The contemplative life directly and immediately occupies itself with the love of God, than which there is no act more perfect or more meritorious. Indeed that love is the root of all merit. When you consider the effect of individual merit upon the vitality of other members of the Mystical Body it is evident that there is nothing sterile about contemplation. On the contrary Saint Thomas's treatment of it in this question shows that the contemplative life establishes a man in the very heart of all spiritual fecundity.* (SSM, 496)

†

St. John of the Cross and the Prayer of Contemplation

Merton's great spiritual master, the teacher to whom he consistently looked, was a sixteenth-century Spaniard named Juan de Yepes y Álvarez, better known by his religious name: Juan de la Cruz, or John of the Cross (1542-1591). It is not surprising that Merton was so attracted to the person and writings of John of the Cross, who was a mystic and a poet par excellence, as well as a saint and a Doctor of the Church. "His teaching is the unvarnished Gospel, neither more nor less," observes Fr. Thomas Dubay, S.M., in *Fire Within* (Ignatius Press, 1989), "and to understand it rightly with neither exaggeration nor diminution we need to see in his manner and deeds how he himself applied it to the concrete circumstances of the daily round. His mode of life is likewise a silent but eloquent testimony of what is indispensable for deep prayer to be given and received" (pp. 32-33).

Merton, in his essay, "St. John of the Cross," wrote, "The life of charity was perfect in the great Carmelite reformer, St. John of the Cross. It was so perfect that is can hardly be said to shine before men. His soul was too pure to attract any attention. ... Let it suffice to say that this Spanish saint is one of the greatest and most hidden of the saints, that of all saints he is perhaps the greatest poet as well as the greatest contemplative, and that in his humility he was also most human ..." (*A Thomas Merton Reader* [Image, rev. ed. 1974], edited by Thomas P. McDonnell; pp. 289, 293).

John was born in 1542 near Ávila. His father died when he was only a few months old, and the family lived in poverty throughout his youth. He attended a Jesuit school from 1559 to 1563, and at the age of twenty-one he became a Carmelite friar. Not long after being ordained a priest, he met Teresa of Ávila, who convinced him to join her in the reform of the Carmelites. However, like many true reformers, he was unpopular with those he wished to reform. In December of 1577, he was kidnapped by a group of Carmelites opposed to his reforms. During his nine months of imprisonment, he was beaten weekly in public and jailed in isolation in a tiny cell. He was finally able to escape in August of 1578. During his imprisonment, John began to compose poems in his mind; he later wrote them down, along with lengthy, formal commentaries on the poems. His poetry is still considered among the finest ever written in Spanish, filled with rich imagery and profound spiritual insights. His major works include *The Ascent of Mount Carmel* (1579-1585), *The Dark Night of the Soul* (1582-1585), *The Spiritual Canticle* (finished in 1591), and *The Living Flame of Love* (finished in 1591).

"The fundamental principle of St. John's theology," states Fr. Jordan Aumann in *Christian Spirituality in the Catholic Tradition* (Ignatius Press/Sheed & Ward, 1985), "is that God is All and the creature is nothing. Therefore, in order to arrive at perfect union with God, in which sanctity consists, it is necessary to undergo an intense and profound purification of all the faculties and powers of soul and body." In *The Living Flame of Love*, John provides this powerful image of the human soul:

> *O lamps of fire!*
> *in whose splendors*
> *the deep caverns of feeling,*
> *once obscure and blind,*
> *now give forth, so rarely, so exquisitely,*
> *both warmth and light to their Beloved. (Stanza 3)*
>
> (St. John of the Cross, *The Collected Works of St. John of the Cross*, trans. Kieran Kavanaugh, O.C.D. and Otilio Rodriguez, O.C.D. [Washington, DC: ICS Publications, 1991], 673.)

These deep caverns, which are infinitely deep and unfathomable, are intellect, will, and feeling. "The capacity of these caverns is deep," he writes in his commentary, "because the object of this capacity, namely God, is profound and infinite."

> *Thus in a certain fashion their capacity is infinite, their thirst is infinite, their hunger is also deep and infinite, and their languishing and suffering are infinite death. Although the suffering is not as intense as is the suffering of the next life, yet the soul is a living image of that infinite privation, since it is in a certain way disposed to receive its plenitude. This suffering, however, is of another quality because it lies within the recesses*

of the will's love; and love is not what alleviates the pain, since the greater the love, so much more impatient are such persons for the possession of God, for whom they hope at times with intense longing." (Stanza 3; par. 22)

(St. John of the Cross, *The Collected Works of St. John of the Cross*, trans. Kieran Kavanaugh, O.C.D. and Otilio Rodriguez, O.C.D. [Washington, DC: ICS Publications, 1991], 681-682.)

The will desires infinite goodness, and it will not rest until it rests in the absolute good of God. The emotions ache with an infinite longing, because they are ordered to the infinity of God. This is why most of us are so restless and dissatisfied. John diagnosed a fundamental spiritual disorder in this way: we try to fill these infinitely deep caverns with the illusory and petty goods of this world, with pleasure, sex, power, praise, comfort. But, as we saw in our discussion of the Beatitudes, this leads to addiction as we try more and more of these unsatisfying goods. Or else, John wrote, we cover the caverns over, pretending that they are not there. We live in a completely superficial way, ignoring the depths within our deepest being.

In order to fulfill these intense longings, we must undergo a purging process, what the spiritual teachers often call the "purgative way." This is how we rid ourselves of attachments to the many and various substitutes for God, what John calls idols, or false gods. He speaks of this spiritual purging as a two-step process. First there is the "dark night of the senses," which is followed by the "dark night of the soul." Fr. Aumann explains:

> *Since any deficiency in the union of love is due to the soul and not to God, St. John concludes that the soul must be completely purified in all of its faculties and powers— those of the sensory order and those that are spiritual—before it can be fully illuminated by the light of divine union. (*Christian Spirituality in the Catholic Tradition, *p.196)*

This purification has nothing to do with a puritanical zeal or with repudiating the goodness of the world. It is, rather, a complete and practical opposition to idolatry. During the dark night of the senses, we learn to not seek ultimate satisfaction in sensible and sensual things; we let go of them and fast from them. John of the Cross, in *Ascent to Mount Carmel*, wrote:

> *For that reason we call this detachment night to the soul, for we are not treating here of the lack of things, since this implies no detachment on the part of the soul if it has a desire for them; but we are treating of the detachment from them of the taste and desire, for it is this that leaves the soul free and void of them, although it may have them; for it is not the things of this world that either occupy the soul or cause it harm, since they enter it not, but rather the will and desire for them, for it is these that dwell within it. (*Ascent of Mount Carmel, *Book 1, ch.3, no. 4)*

During the dark night of the soul, or of the spirit, we let go of even those most rarified things that substitute for God, the concepts and images of the mind. When these purgations are complete, we are ready for the journey into God—that is, to receive the divine and holy gift that God wants to give. Here is what John says in the opening stanza of *The Dark Night of the Soul*:

> *One dark night,*
> *fired with love's urgent longings*
> *— ah, the sheer grace! —*
> *I went out unseen,*
> *my house being now all stilled.*

The stilled house is the purified soul that has passed through the dark night of the senses and the soul. And now it goes out, illumined only by the light in its own heart. This is echoed in St. John's poem "The Living Flame of Love," when he speaks of those infinite caverns—"deep caverns of feeling"— illuminated by the light and heat of God so that they "now give forth, so rarely, so exquisitely, both warmth and light to their Beloved."

In *The Dark Night*, these evocative lines describe the high point of the mystical union:

> *Upon my flowering breast*
> *which I kept wholly for him alone,*
> *there he lay sleeping,*
> *and I caressing him*
> *there in a breeze from the fanning cedars.*

This is the language of a soul in love, drawn upon the rich imagery of the Song of Songs, having found its beloved. And then:

> *I abandoned and forgot myself,*
> *laying my face on my Beloved;*
> *all things ceased; I went out from myself,*
> *leaving my cares*
> *forgotten among the lilies.*

It is hard to find, in all of the world's literature, a more beautiful description of contemplative prayer. This mystical marriage between Christ and the soul, recounted in words as erotically evocative as anything in the Song of Songs. The soul is face to face, mouth to mouth, with the Beloved, in the orientation of adoration. It gives us some glimpse into the radical way of love, purification, and self-gift lived by St. John. As Fr. Dubay notes, "the most important thing about St. John of the Cross was not what he did but what he was. Sheer sanctity was his paramount trait. This man was on fire, utterly absorbed in God" (*Fire Within*, p. 35).

QUESTIONS FOR UNDERSTANDING — Part 1:

1. What are the basic types or forms of prayer? What is the most common type of prayer found in Scripture? Provide some examples. (CCC 2568-2622, 2625-2649; Eph. 6:18)

2. What were some of the obstacles that Thomas Merton had to address and overcome in his journey toward the Church? How did Merton's misconceptions about God hinder his spiritual life?

3. How can our appetites, desires, and interests hinder our prayer life? What did St. John of the Cross teach about this problem?

QUESTIONS FOR APPLICATION — Part 1:

1. What sort of prayer or prayers do you usually engage in?

2. What aspects of Thomas Merton's journey and conversion can you relate to? Do you have questions or concerns that keep you from offering adoration to God more fully and joyfully?

3. St. John of the Cross was both a profound mystic and a brilliant poet. Many of the greatest prayers in the Bible—the Psalms, notably—are poems. Have you ever written a prayer to God in the form of poetry? Consider writing short prayers of adoration or petition in the form of poems or psalms.

PRAYER & THE LIFE OF THE SPIRIT
Episode 9, Part 2

OUTLINE *(Tracks 5-7 on DVD)*

I. St. Teresa of Ávila

    A. Reformer, Doctor of the Church, authority on the theology of prayer

    B. Entered the Carmelite monastery at Ávila in November of 1535

    C. Determined efforts to achieve perfection; serious illness

    D. At the age of forty, began experiencing intense mystical visitations

        1. Lapse into ecstasy; lying still; levitation; "transverberation"

        2. Described in her autobiography, *The Life of Teresa of Jesus*

        3. Other major works: *The Way of Perfection* and *The Interior Castle*

    E. Contemplation for Teresa was an experienced, mutual presence, "an intimate sharing between friends"

    F. "God alone suffices"

II. Prayer of Petition

    A. Petition is a fundamental form of prayer, the most common in Scripture ("Our Father")

    B. Petitionary prayer comes from the deepest part of the heart and soul

    C. "Ask, and it will be given to you; seek, and you will find..." (Mt. 7:7)

    D. God knows what we need, but wishes to hear our requests

    E. St. Augustine: prayer expands our hearts for God's gifts

    F. Jesus's prayer to the Father: "Thy will be done."

III. "They're All Shining Like the Sun"

    A. Merton's last twenty-seven years spent at the Abbey of Gethsemani, writing and praying

    B. To contemplate is to waken the deepest center

    C. Contemplation is not just for mystics but for every Christian

    D. 1950s: Merton in Louisville

PRAYER & THE LIFE OF THE SPIRIT: Lesson 9, Part 2

St. Teresa of Ávila and the Prayer of Adoration

Perhaps the most important figure in the life of John of the Cross was Teresa of Ávila (1515-1582), who "has a double title to the preeminent place she holds in the history of spirituality: reformer of Carmel and unsurpassed authority on the theology of prayer" (Aumann, p. 189). Almost three decades older than John, Teresa was born into nobility and enjoyed a pampered childhood. When she was thirteen, her mother died; Teresa was then sent off to be educated by Augustinian nuns. After managing the family household for a while, she became convinced of her vocation to the religious life, and in November of 1535 she entered the Carmelite monastery at Ávila.

The young nun was determined to achieve perfection, giving herself completely to prayer and spiritual discipline with remarkable fervor. But this intense fervor was not always prudent, and she soon fell very ill. Her health failing, Teresa was eventually taken back to her father's home in July of 1539, and the next month she fell into a coma for four days. She revived, but her legs remained paralyzed for three years. She attributed her eventual cure to St. Joseph, to whom she thereafter had a deep devotion.

And yet, even after her recovery, her spiritual life was marked by mediocrity for quite some time. This changed as she neared the age of forty, and began receiving and experiencing intense mystical visitations. She would sense Jesus Christ and the saints—not with her eyes, but with the imagination and the intellect. She wrote of these experiences in her autobiography, such as this encounter with Christ:

> At the end of two years spent in prayer by myself and others for this end, namely, that our Lord would either lead me by another way, or show the truth of this,—for now the locutions of our Lord were extremely frequent,—this happened to me. I was in prayer one day,—it was the feast of the glorious St. Peter,—when I saw Christ close by me, or, to speak more correctly, felt Him; for I saw nothing with the eyes of the body, nothing with the eyes of the soul. He seemed to me to be close beside me; and I saw, too, as I believe, that it was He who was speaking to me. As I was utterly ignorant that such a vision was possible, I was extremely afraid at first, and did nothing but weep; however, when He spoke to me but one word to reassure me, I recovered myself, and was, as usual, calm and comforted, without any fear whatever. Jesus Christ seemed to be by my side continually, and, as the vision was not imaginary, I saw no form; but I had a most distinct feeling that He was always on my right hand, a witness of all I did; and never at any time, if I was but slightly recollected, or not too much distracted, could I be ignorant of His near presence. (The Life of Teresa of Jesus, ch. XXVII)

During these experiences, Teresa would lapse into ecstasy, sometimes lying still for up to thirty minutes; sometimes she would levitate. She also saw devils from time to time. In some cases, Christ would speak to her; other times she would simply see him. The "transverberation"—that is, a spiritual wounding of the heart—evocative of the mystical marriage, is the most famous of her ecstatic experiences.

The three major works of Teresa are her autobiography, *The Life of Teresa of Jesus*, *The Way of Perfection*, and *The Interior Castle*. When writing about prayer, says Fr. Dubay, Teresa "is charming, simple and profound. For her, contemplation is an experienced, mutual presence, 'an intimate sharing between friends,' a being alone with the God Who loves us. ... For Teresa this indwelling presence is the focal point of prayer: wherever God is, there is heaven, a fullness of glory" (Dubay, 58). Teresa is an exceptional exemplar of the prayer of adoration, which might be described as the prayer of the center. When we adore God, we allow God to take his place at the very center of our lives and hence to become the organizing principle of our lives. John of the Cross referred to the center as the "inner wine cellar," the place of intoxication and the lifting up of the spirits. Teresa referred to it, in her famous book by the same name, as "the interior castle." Think what that term would have meant to a sixteenth-century Spaniard: a place of safety and power.

The *Catechism*, expounding on adoration, states:

> Adoration is the first attitude of man acknowledging that he is a creature before his Creator. It exalts the greatness of the Lord who made us and the almighty power of the Savior who sets us free from evil. Adoration is homage of the spirit to the "King of Glory," respectful silence in the presence of the "ever greater" God. Adoration of the thrice-holy and sovereign God of love blends with humility and gives assurance to our supplications. (par. 2628).

When we are grounded in God, we are linked to the greatness and power that is here and now creating the universe, which is outside of space and time and the vagaries of this life. This center, therefore, is a place of peace around which the whole of one's life can be properly ordered. The centered soul is the beautiful soul, possessing *integritas, consonantia et claritas*—"wholeness, harmony, and brightness" (*Summa Theologiae* I, 39, 8c).

One of Teresa's most well-known pieces of writing is a short poem, titled "Bookmark":

> *Let nothing disturb you,*
> *Let nothing frighten you,*
> *All things are passing away:*
> *God never changes.*
> *Patience obtains all things.*
> *Whoever has God lacks nothing;*
> *God alone suffices.*
> ("Prayer of Saint Teresa of Avila", Accessed at *https://www.ewtn.com/devotionals/prayers/StTeresaofAvila.htm*)

That is a prayer uttered from the security of the interior castle. It is from this center that one can live a life of detachment and acceptance of God's will: whether I have a long life or a short life; whether I'm sick or healthy; whether I'm rich or poor. There, in that center, is where the mystical marriage—the union of God's divine life with our souls—takes place.

Prayer of Petition and Intercession

When most people think of prayer, they don't usually think of the more rarified and mystical forms of prayer practiced by saints such as John of the Cross and Teresa of Ávila. Prayer is often thought of as simply making a request of God. Indeed, prayers of petition are a fundamental form of prayer, of raising our minds and hearts to God. Petitionary prayer, in fact, is the most common sort of prayer in Scripture. The Our Father, for example, is a series of petitions: "Give us this day..."

"The vocabulary of supplication in the New Testament," remarks the *Catechism*, "is rich in shades of meaning: ask, beseech, plead, invoke, entreat, cry out, even 'struggle in prayer.' Its most usual form, because the most spontaneous, is petition: by prayer of petition we express awareness of our relationship with God. We are creatures who are not our own beginning, not the masters of adversity, not our own last end. We are sinners who as Christians know that we have turned away from our Father. Our petition is already a turning back to him" (par. 2629). There is just something elemental and primal about petitionary prayer, which comes from the deepest parts of our heart and soul: "O God, help me!" "Please God, do something!" "O Lord, give her good health!" How many millions of such prayers are uttered in silence and aloud each day?

Jesus exhorted his disciples to persevere in prayer; he tells us the same: "Ask, and it will be given you; seek, and you will find; knock, and it will be opened to you. For every one who asks receives, and he who seeks finds, and to him who knocks it will be opened" (Matt. 7:7-8). Dilemmas emerge and questions arise: if God knows everything, what is the point of telling him what you need? And if God doesn't change, what's the point of asking him for anything? Jesus, after all, did say: "Do not be like them, for your Father knows what you need before you ask him" (Matt. 6:8).

An analogy helps provide perspective on this dilemma. Parents hear requests, even persistent demands, from their children all the time. Some of these are good requests, others are bad. Good parents know what their children need even before the request is made. But this doesn't mean the parents silence their children's requests. Quite the contrary, they wish to hear them, even if they don't respond positively to them.

God, who is portrayed throughout Scripture as a parent and revealed in the New Testament as Father, knows everything, including what we need even before we ask for it. Yet, like a good parent, he wishes to hear our requests. And like a good parent, he doesn't always respond the way we want him to.

St. Augustine taught that God wants us to ask and ask and ask again for certain things so our hearts might expand so as to receive what God really wants to give us. In this way, God is changing us through his invitation to pray persistently. St. Thomas Aquinas points out that our prayer doesn't move God, as God is the unmoved mover. But our prayer, at its best, is God already working and praying through us—that is, God as it were prompting us to order our lives according to his will. "When we share in God's saving love," the *Catechism* teaches, "we understand that *every need* can become the object of petition. Christ, who assumed all things in order to redeem all things, is glorified by what we ask the Father in his name" (CCC 2633).

Which is why all of our prayers should end in the same way as Jesus' great prayer in the Garden of Gethsemane ended: "Thy will be done." Or, in the words of St. Teresa of Ávila: "So I want you to realize with Whom (as they say) you are dealing and what the good Jesus offers on your behalf to the Father, and what you are giving Him when you pray that His will may be done in you: it is nothing else than this that you are praying for" (*The Way of Perfection*, ch. 32; Image Books edition, 1964. Accessed at http://www.ccel.org/ccel/teresa/way.txt).

✝

"They're All Shining Like the Sun"

Thomas Merton spent the last twenty-seven years of his life at the Abbey of Gethsemani, in Kentucky. He wrote numerous books about the spiritual life and contemplative prayer. Yet Merton was always a restless soul, always seeking more radical expressions of the spiritual life. He longed to be a Camaldolese or a Carthusian. Finally, in the mid-sixties, his abbot gave him permission to live in a small hermitage on the grounds of Gethsemani, which was where he spent the last few years of his life.

Merton may have best summed up the nature of contemplation when he wrote, "to contemplate is to find that place in you where you are here and now being created by God." Or it is to awaken to that deepest center—what Merton called "the virginal point"—where we can say, with St. Paul, "it is no longer I who live, but Christ who lives in me" (Gal. 2:20). Contemplation is not just for the mystics and the spiritual athletes, but is at the heart of every Christian's life. It is the reorganization of one's life around a new divine center.

In the mid 1950s, after some fifteen years in the monastery, Merton went into Louisville on some practical business. He found himself in the center of the city, at the corner of 4th and Walnut Streets. As he stood there watching the crowds of ordinary people go by, he was struck by how much he loved them, how connected to them he felt. It was, he said, "like waking from a dream of separateness." What he had discovered, of course, was the consequence of contemplation. Once one has found the place where he is—here and now—being created by God, he finds the place that connects him to everyone else and everything else in the cosmos. As a monk and a mystic, Merton could see this. His account reaches its emotional climax when he says, "there is no way of telling people that they are all walking around shining like the sun" (Thomas Merton, *Conjectures of a Guilty Bystander* [New York: Image Books, 1966], p. 155).

QUESTIONS FOR UNDERSTANDING — Part 2:

1. What is the "interior castle" that St. Teresa of Ávila described? What are some of the methods or techniques she employed in order to pray more deeply?

2. In what ways is the "Our Father" a prayer of petition? Why did Jesus give his disciples that prayer? If prayer cannot change God, what is prayer really meant to accomplish? (CCC 2629, 2632, 2761-62, 2771)

QUESTIONS FOR APPLICATION — Part 2:

1. What are the distractions that most hinder your prayer life? What are some ways you can change your routine or practice of prayer to lessen those distractions?

2. Consider spending 15-30 minutes reading and reflecting on St. Teresa of Ávila's prayer-poem, "Bookmark." Ask yourself: What disturbs me? What frightens me? Do I act and think as though God alone suffices?

3. Is there something you wish to ask or entreat of God, but haven't? Seek to offer that prayer of petition—and to pray at the same time for the needs of three other people.

TERMS & NAMES

Adoration: To worship, exalt, praise, and acknowledge God for who he is. "To adore God is to acknowledge, in respect and absolute submission, the 'nothingness of the creature' who would not exist but for God. To adore God is to praise and exalt him and to humble oneself" (CCC 2097).

Carmelites: A contemplative, ascetical order first founded in the late twelfth century, originally for men only. Communities of women were incorporated into the order in 1432, and lay people became affiliated with the order. Teresa of Ávila and John of the Cross were key reformers in the order, establishing the Discalced Carmelites, who did not wear sandals and observed a more ascetic way of living.

Clark, Lord Kenneth (1903-1983). A British author and art historian who is famous for his BBC Television series, *Civilisation*.

Contemplation/contemplative prayer: To reflect, ponder, and focus upon God, opening one's soul to him. "Contemplative prayer seeks him 'whom my soul loves.' It is Jesus, and in him, the Father. ... Contemplative prayer is a *communion* in which the Holy Trinity conforms man, the image of God, 'to his likeness.' ... Contemplation is a *gaze* of faith, fixed on Jesus" (CCC 2709, 2713, 2715).

Francis de Sales, Saint (1567-1622). Bishop of Geneva, Doctor of the Church, theologian, apologist, and a leader in the Counter-Reformation. His most famous writings are *Introduction to the Devout Life* and *Treatise on the Love of God*, both classics of Catholic spirituality.

Ipsum esse subsistens: The subsisting 'to be,' Being itself.

John XXIII, Saint (1881-1963 A.D.). The Italian pope who called the Second Vatican Council.

Petition/petitionary prayer: To request and ask of God, to "beseech, plead, invoke, entreat, cry out" for his aid, assistance, mercy, and love. "Christian petition is centered on the desire and *search for the Kingdom to come*, in keeping with the teaching of Christ" (CCC 2629, 2632).

Sainte-Chapelle ('Holy Chapel'): A Gothic chapel in the heart of Paris sponsored by St. Louis IX of France. It was built to house relics, most significantly the Crown of Thorns.

The Seven Storey Mountain: The spiritual autobiography of Thomas Merton, a Trappist Monk. It was an instant success upon its release in 1948.

Lesson 10

WORLD WITHOUT END
The Last Things

"The great wheel of the north rose window, with its myriad parts in
harmonious interconnection and with the sunlight shining through it, certainly
qualifies as a beautiful thing. But its beauty is in service of a higher good,
for it is meant to be a foretaste of the beauty of the beatific vision."

- Bishop Robert Barron

North Rose Window. Notre-Dame Cathedral. Paris, France.

THE LAST THINGS
Episode 10, Part 1

OUTLINE *(Tracks 1-4 on DVD)*

I. **Eschatology: The Last Things**

    A. The four last things: death, judgment, hell, and heaven

    B. Eschatology (*eschata*), means "the final things"

        1. General eschatology: the "big picture" and the end of time

        2. Individual eschatology: each person's afterlife, final destination

    C. Church teaching on heaven, hell, and purgatory are fascinating to some, upsetting to many others

    D. Popular culture has many references to the afterlife, ghosts, angels

II. **Beginning with Dante**

    A. *The Inferno*: Dante is led through Hell by the poet, Virgil

    B. The Devil is not in flames, but encased in ice, with wings and three faces

    C. Hell is full of sadness, self-absorption, isolation, loneliness

    D. Why is Satan in Hell? He chose it

    E. Hell is the state that follows from refusing divine love

    F. C.S. Lewis: the love of God lights up the fires of Hell

    G. *Catechism*: Hell "consists of eternal separation from God" (par. 1057)

III. **Purgatory**

    A. Often dismissed as "medieval" or "superstitious"

    B. *Catechism*: purgatory is for those who "die in God's grace and friendship" but need to be fully purified (par. 1030)

    C. Mortal and venial sins (1 Jn. 5:16-17)

    D. Purgatory is not a destination, but a continuation and completion of sanctification

    E. C. S. Lewis: Purgatory is the washroom of heaven

    F. Biblical foundations

        1. 2 Macc. 12:40-46: Prayers for the dead

        2. Mt. 12:32: Forgiveness in this age and the age to come

        3. 1 Cor. 3: The fire will test the work of each man

    G. Dante: Mount Purgatory and the seven deadly sins

✠

THE LAST THINGS: Lesson 10, Part 1

Eschatology: The Last Things

"God is the 'last thing' of the creature. Gained, he is paradise; lost, he is hell; examining, he is judgment; purifying, he is purgatory."
— Hans Urs von Balthasar, *Explorations in Theology I: The Word Made Flesh* (Ignatius Press, 1989), p. 260.

"The world is only peopled to people heaven."
— St. Francis de Sales, *Letters to Persons in the World* (2.32)

"The Kingdom of God is a gift, and precisely because of this, it is great and beautiful, and constitutes the response to our hope. And we cannot— to use the classical expression— 'merit' Heaven through our works. Heaven is always more than we could merit, just as being loved is never something 'merited,' but always a gift."
— Pope Benedict XVI, *Spe Salvi*, sec. 35.

"The four last things to be ever remembered," states the *Penny Catechism*, "are Death, Judgment, Hell, and Heaven" (Tan Books, rep. ed. 2009, p. 55). The study of these things is called eschatology, which comes from the Greek word, *eschata*, which means "the final things." Traditionally, eschatology is divided into two parts: individual eschatology and general eschatology. The latter is what might be called the cosmic perspective—the big picture about history, the end of time, and the manifestation of the new heavens and new earth. Individual eschatology, as its name indicates, focuses on what awaits each man after his death.

The Church's teachings about hell, purgatory, and heaven are both fascinating and objectionable to many people. While purgatory is often misunderstood as a second chance or as a part of Hell (it is neither), it is Hell that garners the most criticism and objections. "If there is any subject which is offensive to modern sentimentalists," wrote Archbishop Fulton Sheen wrote in the 1930s, "it is the subject of hell. Our generation clamors for what the poet has called 'a soft dean, who never mentions hell to ears polite,' and our unsouled age wants a Christianity watered so as to make the Gospel of

Christ nothing more than a gentle doctrine of good will, a social program of economic betterment, and a mild scheme of progressive idealism" (*The Hymn of the Conquered* [Our Sunday Visitor, 1933], p. 93).

And so many people ask, "How can an all-good and all-loving God possibly send anyone to eternal torture and torment?" It is also common for skeptics and "enlightened" moderns to dismiss, or even scoff at, the belief in heaven. How can any educated, sensible person believe that there exists, somewhere "up there," a place of perfect happiness and joy? Isn't that simply a childish way of avoiding reality and creating a fantasy that hinders real progress and authentic personal fulfillment? In addition, even many Christians roll their eyes at the doctrine of purgatory, finding it bizarre and arbitrary, lacking (so they say) any real biblical foundation.

Yet, strangely enough, our culture seems obsessed with the topics of heaven, hell, and the afterlife. Countless novels, films, and television dramas fixate on the question of what happens after death. Ghost stories are consistently popular, for they seem to provide a glimpse into the next world. Angels are equally popular for similar reasons, the subject of television shows and stories about miraculous or unexplained events. Several years ago, *Time* magazine featured a story and an opinion poll on angels. The poll revealed that 69% of respondents believed in the existence of angels. However, only 49% believed in the existence of fallen "angels or devils." Not surprisingly, people are often far more accepting of heaven or some vague realm of eternal comfort than of a corresponding destination of suffering and spiritual anguish.

What, then, does the Catholic Church teach about the "last things," especially about heaven, purgatory, and hell?

†

Beginning with Dante

T. S. Eliot remarked that Western literature is divided between two great thinkers and authors, Shakespeare and Dante, with all the rest being secondary. How fascinating that the most important work—*The Divine Comedy*—of the greatest poet in the Western literary tradition is about heaven, hell, and purgatory. "The poem," explains literary critic Lucy Beckett in her study, *In the Light of Christ* [Ignatius Press, 2006], "is like no other written before or since. It is set in the year 1300, when Dante, on the edge of the exile that colours the whole poem, was thirty-five, mid-way through the biblical lifespan of a man: 'Halfway along the path that is our life,' as the first line says" (p. 181).

Dante's poem is obviously a work of creative imagination, filled with numerous and complex allusions, so it needn't be taken literalistically in order to recognize that it is also filled with sound theology. *The Divine Comedy* "is an allegory of that multiplicity of perfections to which our understanding is debtor and our charity creditor. In Hell we see perfection in the breach. In Purgatory we see it painfully being reconstructed. In Paradise we see it once more attained" (*Sources and Resources: The Literary Traditions of Christian Humanism* [The Newman Press, 1960], by Barry Ulanov, p. 118).

The poet's first stop is *Inferno*, or Hell. Dante is led through Hell by the Roman poet Virgil. They move downward through the topography of Hell, winding their way to the bottom, on an ever narrower path, until they come to the very bottom. There they see Satan, or Lucifer. There is a tendency in much literature to romanticize Satan, or portray him in terms of power and cleverness, but Dante is intent on a far more theologically precise portrayal:

> *With fear I set these words in verse! It was*
> *where the shades are all covered up in ice,*
> *and clearly seen, like wisps of straw in glass.*
>
> *Some souls lie prone and some stand straight; of those*
> *some have their heads up, other have their soles,*
> *and some bend over, face to feet, like bows.*
>
> *When we'd walked far enough to reach the place*
> *where my instructor thought it well to show me*
> *the creature who once had the lovely face,*
>
> *He stopped me, stepped away from where I stood,*
> *saying, "Behold there, Dis [Satan]! Behold the place*
> *where you must arm yourself with fortitude. ..."*

(Canto 34, lines 10-21; translation by Anthony Esolen [The Modern Library, 2005], p. 351).

The Devil, we read, is not standing in flames, but is stuck in ice, completely frozen in place. St. Augustine defined sin as being *incurvatus in se* (caved in on oneself). We are meant to break out of the narrow confines of the self and to mix with the world; we are hungry for the fullness of being. To sin is, voluntarily, to turn away from this and to reign as the sovereign of your little kingdom, which is precisely as big as your own ego.

Dante portrayed Satan has having great wings, like a bat. Why? Because we are meant to fly! Sin is a heaviness that weighs us down, that keeps us from being what we really are—and are called to be, by God's grace. Dante writes, "I saw three faces in his head, how great a marvel it appeared to me!" These three faces are a perverted mimicry of the Three Divine Persons, the Trinity. Satan dared to grasp at godliness, to ascend the throne of heaven, but of course failed. All of us, being sinners, think we are God in some form or fashion, convinced that the world revolves around us, our needs, and our desires. Hell, as C. S. Lewis describes it in *The Great Divorce*, is a state of complete self-absorption and intense loneliness, narcissism taken to its furthest and logical end: "Every shutting up of the creature within the dungeon of its own mind—is, in the end, Hell." (*The Great Divorce* [Macmillan, 1946], p. 69).

From Satan's six eyes, Dante wrote, come tears: "With his six eyes he wept, and down three chins / dribbled his tears and slaver slick with blood" (p. 355). There is a profound and immense sadness in sinfulness, being self-absorbed and stuck in the narrow confines of the ego. There is nothing glamorous about sin and evil, for evil is depressing, soul-shrinking, and finally powerless. When Virgil and Dante approach Satan, the fallen angel does nothing to stop them. Like someone caught in a deep depression, he doesn't even notice them—such is the total self-absorption of Hell. When we, in this life, experience the coldness of isolation and the dark terrors of loneliness, we have a small taste of Hell.

CATHOLICISM

Why is Satan in Hell? After all, he was a most glorious creature of God, an angel of great power and beauty. The answer is both simple and mysterious: he chose Hell. He refused to serve God, seeking false freedom, and ended up ruling the tiny kingdom of the ego. God respected his freedom to so choose. This helps to clarify how the existence of Hell can be reconciled with the divine goodness and love of the Creator. "God our Savior," wrote the Apostle Paul, "... desires all men to be saved and to come to the knowledge of the truth" (1 Tim. 2:3-4). God wants all men to share in his divine life. But God's life is love, and love is not really love unless it is freely given and freely received. Love cannot be forced or coerced.

So Hell is the state that follows from having refused divine love. It is the state of those persons who reject a right relationship with God and insist upon their own autonomy from God, turning their back on his supernatural life. This rejection of supernatural life and love is the embrace of supernatural anguish and death.

Taking up the more traditional metaphor of flames, C. S. Lewis said that the love of God lights up the fires of Hell. He meant that the refusal to accept the divine light burns us, the way that the bright light of day would burn the eyes of those who had been sunk for days in a cave. While the fire of God's divine love animates those who receive it, it torments those who reject it. Or, as the *Catechism* states, "Hell's principal punishment consists of eternal separation from God in whom alone man can have the life and happiness for which he was created and for which he longs" (par. 1057).

†

Purgatory

If Hell is the most criticized doctrine in Catholic eschatology, purgatory isn't far behind. It is routinely dismissed as "medieval" and "superstitious," an unnecessary holdover from the Middle Ages that supposedly lacks biblical support and serves no useful purpose. But purgatory—or, rather, the agitated response to it—is an excellent example of what Fulton Sheen meant when he wrote, "There are not over a hundred people in the United States who hate the Catholic Church. There are millions, however, who hate what they wrongly believe to be the Catholic Church—which is, of course, quite a different thing" (Preface to *Radio Replies* [TAN, 1979; vol. 1], by Rumble and Cary, p. ix).

It is undoubtedly the case that the vast majority of those who denounce the doctrine of purgatory are unable to correctly describe or explain what the Catholic Church really teaches about it. Here is what the *Catechism* says of purgatory:

> *All who die in God's grace and friendship, but still imperfectly purified, are indeed assured of their eternal salvation; but after death they undergo purification, so as to achieve the holiness necessary to enter the joy of heaven. The Church gives the name* Purgatory *to this final purification of the elect, which is entirely different from the punishment of the damned.* (pars. 1030-31)

One key to comprehending the Church's teaching about purgatory is to recognize a distinction made in 1 John:

IF ANY ONE SEES HIS BROTHER COMMITTING WHAT IS NOT A MORTAL SIN, HE WILL ASK, AND GOD WILL GIVE HIM LIFE FOR THOSE WHOSE SIN IS NOT MORTAL. THERE IS SIN WHICH IS MORTAL; I DO NOT SAY THAT ONE IS TO PRAY FOR THAT. ALL WRONGDOING IS SIN, BUT THERE IS SIN WHICH IS NOT MORTAL. (1 JN. 5:16-17)

There are mortal sins and non-mortal, or venial, sins. The former are those sins that definitively rupture one's relationship with God, and so destroy the divine life in us. There are other sins, less grave but still sins, which compromise and harm our relation to God, but do not destroy it outright. These venial sins (from the Latin, *venia*, meaning "pardonable") still affect the soul negatively, producing, as it were, a scar. The self-absorption of these sins leaves a mark on us, warping and twisting us, even if slowly. This warping and twisting needs to be corrected. This correction can and should, of course, begin here and now, through acts of penance, self-denial, fasting, and prayer, which "untwist" us and shape us back in the right direction.

But if someone dies with God's divine life in her—that is, in friendship with God—yet is still in need of spiritual cleansing, purgatory is her destination. Yet it is not a permanent destination, for it is actually a continuation and fulfillment of God's preparation of our souls for eternal communion, or beatitude, with him. This is not the same as saying someone can be "saved" after they have died, as if they have a second chance after death. On the contrary, it is a recognition that those who are saved—those who partake in God's divine nature (2 Pet. 1:4; CCC 2009)—might not yet be completely perfect and holy. And since nothing unclean or unholy can enter into heaven (cf. Rev. 21:27), Christ continues his work of sanctification beyond the grave.

As C. S. Lewis described it, purgatory is the anteroom, or washroom, of heaven, in which those who are saved are washed, cleansed, and completely purified. This is not, over against common stereotypes, a "place" of gloom or despondency, but of joy. Yes, being purified is painful, as we know even here on earth, but it is a joyful pain. Put another way, purgatory is training for heaven. "By no means will any of us enter heaven, or even want to enter there," notes Fr. Anthony Zimmerman, "unless our characters are in perfect shape, and our deficits are paid up in full. Purgatory is the service shop where repair work is done, and where books are balanced" ("Purgatory: Service Shop for Heaven" [*Purgatory, Workshop for Heaven*, June 1999; accessed at https://www.ewtn.com/library/Theology/PURGATRY.HTM.

Consider this analogy: Think of someone who is very self-absorbed, superficial, and spiritually undeveloped. Now imagine that person brought to Calcutta to live and work with Mother Teresa's sisters. He would be, in a sense, in heaven, but he would be so unready for this life that it would awaken deep anxiety and resistance in him. If he was open to it, he would pass through a period of adjustment, preparation, and conversion. At the end of this process, he would be able to give himself to the life of the sisters.

What of the biblical foundations for purgatory? While the word "purgatory" is not found in the Bible, the idea certainly is. For example, the idea of praying for the dead is evident in 2 Maccabees, when Judas Maccabeus, after a battle, examines the corpses of the fallen Jews. On the persons of some of the dead, he finds idolatrous amulets and guesses that this is the reason for their deaths. But then he urges that prayers and sacrifices be offered on their behalf (2 Macc. 12:42-46). How would this make sense unless those souls were in something like a purgatorial state?

CATHOLICISM

Jesus stated, "And whoever says a word against the Son of man will be forgiven; but whoever speaks against the Holy Spirit will not be forgiven, either in this age or in the age to come" (Matt. 12:32). The "age to come" is likely the afterlife, suggesting that some sins can be forgiven and cleansed after death. In Paul's first letter to the Corinthians there is a discussion of good works and the foundations upon which they are built. "Now if any one builds on the foundation with gold, silver, precious stones, wood, hay, stubble," says Paul, "each man's work will become manifest; for the Day will disclose it, because it will be revealed with fire, and the fire will test what sort of work each one has done" (1 Cor. 3:12-13). The fire will, in some cases, burn up a man's work and "he will suffer loss, though he himself will be saved, but only as through fire" (1 Cor. 3:15). This is what the mystics often call the "fire of love"—the divine fire that torments those who have chosen to be separated from it and animates those who have chosen God. Or, as Eliot put it in *The Four Quartets*, "The only hope, or else despair / Lies in the choice of pyre or pyre— / To be redeemed from fire by fire" ("Little Gidding," IV).

Dante, not surprisingly, is a helpful guide when it comes to purgatory. Once Dante and Virgil had descended all the way through Hell, they came out the other side of the earth and saw the mountain of purgatory. Dante imagines it as a seven-storey mountain, with each level corresponding to one of the deadly sins: pride, envy, anger, sloth, avarice, gluttony, and lust. On each level of Mt. Purgatory the souls are exercised, punished, and cajoled out of the corresponding sin. For example, the prideful (on the first level) must carry heavy stones. Why? Because they had exalted themselves in life, so now they are pressed down to the ground. The envious are punished on the second level by having their eyelids sewn shut, for throughout their earthly lives they had always looked anxiously at the achievements of others, harboring envy. The slothful are made to run and the gluttonous are starved. "We can infer," wrote St. John of the Cross, "the manner in which souls suffer in purgatory. The fire, when applied, would be powerless over them if they did not have imperfections from which to suffer. These imperfections are the fuel that catches on fire, and once they are gone there is nothing left to burn" (*The Dark Night of the Soul*, Bk. 2, Ch. 10, sec. 5).

When is a person released from purgatory? As St. John's remark indicates, when the imperfections are gone and the souls are ready for the banquet of heaven. In *The Divine Comedy*, each individual soul realizes this moment, for only the person in purgatory knows when he is ready for full participation in God's boundless love and perfect life.

QUESTIONS FOR UNDERSTANDING — Part 1:

1. What are the four "last things"? What is the difference between general eschatology and individual eschatology?

2. What is the theological basis for Dante depicting the Devil stuck in ice in the very bottom recesses of hell? What other details are based upon Catholic teaching about hell? (CCC 1033-1037)

3. What is the relationship between love, free will, and hell? (CCC 1036-37, 1057)

4. What are three faulty understandings of purgatory? What are three correct metaphors or descriptions of purgatory? (CCC 1030-1031)

5. How is purgatory a continuation and fulfillment of Christ's work of salvation? What Scriptural evidence is there for a belief in purgatory? (CCC 1987; 2 Macc. 12:40-46; Mt. 12:32; 1 Cor. 3:12-13, 15)

QUESTIONS FOR APPLICATION — Part 1:

1. What are some of the misconceptions or misunderstandings that exist about the "last things"? What understanding of Catholic teaching have you gained that might clear these up?

2. Which do you find more interesting: individual eschatology or general eschatology? Why might it be important to keep the two in balance and in proper relationship to each other?

3. If you were asked to explain the difference between purgatory and hell, how would you respond? Which of the two do you think is more difficult to explain? Why?

THE LAST THINGS
Episode 10, Part 2

OUTLINE *(Tracks 5-6 on DVD)*

I. Angels and Devils

    A. Angels

    B. Devil

II. Heaven

    A. Heaven is communion of life and love with the Trinity (CCC 1024)

    B. Faith, hope, love—"the greatest of these is love" (1 Cor. 13:13)

    C. No need for faith (beatific vision) or hope (realized) in heaven

    D. Many different images and descriptions of heaven

        1. The beatific vision: perfect happiness

        2. Unending beauty

        3. Household of God, communion of saints

        4. The heavenly Jerusalem, a city of life

THE LAST THINGS: Lesson 10, Part 2

Angels and Devils

"They are intellectual natures, at the peak of creation..."
- St. Thomas Aquinas

The great Nicene Creed of the Church professes that we believe in things visible and invisible. In other words, there is a reality that extends beyond what is immediately apparent to the physical senses. Perhaps the most popular example of these invisible realities are the mysterious creatures that are identified as the angels (CCC 328).

While the creatures that we call "angels" are known as such, the *Catechism of the Catholic Church* offers an interesting distinction. The word "angel" is really what these creatures do— "angel" designates their mission, which is to act in the corporeal world as emissaries of God. This mission is readily apparent from the manner in which the angels are identified in the Scriptures. The *Catechism* provides this insight:

> *Angels have been present since creation and throughout the history of salvation, announcing this salvation from afar and near and serving the accomplishment of the divine plan: they closed the earthly paradise; protected Lot; saved Hagar and her child; stayed Abraham's hand; communicated the law by their ministry; led the people of God, announced births and callings; and assisted the prophets, just to cite a few examples. Finally, the angel Gabriel announced the birth of John the Baptist and that of Jesus himself.* (CCC 332)

Saint Thomas Aquinas considered the mission of these spiritual creatures to be to inform humanity of divine realities and so lead people to God.

If angel denotes the mission of these creatures, what precisely *are* they? These creatures are spirits, which means that they are incorporeal beings of intellect and will, immortal by nature, and possessing abilities that exceed that of corporeal creatures. These spirits are not, as some propose, the souls of deceased humans, but are a distinct type of created beings. The *Catechism* clarifies:

> *The profession of faith of the Fourth Lateran Council (1215) affirms that God "from the beginning of time made at once out of nothing both orders of creatures, the spiritual and the corporeal, that is, the angelic and the earthly..."* (CCC 327)

The interactions of these spirits with humanity are enveloped in mystery. While the *Catechism* records the positive interventions of angels as they act to announce the great events of salvation history, the Scriptures record other angelic actions which are much more upsetting and off-putting. Angels announce the doom of Sodom and Gomorrah (Gen. 19). Angels act to bring terrifying chastisement upon both Israel and their enemies (2 Sam. 24, 1 Chr. 21, 2 Kgs. 19). Thus we can understand the response of both the shepherds (Lk. 2:9) and the Mother of God (Lk. 1:30) to the appearances of angels as being one of fear. These spirits are not the charming entities that have been popularized by some of the imagery of the culture, but are fierce creatures of incredible presence and power.

Not all of these spirits are servants of the Lord. The Church is clear that some of these creatures have refused to serve God and are the enemies of the Lord and his creation. Their wills express themselves in malevolent actions, and their intellects have been perverted by their opposition to God:

> *Behind the disobedient choice of our first parents lurks a seductive voice, opposed to God, which makes them fall into death out of envy. Scripture and the Church's Tradition see in this being a fallen angel, called "Satan" or the "devil". The Church teaches that Satan was at first a good angel, made by God: "The devil and the other demons were indeed created naturally good by God, but they became evil by their own doing."* (CCC 391)

Humanity should not be dismissive concerning the influence and power of the devil and other fallen spirits. The rebellious angels did not lose the power of their incorporeal nature and because of this they remain capable of inflicting great harm, singling out for their particular attention all that is loved by God. Since they cannot hurt the Lord, they have turned in anger against his creation, especially against humanity. And yet, the Church assures us:

> *The power of Satan is, nonetheless, not infinite. He is only a creature, powerful from that fact he is pure spirit, but still a creature. He cannot prevent the building up of God's reign. Although Satan may act in the world out of hatred for God and his kingdom in Christ Jesus, and although his action may cause grave injuries—of a spiritual nature and, indirectly, even of a physical nature—to each man and to society, the action is permitted by divine providence which with the strength and gentleness guides human and cosmic history.* (CCC 395)

†

Heaven

"This perfect life with the Most Holy Trinity—this communion of life and love with the Trinity, with the Virgin Mary, the angels and all the blessed—is called 'heaven,'" states the *Catechism*. "Heaven is the ultimate end and fulfillment of the deepest human longings, the state of supreme, definitive happiness" (par. 1024). In coming to the topic of heaven, we come to the end, the goal of this series. Heaven is the goal of the Faith. Everything we have talked about—God, Jesus, the Church, the sacraments, revelation, the saints, the liturgy—points to and culminates in heaven.

God's desire for his creatures and his creation is to share in his Trinitarian life, the life of perfect love. Heaven *is* love, love in the fullest sense—love completed. In a well-known and oft-quoted passage, the Apostle Paul wrote, "So faith, hope, love abide, these three; but the greatest of these is love" (1 Cor. 13:13). In heaven, there will be no need for faith, for we will be face to face with the object of faith; there will be no need for hope, for all hope will be fulfilled. But love will stay, for the life of heaven is love.

There are many different descriptions and images of heaven, in both the Bible and within the tradition. Each is inadequate, but each gives us a small taste, of what heaven is. One of those descriptions is "beatific vision," that is, the vision that makes us finally and fully happy. Thomas Aquinas says the spirit of man is structured in such a way that it moves outward toward the true, the good, and the beautiful. It longs for these realities; it seeks them in every situation. When the mind finds something true, it rejoices; when the will finds something good, it rejoices; when the soul finds something beautiful, it rejoices. And yet the mind, the will, and the soul are not satisfied in this life; they long and thirst for more. "The beatific vision, in which God opens himself in an inexhaustible way to the elect, will be the ever-flowing well-spring of happiness, peace, and mutual communion" (CCC 1045).

Heaven is beautiful, beyond anything that can be imagined or described. Thomas Aquinas said that three things are required for the beautiful: *integritas, consonantia et claritas*, wholeness, harmony, and brightness. Heaven's beauty, St. Bernard of Clairvaux said, cannot be taken in all at once. Rather, the more we see, the more we desire to see; the more we understand, the more we want to understand; the more we explore, the more we wish to explore. It's no accident that, in *The Divine Comedy*, St. Bernard is the guide who ushers Dante in to a vision of God. Dante sees what appears to be a white rose, made up of all of the saints and angels clustered around God:

> *So now, appearing to me in the form*
> *of a white rose was Heaven's sacred host,*
> *those whom with His own blood Christ made His bride,*
>
> *while the other host—that soaring see and sing*
> *the glory of the One who stirs their love,*
> *the goodness which made them great as they are, ...*
>
> *This unimperiled kingdom of all joy*
> *Abounding with those saints, both old and new*
> *Had look and love fixed all upon one goal.*
> *O Triune Light which sparkles in one star*
> *Upon their sight, Fulfiller of full joy!*
> *Look down upon us in our tempest here!*
>
> (*Paradiso,* Canto XXXI, 1-6, 25-30; translated
> by Mark Musa [Penguin Classics, 1986])

This vision of the community of the saints and angels provides another important clue: heaven is never experienced alone. To love God is to love all those things and people loved by God. The Church is the "household of God," (1 Tim. 3:15) and in heaven the Church Triumphant is like a glorious and bustling household, where everyone has a distinctive task and where everyone works together in harmony. "Heaven is a stranger to isolation," wrote Joseph Ratzinger, "It is the open society of the communion of saints, and in this way the fulfillment of all human communion" (*Eschatology: Death and Eternal Life* [CUA Press, 1988], p. 235).

Another great, biblical image for heaven is that of the city, the heavenly Jerusalem. Again, there is nothing passive or individualistic about this, for cities are filled with life and communal activities and festivity. Similarly, you can think of heaven as a game, with many participants gathered together around a common purpose, their energies and powers engaged.

But the best image for heaven is given in the fourth and fifth chapters of the Book of Revelation: "After this I looked, and lo, in heaven an open door! And the first voice, which I had heard speaking to me like a trumpet, said, 'Come up hither, and I will show you what must take place after this'" (Rev. 4:1). John the Revelator is taken up in the Spirit and stands in heaven, gazing upon the throne, and the one "who sat there appeared like jasper and carnelian, and round the throne was a rainbow that looked like an emerald" (Rev. 4:3). Surrounding the central throne, the seat of God, are twenty-four thrones on which sit twenty-four "elders" (Rev. 4:4). The term John uses is *presbyteroi*, or priests. They are clothed in white robes and wear crowns on their heads.

John then saw a seven branched candlestick, much like the Menorah in the temple, and four "living creatures"—like a man, an eagle, a lion, and a calf—and they were singing unceasingly: "Holy, holy, holy is the Lord God almighty." And then, at the climax of this heavenly liturgy, a sacred text—a scroll sealed with seven seals—is brought forth. Who will open it? John despairs that anyone can be found. But his fears are unfounded:

> AND BETWEEN THE THRONE AND THE FOUR LIVING CREATURES AND AMONG THE ELDERS, I SAW A LAMB STANDING, AS THOUGH IT HAD BEEN SLAIN, WITH SEVEN HORNS AND WITH SEVEN EYES, WHICH ARE THE SEVEN SPIRITS OF GOD SENT OUT INTO ALL THE EARTH; AND HE WENT AND TOOK THE SCROLL FROM THE RIGHT HAND OF HIM WHO WAS SEATED ON THE THRONE" (REV. 5:6-7)

This is Jesus, the Lamb of God who was crucified and now stands risen from the dead. When he appears, the elders take up bowls of incense and sing a hymn, "Worthy art thou to take the scroll and to open its seals, for thou wast slain and by thy blood didst ransom men for God from every tribe and tongue and people and nation, and hast made them a kingdom and priests to our God, and they shall reign on earth" (Rev. 5:9-10).

What does this resemble? What does it bring to mind? A figure seated upon a central chair, with priests in white robes and wearing crowns gathered around him? Candles, incense, singing, and the introduction of a sacred text? And the appearance, at the culmination of the ceremony, of the Lamb of God?

Yes, what is being described here is the Mass. The Mass is not simply a gathering of the earthly community, nor is it merely a fellowship meal. The Mass is an opening into heaven, the door through which we gaze into the eternal worship of the angels and the saints. As we sing, "Holy, holy, holy," we join our voices to those of the angels: "May our voices be one with theirs." At the "Lamb of God," we participate even now in the heavenly worship of the Lamb of God, which never ends. When we hear the Word of God here below, we listen to the eternal proclamation of the Word in heaven:

In the earthly liturgy we take part in a foretaste of that heavenly liturgy which is celebrated in the holy city of Jerusalem toward which we journey as pilgrims, where

Christ is sitting at the right hand of God, a minister of the holies and of the true tabernacle; we sing a hymn to the Lord's glory with all the warriors of the heavenly army; venerating the memory of the saints, we hope for some part and fellowship with them; we eagerly await the Saviour, Our Lord Jesus Christ, until He, our life, shall appear and we too will appear with Him in glory. (Sacrosanctum Concilium, sec. 8)

Notre-Dame Cathedral, Paris:

"I don't know any place on earth that better symbolizes the beatific vision than the north rose window at Notre-Dame Cathedral in Paris. I first saw this window on a June day in 1989, just after I had arrived, jet-lagged and confused, to begin my doctoral studies. I was so mesmerized by this sight that I returned here every day until I went home for Christmas vacation. What drew me to this place? Well, this is much more than a compellingly beautiful arrangement; it is meant to evoke the vision of heaven. It is, of course, a circle, that mysterious shape that has no beginning and no end and is hence evocative of eternity. Also, the predominance of the numerical theme of eight, also evocative of that which stands outside of time."

- Bishop Robert Barron, Episode 10 of *CATHOLICISM,* "World Without End: The Last Things"

QUESTIONS FOR UNDERSTANDING — Part 2:

1. What are angels and how are they different than human beings? Can a human become an angel after he/she dies? (CCC 329-330; Heb 1:14)

2. Who leads the fallen angels and what is his power on earth? (CCC 391-395)

3. What are some descriptions of heaven found in Scripture? In Tradition? How would you explain the term "beatific vision"? (CCC 1024-27, 1045, 1326)

QUESTIONS FOR APPLICATION — Part 2:

1. We are exhorted by the Church to pray for those who have died. This week, consider praying for someone who has died recently.

2. Read chapters 4 and 5 of the Book of Revelation. Where do you see parallels between these Scripture passages and the Mass?

TERMS & NAMES

de Chardin, Teilhard (1881-1955). A French Jesuit priest and philosopher trained as a paleontologist and geologist who integrated theology and certain aspects of evolution.

Eliot, T.S. (1888-1965). An American-born British playwright, literary critic, and poet. He is one of the most important poets of the twentieth century. He identified himself as Anglo-Catholic. His poem *The Wasteland* (1922) is a modernist masterpiece.

Freud, Sigmund (1856-1939). An Austrian neurologist and the founder of psychoanalysis. His work drew attention to the vastness of the unconscious mind and its tremendous influence on consciousness. Freud believed religion was a form of wish fulfillment.

Marx, Karl (1818-1883). A German philosopher, sociologist, economic historian, journalist and socialist whose ideas are behind Communism and other forms of Marxism. He believed that religion is the "opium of the people." It is the drug of the "oppressed creature" and once people find liberation they will cast off religion since they have no need of it anymore.

Sheen, Archbishop Fulton (1895-1979). Popular American priest and preacher, author, and philosopher. He is considered by many to be the most influential Catholic in the Unisted States in the twentieth century. Millions watched his popular television series "Life is Worth Living" every week and listened to his radio program, "The Catholic Hour." He wrote dozens of books on numerous topics, including Jesus, Mary, spirituality, politics, philosophy, and marriage.

Virgil (70 B.C.-19 B.C.). Full name, Publius Vergilius Maro. One of the greatest of the ancient Roman poets. His three major works were the *Eclogues* (or *Bucolics*), the *Georgics*, and the *Aeneid*, an epic poem about Rome. He also wrote several minor poems.

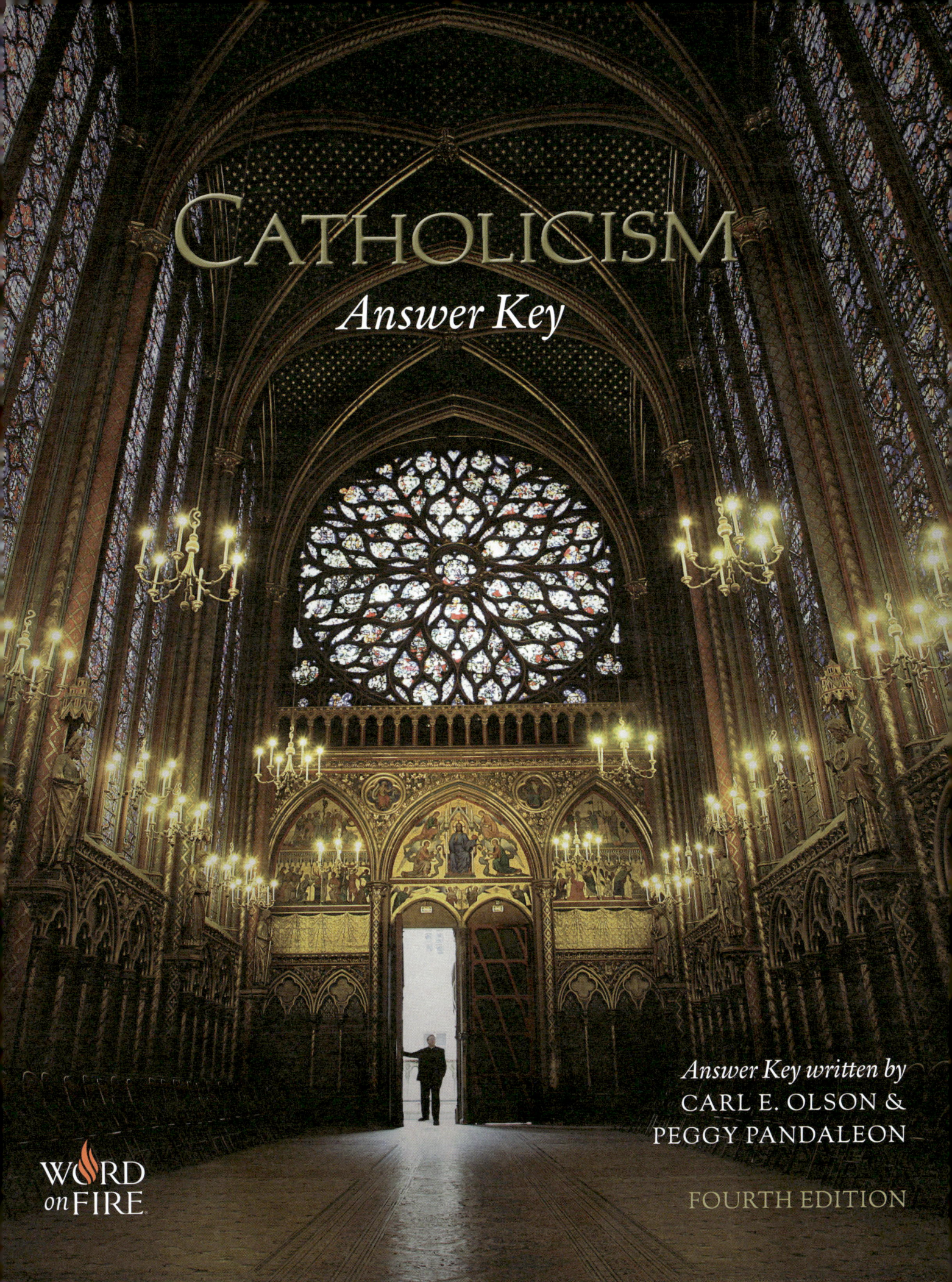

CATHOLICISM
Answer Key Table of Contents

The Answer Key is provided to add insight to the group discussion. Do not present the Answer Key as the standard to which the group is supposed to attain. It is much more detailed and brings in information from sources not available to the group.

AMAZED & AFRAID: Lesson 1, Part 1

1. **Bishop Barron says that the "essence of humor is the coming together of opposites—the meeting of incongruous things." How is "divine humor" or "sacred jest" revealed in the Incarnation? (CCC 461, 463)**

The Incarnation is a deep mystery that is filled with rich humor, what G. K. Chesterton called "that sacred jest" upon which "the whole of Christianity doth rest." It is rooted in the improbable and astounding belief that the God who created the cosmos and the world would willingly be born as a baby into that same cosmos and world. In *The Everlasting Man*, his reflection on the meaning of the Incarnation, Chesterton wrote of the humorous paradox "that the hands that had made the sun and stars were too small to reach the huge heads of the cattle." He wrote:

> *Upon this paradox, we might almost say upon this jest, all the literature of our faith is founded. It is at least like a jest in this, that it is something which the scientific critic cannot see. He laboriously explains the difficulty which we have always defiantly and almost derisively exaggerated; and mildly condemns as improbable something that we have almost madly exalted as incredible; as something that would be much too good to be true, except that it is true...Any agnostic or atheist whose childhood has known a real Christmas has ever afterwards, whether he likes it or not, an association in his mind between two ideas that most of mankind must regard as remote from each other; the idea of a baby and the idea of unknown strength that sustains the stars.*

In the Incarnation, humanity and divinity exist, in their fullness, in perfect relationship to one another. There is no competition between the two; they exist in what the Tradition calls the hypostatic union. This is the "sacred jest" that continues to surprise everyone, and it a reason why Dante titled his great poem the *Divina Commedia*.

For further reference, see CCC 456-483.

2. **What is the significance of St. Paul and other New Testament writers describing Jesus as Lord? What are the Old Testament roots of that title? How would most first century Greeks or Romans respond to the statement, "Jesus is Lord"? (CCC 446, 448, 450)**

Ancient Greeks and those in the larger Hellenistic world used the word kyrios to refer to a superior, ruler, or leader; the Romans used the word for their emperors. St. Paul was certainly aware of that usage, but his use of the word was grounded in Jewish tradition. Jews of his time largely refused to pronounce the Hebrew name for God (*Yahweh*), instead substituting other names, the most common substitute being *Adonai*, meaning "Lord," translated to kyrios in the Septuagint, the Greek translation of Scripture. The term was a favorite of St. Paul, who calls Jesus *Kyrios* some 180 times in his letters.

The *Catechism* further explains the historical background:

In the Greek translation of the Old Testament, the ineffable Hebrew name YHWH, by which God revealed himself to Moses, 59 is rendered as Kyrios, "Lord". From then on, "Lord" becomes the more usual name by which to indicate the divinity of Israel's God. The New Testament uses this full sense of the title "Lord" both for the Father and - what is new - for Jesus, who is thereby recognized as God Himself. (par. 446)

First-century Greeks and Romans would have responded to the Christian description of Jesus as "Lord" with astonishment and even scorn. Referring as "Lord" to a crucified criminal—as they understood Jesus to be—would have been amusing at best, but mostly outrageous. But for Christians, the title of "Lord" was a recognition of the divinity, power, majesty, and glory of Jesus Christ:

By attributing to Jesus the divine title "Lord", the first confessions of the Church's faith affirm from the beginning that the power, honor and glory due to God the Father are due also to Jesus, because "he was in the form of God", and the Father manifested the sovereignty of Jesus by raising him from the dead and exalting him into his glory (CCC 449).

For further reference, see CCC 202, 206-09, 446-451.

3. **What place does the Incarnation have in the beliefs of the Catholic Church? How does the Incarnation distinguish Jesus Christ from men such as Buddha, Mohammed, or Confucius? What options are available when one has to decide who Jesus Christ is? (CCC 423, 430-445)**

The Incarnation is, along with the Trinity, a central dogma of the Church and a foundational claim of Christianity. "Belief in the true Incarnation of the Son of God", states the *Catechism*, "is the distinctive sign of Christian faith", for it is an "unique and altogether singular event" (pars. 463, 464). It is in and through the Incarnate Word, embodied in a particular man from Nazareth during the reign of Caesar Augustus and crucified under Pontius Pilate, that we see the face of God.

In identifying Jesus as God Incarnate, Christianity makes a unique and shocking claim. No other religion identifies its founder with God. After all, Buddha, Mohammed, Confucius, and other religious founders and leaders did not claim to be God, the Son of God, or divine. They did not say, as did Jesus Christ, that they were the Truth, the Way, and the Life (Jn. 14:6). In comparison to other religions, Christianity is strange in its claim that the truth, beauty and good have become incarnate and enfleshed in Jesus Christ and we have touched him with human hands (see Bishop Barron's *Priority of Christ*, p. 176).

Jesus does not allow for any middle ground when it comes to his identity, which is intimately connected with his mission as Messiah: "Whoever is not with me is against me, and whoever does not gather with me scatters" (Mt. 12:30). After Jesus was arrested, the Sanhedrin asked him if he was the Messiah. He responded, "If I tell you, you will not believe, and if I question you will not respond. But from this time on the Son of Man will be seated at the right hand of the power of God." They then asked, "Are you the Son of God?" He replied to them, "You say that I am" (Lk. 22:67-70). Christ's identity is the hinge upon which everything turns, for if he is who he says he is we have to devote our whole lives to him. If he isn't, then he is a either a liar or a lunatic, as C. S. Lewis famously argued in *Mere Christianity*:

A man who was merely a man and said the sort of things Jesus said would not be a great moral teacher. He would either be a lunatic—on the level with a man who says he is a poached egg—

or he would be the devil of hell. You must take your choice. Either this was, and is, the Son of God, or else a madman or something worse. You can shut Him up for a fool or you can fall at His feet and call Him Lord and God. But let us not come with any patronizing nonsense about His being a great human teacher. He has not left that open to us.

For further reference, see CCC 422-24, 461-69, 430-45.

AMAZED & AFRAID: Lesson 1, Part 2

1. **What were the four central tasks expected of the Messiah by most first century Jews? Where did those tasks originate and what are some examples of how they were expressed?**

The four tasks expected of the Messiah, as described in the Torah (the Law), the Prophets, and the Psalms, were:

1. **Gathering the Tribes**
2. **Cleansing the Temple of God**
3. **Dealing with the Enemies of Israel**
4. **Reigning as Lord of the Nations**

These four tasks are closely connected with the inauguration of the Kingdom of God. The Torah the Prophets, and the Psalms convey the longing of the people of Israel for the fulfillment of the promises of the covenants. Moses and the various mediators between the people and God after him—judges, prophets, kings—were not capable of bringing about this fulfillment. Israel needed a mediator who could; this mediator was believed to be the Messiah. Christians believe that Christ, the messiah, is the perfect mediator who fulfills his messianic mission in his life, death and resurrection.

An example of this can be seen in how Jesus' identified himself with the Temple, including his cleansing of the Temple. The first Temple has been destroyed by the Babylonians in 587 B.C. The prophet Ezekiel wrote of his vision of a new Temple (Ezek. 40-48), drawing upon imagery found in Genesis 2: pure water, abundance, fruitful trees. This heavenly Temple would descend from heaven so that God could dwell among men.

The new Temple of God did come down from heaven, and it dwelt among man (Jn. 1:14)—as a man, the Messiah, who is the true Temple. That Temple, Jesus Christ, would cleanse the Temple built of stone as a sign of God's desire for holiness (which he perfectly fulfilled) and a sign of his own death: "Destroy this temple and in three days I will raise it up" (Jn. 2:13-22). Thus, the destruction of the Temple one generation from the death and Resurrection of Christ was a sign the beginning of a new era in God's work of salvation had begun.

For further reference, see CCC 576, 583-586, 590, 737, 994.

2. **Why did the tribes of Israel need to be gathered? How did Jesus go about doing this? (CCC 541, 542)**

Because of their failure to keep the Law and to observe the commandments, the Israelites had been scattered far and wide by war, persecution, and exile. First-century Jews believed, based on the Pentateuch and the prophets, that a central task of the Messiah was to bring about the gathering and reunification of the people of Israel (cf. Deut. 30:1-3). When Jesus announced the Kingdom of God, listeners heard a promise of national restoration Davidic in nature and scope. But Jesus went even deeper, to the real root of the problem: sin.

This gathering was focused in the new covenant established by Jesus—through his salvific work and his person—so that a new Israel, the Church, could unite all the tribes, nations, and peoples of the earth in the love of the Father, the life of the Son, and the power of the Holy Spirit. The very first paragraph of the *Catechism* expresses this essential truth: "God, infinitely perfect and blessed in himself, in a plan of sheer goodness freely created man to make him share in his own blessed life. For this reason, at every time and in every place, God draws close to man. He calls man to seek him, to know him, to love him with all his strength. He calls together all men, scattered and divided by sin, into the unity of his family, the Church. To accomplish this, when the fullness of time had come, God sent his Son as Redeemer and Saviour. In his Son and through him, he invites men to become, in the Holy Spirit, his adopted children and thus heirs of his blessed life" (CCC, par. 1).

For further reference, see CCC 1, 56, 257-60, 764-66.

3. **What was the purpose of the Temple within ancient Judaism? How did Jesus identify himself with the Temple? (CCC 2099, 2100, 1179, 1197)**

The central place of the Temple in ancient Judaism cannot be emphasized enough. The Temple was a barometer of the health of the covenantal relationship between God and the people. It was where man, through praise and sacrifice, was ordered both toward and into communion with God. The interior of the Temple was meant to evoke the Garden of Eden, for in Eden, prior to the Fall, man enjoyed a perfect adoration of God. In Eden, man was fully alive—and restoring and obtaining this blessed state was the purpose of the Temple.

The worship of God in the Temple was offered in the form of sacrifice for it was sacrifice that established communion with God. It was a way of offering a gift back to the One who is Creator and Gift-giver in humility and thanksgiving. It was a key part of the "logic" of reestablishing communion with God, a cultivation of a spirit of gratitude. In offering himself as a sacrifice, Jesus Christ gave to God the Father the gift of his Person, drawing humanity into the divine life of the Trinity, the perfect self-gift of divine Persons and the origin of all life, both natural and supernatural. "Destroy this temple," Jesus said, "and in three days I will raise it up" (Jn. 2:19).

Through his death and Resurrection, the Incarnate Word—as mediator between God and man—restores communion so that mankind can be saved. Jesus, in other words, is the perfect and final Temple, as well as the sacrificial lamb and the high priest. "Christ is the true temple of God, 'the place where his glory dwells'; by the grace of God, Christians also become temples of the Holy Spirit, living stones out of which the Church is built" (CCC 1197).

For further reference, see CCC 606-18.

4. **What enemies did Jesus conquer and how did he do battle? (CCC 559, 550, 635)**

The Messiah was expected to gather together the scattered people, so he had to destroy those who had scattered the people of God; he had to be a warrior who would fight against sin and every form of dissolution and antagonism that separates man from God.

In fighting the demonic forces, Christ chose the way of humility. He didn't use or rely upon military might and political power. Rather, he came with a host of angels and a band of shepherds whose power was in their song of praise to the Lord and in the revelation of his divine Person. As the Son of David, it was expected that the Messiah would be a Davidic warrior. But, unlike his forefathers, Jesus Christ did not fight physical enemies such as pharaohs, kings and emperors, but the very Enemy himself: Satan.

For further reference, see CCC 272, 538-40, 566, 638.

5. **Why did Jesus die on the cross? What did he accomplish, fulfill, and embody in being crucified? (CCC 599, 613, 614, 614, 616, 618, 622, 623)**

In taking on the sins of the world by dying on the cross, Jesus took on all forms of human dysfunction, discord, depravity, and despair. On the cross, Jesus lived out what he had proclaimed in the Beatitudes in the Sermon on the Mount: "Blessed are the poor in spirit, for theirs is the kingdom of heaven. Blessed are those who mourn, for they shall be comforted. Blessed are the meek, for they shall inherit the earth" (Matt. 5:3).

Jesus overcame evil through non-violence; he conquered death by his death. He took upon himself the sin of the world in order to interrupt the terrible cycle of violence and blindness that engulfs mankind, thereby liberating all of us from our attachment to sin. The goal of Christ's crucifixion is that man can be restored to communion with God, sharing by grace in the sonship that Jesus has by nature: "I have been crucified with Christ; it is no longer I who live, but Christ who lives in me; and the life I now live in the flesh I live by faith in the Son of God, who loved me and gave himself for me" (Gal. 2:19-20).

For further reference, see CCC 456-60, 608-18.

6. **Why is the historical and physical nature of the Resurrection so important to Christians? What is an historical argument in favor of the Resurrection? (CCC 638, 639, 643, 644, 645)**

St. Paul explained the importance of the Resurrection in all-or-nothing terms:

> But if there is no resurrection of the dead, then Christ has not been raised; if Christ has not been raised, then our preaching is in vain and your faith is in vain. We are even found to be misrepresenting God, because we testified of God that he raised Christ, whom he did not raise if it is true that the dead are not raised. For if the dead are not raised, then Christ has not been raised. If Christ has not been raised, your faith is futile and you are still in your sins." (1 Cor. 15:13-17)

Although the Resurrection of Jesus Christ from the dead is beyond human comprehension, it is not symbolic or metaphorical in nature. It "cannot be interpreted as something outside the physical order, and it is impossible not to acknowledge it as an historical fact" (CCC 643).

It is the event that gives meaning to the whole; if there were no resurrection, Christ's death would have been a tragedy, but hardly an event worth putting at the center of our lives. But the Resurrection gives joyful meaning to the totality of things.

St. Cyril of Jerusalem, writing some 1700 years ago, wrote that when Peter and John first ran to the empty tomb they did not, at that very moment, "meet Christ risen from the dead, but they infer his resurrection from the bundle of linen clothes" and connected that physical fact to Jesus' own words and the prophecies of Scripture. "When, therefore, they looked at the issues of events in the light of the prophecies that turned out true, their faith was from that time forward rooted on a firm foundation" (*Commentary on the Gospel of John*, 12). What the two men saw was unexpected and astounding, but they didn't give themselves over to irrational judgments or emotional conjectures, but began to logically put together the pieces of the prophetic puzzle.

This is a powerful explanation for the birth and growth of Christianity in the first century. Scripture scholar N. T. Wright argues that it is impossible to explain the emergence of Christianity without the fact of the Resurrection. There were many messianic movements that came on the scene and shortly passed away during the first century. What distinguished the movement founded by a carpenter's son from Nazareth? Peter provides a strong answer in his testimony to the centurion Cornelius: "And we are witnesses to all that he did both in the country of the Jews and in Jerusalem. They put him to death by hanging him on a tree; but God raised him on the third day and made him manifest; not to all the people but to us who were chosen by God as witnesses, who ate and drank with him after he rose from the dead. And he commanded us to preach to the people, and to testify that he is the one ordained by God to be judge of the living and the dead" (Acts 10:39-42). The disciples really did believe that Jesus rose from the dead—not despite the evidence, but because of the evidence and their personal encounter with the risen Lord.

For further reference, see CCC 638-58, 988-1004.

7. **Who was the first evangelist for the crucified Messiah? What is the irony of that fact? (CCC 306, 307)**

The Roman governor, Pontius Pilate, in placing the sign over Jesus on the cross—"Jesus of Nazareth, the King of the Jews" (Jn. 19:19)—unwittingly became the first evangelist for the crucified Messiah. "Before Pilate, Christ proclaims that he 'has come into the world, to bear witness to the truth.'" (CCC, par. 2471). Pilate, although he would not knowingly acknowledge the truth, still bore witness to the truth in having the sign posted over Jesus' head. Thus, the man who sentenced Jesus to death on the cross also proclaimed to the world that Jesus was the King of the Jews.

All men are created by God and all men will, in the end, carry out his purposes, even if we are not aware of our role in his providential plan. Jesus is the Lord in that he governs the cosmos; all creatures are mysteriously involved in accomplishing his purposes. And, in the end, all men will have to face the truth about Jesus, "for it is written, 'As I live, says the Lord, every knee shall bow to me, and every tongue shall give praise to God.' So each of us shall give account of himself to God" (Rom. 14:11-12; Phil. 2:9-11). God will, of course, respect the freely made choices of man, but man will have to admit, in the end, the One who is the Creator, Savior, and Lord of all men.

For further reference, see CCC 669, 678-82.

THE TEACHINGS OF JESUS: Lesson 2, Part 1

1. **How does the Catholic Church teach that Jesus is completely unique in his person and work? (CCC 454, 464, 614, 617)**

The uniqueness of Jesus is rooted in who he is and what he has done. Both of these are rooted in the fact that he is completely divine—he is truly God—and completely human. He is the Incarnate Word of God, who became man for the salvation of all men: "And the Word became flesh and dwelt among us, full of grace and truth; we have beheld his glory, glory as of the only Son from the Father" (Jn. 1:14).

The Catechism of the Catholic Church highlights the singular relationship that Jesus Christ has with the Father: "The title 'Son of God' signifies the unique and eternal relationship of Jesus Christ to God his Father: he is the only Son of the Father (Jn 1:14, 18; 3:16, 18); he is God himself (Jn 1:1). To be a Christian, one must believe that Jesus Christ is the Son of God (Acts 8:37; 1 Jn 2:23)" (par. 454). The *Catechism* further notes, "The unique and altogether singular event of the Incarnation of the Son of God does not mean that Jesus Christ is part God and part man, nor does it imply that he is the result of a confused mixture of the divine and the human. He became truly man while remaining truly God. Jesus Christ is true God and true man" (CCC 464).

Because Jesus Christ alone is truly God and man—two natures, one Person—he alone is able to bridge the chasm between God and man brought about by the sin of the first Adam. The new Adam came in order to offer himself as a sacrifice that brings reconciliation between God and man, a sacrifice made freely and out of love (see CCC, par. 614). "The Council of Trent emphasizes the unique character of Christ's sacrifice as 'the source of eternal salvation' and teaches that 'his most holy Passion on the wood of the cross merited justification for us.' And the Church venerates his cross as she sings: 'Hail, O Cross, our only hope.'" (CCC 617).

Dominus Iesus, the Congregation for the Doctrine of the Faith's document "On the Unicity and Salvific Universality of Jesus Christ and the Church" (August 2000), comments at length about the uniqueness of Christ and his saving work. It emphasizes that Christ is the unique mediator between God and man:

> *The Church's Magisterium, faithful to divine revelation, reasserts that Jesus Christ is the mediator and the universal redeemer: "The Word of God, through whom all things were made, was made flesh, so that as perfect man he could save all men and sum up all things in himself. The Lord...is he whom the Father raised from the dead, exalted and placed at his right hand, constituting him judge of the living and the dead". This salvific mediation implies also the unicity of the redemptive sacrifice of Christ, eternal high priest (Heb 6:20; 9:11; 10:12-14) (par. 11; see especially, pars. 5-15).*

2. **Read Luke 6 and Matthew 5-7. In what ways are the two versions of the Sermon on the Mount similar and different?**

The Sermon recorded in the Gospel of Matthew, in chapters 5 through 7, is obviously longer than the Sermon found in the Gospel of Luke (6:17-49) and includes much unique material. For example, Luke 6 does not contain verses that parallel what is found in Matthew 5:16-24, 33-37; 6:1-8, 14-18; 7:6, while other passages from Matthew 5-7 have parallels in other chapters of the Gospel of Luke. While there were attempts over the centuries to demonstrate that the two versions of the Sermon on the Mount were gleaned from the same sermon, most commentators now believe that Jesus very likely gave several sermons touching on the same themes and using the same basic concepts, examples, and language. It is also widely recognized that the Evangelists chose statements and discourses to be worked into a larger framework, with particular theological emphases in mind and oriented toward specific audiences. Matthew was writing for a Jewish audience while Luke, who was not Jewish, was writing for a mostly Gentile audience. This can be seen in how Matthew almost always uses the term "kingdom of heaven", since it was more acceptable to Jewish readers than "kingdom of God", used by Luke.

This also explains why Matthew has so many overt references to the Old Testament, especially to the Law (notably Matt. 5:17-18) and to interpretations of the Law, as when Jesus states, several times, "You have heard that it was said… But I say to you…". In this way Jesus is clearly presented as the new Moses giving the new Law, a matter of great significance to Jewish readers but of less importance to Gentiles.

3. **How does the Sermon on the Mount express and fulfill the commandments of the Law? What are some of the key connections between the Sermon on the Mount and the Law? (CCC 1965, 1968)**

The Sermon on the Mount is given by the lawgiver, Jesus Christ, who is in both word and deed the perfect fulfillment of the Law: "Think not that I have come to abolish the law and the prophets; I have come not to abolish them but to fulfil them" (Matt. 5:17). The New Law given by Christ is the "law of the Gospel", and "is the perfection here on earth of the divine law, natural and revealed. It is the work of Christ and is expressed particularly in the Sermon on the Mount" (CCC 1965). Jesus, in reinterpreting the Law, plumbs its depths and reveals the radical orientation toward God's will, mercy, and love that informs the Law but which cannot be freed, so to speak, without his interpretation and example.

The *Catechism* remarks upon the deeply significant relationship between the Old Law and the New Law:

> *The Lord's Sermon on the Mount, far from abolishing or devaluing the moral prescriptions of the Old Law, releases their hidden potential and has new demands arise from them: it reveals their entire divine and human truth. It does not add new external precepts, but proceeds to reform the heart, the root of human acts, where man chooses between the pure and the impure, where faith, hope, and charity are formed and with them the other virtues. The Gospel thus brings the Law to its fullness through imitation of the perfection of the heavenly Father, through forgiveness of enemies and prayer for persecutors, in emulation of the divine generosity. (CCC 1968)*

Jesus purposefully goes up the mountain to give his Sermon (Matt. 5:1), making a clear connection to Moses' ascent up Mount Sinai to receive the Law from God. Throughout the Old Testament, mountaintops are places where man encounters God—where God reveals something about himself, his Law, his plan for man. Jesus, in going up on the mountain, presents himself as the New Moses, the giver of a new and perfect law. "Jesus sits on the cathedra of Moses," explains Pope Benedict XVI in *Jesus of Nazareth*, "But he does so not after the manner of teachers who are trained for the job in a school; he sits there as the greater Moses, who broadens the Covenant to include all nations. The mountain, then, is 'the new and definitive Sinai.'" The Holy Father further notes, "Jesus understands himself as the Torah."

In sum, the Son of God is the lawgiver, the New Moses, the fulfillment of the Old Law, and the perfect personification of the New Law.

For further reference, see CCC 1961-86.

4. **What is the meaning of "happy" or "blessed" as used in the Sermon on the Mount? How is the biblical concept of happiness different from happiness as most people understand it today? (CCC 1716-29)**

The word "happy," or "blessed" (*makarios* in Greek; *beatitudo* in Latin) is often misunderstood, especially since "happy" connotes a temporary, emotional state. But true happiness is spiritual and moral; it is not based on external events but on the certainty of God's gift of grace and our participation in the divine life. As Mark Brumley notes, "The saints in heaven are supremely happy, because they're with God, the source of all happiness. We call their happiness beatitude, and we speak of the beatific vision of God, which the saints enjoy. ("The Blessings & Curses of the Beatitudes," *The Catholic Faith* [September/October 2001]).

This blessedness and happiness is joyful, for it flows from the life of God and is, in fact, the great gift of divine life. In addition, it refers to a path or promise that leads to rest and consolation, especially for those who are distressed and afflicted.

The beatitudes draw deeply from the Old Testament—especially from the Psalms and Wisdom literature—which contains forty-five beatitudes, usually introduced with the preface, "Blessed is the one..." The first Psalm, for example, opens with such a statement: "Happy those who do not follow the counsel of the wicked ... Rather, the law of the Lord is their joy" (Ps 1:1a, 2a). These Old Testament passages usually depict blessings in primarily temporal, material terms: land, health, and so forth. But the eight beatitudes uttered by Jesus in the Sermon on the Mount refer to blessings that begin in this life but will be fully realized in the kingdom of heaven. "They express the vocation of the faithful associated with the glory of his Passion and Resurrection; they shed light on the actions and attitudes characteristic of the Christian life; they are the paradoxical promises that sustain hope in the midst of tribulations; they proclaim the blessings and rewards already secured, however dimly, for Christ's disciples; they have begun in the lives of the Virgin Mary and all the saints" (CCC 1717).

For further reference, see CCC 459, 581, 1716-29.

5. **What are some of the paradoxical qualities of the beatitudes? How do they contrast with a worldly desire for power, honor, pleasure, and wealth? (CCC 1719, 1722, 1723)**

The beatitudes go very much contrary to our natural understandings of happiness, peace, and perfection; they are especially contrary to the priorities and desires of the world, which focuses on transitory passions and passing pleasures. It is paradoxical to the hear that those who mourn, hunger, thirst, and are persecuted will be comforted, satisfied, and enter the kingdom of heaven. It is paradoxical to hear that abandoning oneself to God's will and dying to our own desires will lead to eternal joy and perfect fulfillment. This paradox rests on the simple fact that if we allow good things—money, food, entertainment—to be the goal of our lives, then we will ultimately lose the gift of the greatest good: God's own divine life. "The Beatitudes reveal the goal of human existence, the ultimate end of human acts: God calls us to his own beatitude" (CCC 1719). This beatitude—this blessing and joy—"surpasses the understanding and powers of man" (CCC 1722), and so seems pointless and illogical to those who live only for what can be seen, grasped, and had in this world.

For further reference, see CCC 1716-29.

1. **What is the relationship between the Sermon on the Mount and Christ's death on the Mount of Calvary?**

The Sermon on the Mount presents an understanding of God, blessings, holiness, and law that reveals the perfection of Jesus Christ and the failings of those to whom he is preaching. This is in turn creates tension and conflict, finally resulting in the arrest, torture, and execution of Jesus, which in turn reveals exactly how perfectly he lived the very things he taught. He is the perfect model of meekness, humility, purity, and holiness; he is the one who is persecuted for righteousness' sake. This, in turn, reveals a third fact: man's desperate need to enter the kingdom of heaven, which can only be done through embracing the cross of the Crucified One.

Archbishop Fulton Sheen, in his *Life of Christ* (New York, 1958), wrote, "He who climbed the first to preach the Beatitudes, necessarily climbed the second to practice what He preached. ... The Sermon on the Mount cannot be separated from His Crucifixion, any more than day can be separated from night." (p. 115). St. Thomas Aquinas said the beatitudes are best exemplified in Christ crucified, so that men will be happy only if they despise what Jesus despised on the cross and if they love what he loved.

The message of the Sermon is the reformation of man's heart through forgiveness, faith, and Jesus' gift of eternal life. The Son of God not only preached the beatitudes, he lived them out in his Passion. Fully human and fully divine, he showed how the New Law is given and how the divine life is lived.

For further reference, see CCC 272-3, 571-82, 606-14, 1961-86.

2. **What does it mean to "love your enemy"? How is this a radical teaching? (Matt. 5:38-39, 44-45; Matt 26:52)**

Loving your enemy—especially those who seek to destroy us—is the greatest test of love. It is not a matter of emotion or feelings. It requires willing the good for the one who will not respond in kind. The Old Law had set limits on retribution; it had presented a form of justice that was quite radical for its time. The New Law goes much further: "You have heard that it was said, 'An eye for an eye and a tooth for a tooth.' But I say to you, Do not resist one who is evil. But if any one strikes you on the right cheek, turn to him the other also..." (Matt. 5:38-39).

This is not an encouragement to passivity in the face of violence, but is a new and provocative form of resistance. It rejects the two normal responses to unjust aggression, which are to either fight or flee, neither of which is ultimately effective. Slapping someone on the right cheek was a blatant gesture of contempt, requiring the back of one's hand. To fight back would make the situation worse; to run away would encourage and confirm the attacker in his violence. A perfect example of rejecting either response is seen in how Jesus reacted in the garden when he was being arrested. He did not attempt to escape, nor did he allow Peter to defend him with the sword: "Put your sword back into its place; for all who take the sword will perish by the sword" (Matt. 26:52).

This is the climax of the Sermon on the Mount because it concretely puts into action what is indicated in a more theological way by Jesus' astounding statement, "You, therefore, must be perfect, as your heavenly Father is perfect" (Matt. 5:48). God is love; he is perfect love. He loves all of mankind, despite their many sins and evil actions. So those who wish to be sons and daughters of God, who seek the kingdom, must also love all men.

For further reference, see CCC 1929-33, 2013, 2303.

3. **What does the Parable of the Prodigal Son teach about the mercy of God the Father and the divine communion in which each of us is called to share? (1 Tim. 2:4; 2 Peter 1:4)**

Pope John Paul II, in *Dives in Misericordia*, his encyclical on the mercy of God, wrote that although the word "mercy" does not appear in the parable, "it nevertheless expresses the essence of the divine mercy in a particularly clear way" (par. 5). This is especially evident in how the father receives back his son with open arms and a loving heart, even though the son had spurned him and wasted his inheritance. This mercy is not rooted in emotions or subjectivity, but in the unrelenting, self-sacrificial love of God for man. "The father of the prodigal son is faithful to his fatherhood," wrote John Paul II, "faithful to the love that he had always lavished on his son. This fidelity is expressed in the parable not only by his immediate readiness to welcome him home when he returns after having squandered his inheritance..." (par. 6). Just as the father in the parable desires full and true communion with his wayward son, God the Father "desires all men to be saved and to come to the knowledge of the truth" (1 Tim. 2:4), that they "may escape from the corruption that is in the world because of passion, and become partakers of the divine nature" (1 Pet. 2:4).

For further reference, see CCC 52, 210-11, 257-60, 460, 1431.

THE INEFFABLE MYSTERY OF GOD: Lesson 3, Part 1

1. **Why do you think God spoke to Moses from a burning bush? In what two ways did God identify himself to Moses? (Ex. 3:1-14)**

We can only speculate as to why God chose to speak from a burning bush. It could be that God was showing how he is both accessible and yet beyond comprehension; he wished to capture the attention of Moses, but not to frighten him. Certainly the mystery of God was brought to the fore by the use of an ordinary bush being engulfed (but not burnt up) by extraordinary fire. In a certain way, it foreshadows the Incarnation: God, the creator of all things, becomes a creature in the person of Jesus Christ. Both the burning bush and the Incarnation reveal the humility of God, who is willing to meet man where he is at—and yet rightly demands in love that man acknowledge who he is, "the First and the Last, the beginning and the end of everything" (CCC 198).

God identified himself first by saying, "I am the God of your father, the God of Abraham, the God of Isaac, and the God of Jacob" (Ex. 3:6). Later, when Moses asks what name he shall use in speaking of God to the people of Israel, God declares, "I AM WHO I AM." And he said, "Say this to the people of Israel, 'I AM has sent me to you.'" (Ex. 3:14).

For further reference, see CCC 205-09.

2. **God said to Moses, "I Am Who I Am." What does the name suggest or indicate about God? (CCC 206, 207, 213)**

The name "*Ehyeh-Asher-Ehyeh*" is very difficult to translate, and so has been rendered in a number of ways: "I am that I am" and "I will be what I will be" and "I will be because I will be" and even simply, "to be". The name reveals a deity whose personality is known only to the extent he wishes to reveal himself: He is the One who is.

The *Catechism* notes that the name is, in a sense, the refusal of a name, emphasizing that God is: "infinitely above everything that we can understand or say: he is the 'hidden God', his name is ineffable, and he is the God who makes himself close to men. ... The revelation of the ineffable name 'I Am who Am' contains then the truth that God alone IS." (CCC 206, 213). The Israelites honored this mysteriousness, hidden nature of God by using the unpronounceable name, what is called the Tetragrammaton: YHWH. This name, "Yahweh," translated as "Lord," appears over 5,400 times in the Old Testament.

For further reference, see CCC 205-13.

3. **Explain the difference between God as a being and God as being itself. (CCC 213)**

The *Catechism* states, "God is the fullness of Being and of every perfection, without origin and without end. All creatures receive all that they are and have from him; but he alone is his very being, and he is of himself everything that he is" (CCC 213). If God were a being, he would be just one thing among many other things. Instead, God is *ipsum esse*—that is, "being itself." This means that God is completely unique, completely other, and completely sufficient unto himself. He is not created; he is not dependent in any way on anything or anyone. If, however, he were a being, he would have to be dependent on something, not completely sufficient by himself. Which in turn would mean that God is limited and therefore not omnipotent and omniscient. But God, wrote St. John of Damascus in his *Exposition of the Orthodox Faith*, "does not belong to the class of existing things: not that He has no existence, but that He is above all existing things, nay even above existence itself" (1.4).

For further reference, see CCC 36-43, 212-27.

4. **What are the five ways Aquinas stated that the existence of God can be demonstrated? Which, for you, is the most understandable of the "five ways"? The most difficult? Why? (CCC 31)**

The "five ways" of St. Thomas are:

1. Argument from motion
2. Argument from efficient causes
3. Argument from contingency
4. Argument from the gradation of being
5. Argument from design

As Bishop Barron notes in *Thomas Aquinas: Spiritual Master* (Crossroad: New York, 1996, 2008), these five ways are often misunderstood: "For some they provide a rational foundation for religious belief, and for others they represent the pathetic and arrogant human attempt to capture God in a net of concepts and logical necessities" (p. 62). But neither of these perceptions is accurate, notes Dr. Edward Feser in *Aquinas: A Beginner's Guide* (Oneworld, 2009), for the five ways "are summaries. Aquinas never intended for them to stand alone ... The Five Ways themselves are merely short statements of arguments that would already have been well known to the readers of Aquinas's day, and presented at greater length and with greater precision elsewhere." Put another way, these are paths pointed out by the spiritual master who has already walked upon them. The *Catechism*, speaking more generally about such "ways" or "proofs", states, "These are also called proofs for the existence of God, not in the sense of proofs in the natural sciences, but rather in the sense of "converging and convincing arguments", which allow us to attain certainty about the truth" (CCC 31).

For further reference, see CCC 32-38, 50.

THE INEFFABLE MYSTERY OF GOD: Lesson 3, Part 2

1. **What does it mean to call God "Father"? (Matt. 28:19; CCC 238-239)**

The *Catechism* points out many religions throughout time have referred to God as "Father", but that for the people of Israel, "God is called 'Father' insomuch as he is Creator of the world. Even more, God is Father because of the covenant and the gift of the law to Israel, 'his first-born son'" (CCC 238). It further states that the Judeo-Christian use of "Father" to refer to God indicates key beliefs: "that God is the first origin of everything and transcendent authority; and that he is at the same time goodness and loving care for all his children" (CCC 239).

In an essay titled, "Father, Son, and Spirit–So What's In A Name?" from the collection, *The Politics of Prayer: Feminist Language and the Worship of God* (Ignatius Press, 1992), Deborah Belonick reflects on the importance of calling God "Father", drawing upon the work of St. Gregory of Nyssa:

> *First, said Gregory, there was no more adequate theologian than the Lord himself, who without compulsion or mistake designated the Godhead "Father, Son, and Holy Spirit" (See Mt 28:19).*
>
> *Further, Gregory said, these names are not indications that God is a male or a man; for God transcends human gender. Rather, these names imply relationships among the Persons of the Trinity and distinguish them as separate Persons who exist in a community of love. The names lead us to contemplate the correct relationships among the three Persons; they are clues to the inner life of the Trinity. ...*

Of particular interest in our own day is Gregory's explanation of the term "Father", which is under scrutiny by feminist theologians as a harmful metaphor that resulted from a patriarchal church structure and culture.

The name "Father", said Gregory, leads us to contemplate (1) a Being who is the source and cause of all and (2) the fact that this Being has a relationship with another person—one can only be "Father" if there is a child involved. Thus, the human term "Father" leads one naturally to think of another member of the Trinity, to contemplate more than is suggested by a term such as "Creator" or "Maker". By calling God "Father", Gregory notes, one understands that there exists with God a Child from all eternity, a second Person who rules with him, is equal and eternal with him.

The name "Father", then, does not mean that God is male, but that he "God possesses a generative characteristic, for which the best analogy in the human realm is that of a human father generating seed." This can be seen clearly in St. Paul's letter to the Ephesians: "For this reason I bow my knees before the Father, from whom every family [*patria*, fatherhood] in heaven and on earth receives its true name" (Eph 3:14-15).

For further reference, see CCC 232-248, 261-264.

2. **If God is provident and all-knowing, why is there suffering and evil? (CCC 309-314)**

The question of evil is the most difficult and sobering questions faced by Christians. The *Catechism*—in answering the question, "Why does evil exist?"—states that the answer cannot be summed up in a single thought, but involves the entire Christian message, in all of its fullness:

> *To this question, as pressing as it is unavoidable and as painful as it is mysterious, no quick answer will suffice. Only Christian faith as a whole constitutes the answer to this question: the goodness of creation, the drama of sin and the patient love of God who comes to meet man by his covenants, the redemptive Incarnation of his Son, his gift of the Spirit, his gathering of the Church, the power of the sacraments and his call to a blessed life to which free creatures are invited to consent in advance, but from which, by a terrible mystery, they can also turn away in advance. There is not a single aspect of the Christian message that is not in part an answer to the question of evil.* (CCC 309)

An important part of this message is that evil is not the existence of something, but the deprivation, or lack, of what ought to be—the privation of being or of good. In addition, God's gift of free will is another key part of the big picture. If man is created in love in order to share in the life and love of God, he must be free to choose or reject that love, for man innately recognizes that love involves the free gift of oneself. In other words, love opens the door to rejection, for it involves a true choice. Another part is the challenging belief that God allows evil so as to bring about a greater good.

Finally, in contemplating the problem of evil, man is called to recognize that the greatest act of evil ever committed was the crucifixion of the holy and blameless Son of God. The Cross, considered in all of its bloody horror and injustice, reveals the heart of God, who desires to save man from sin, suffering, and death.

For further reference, see CCC 302-14.

3. **How has the Trinity been revealed to us? (CCC 261, 237, 244, Mt. 3:16-17, Mt. 28:19)**

The Trinity is "the central mystery of the Christian faith and of Christian life. God alone can make it known to us by revealing himself as Father, Son and Holy Spirit" (CCC 261). It is not conceived or appropriated by natural reason, though it is not contrary to reason; it is a mystery transcending mere human logic and knowledge. It was revealed through the person, teachings, and actions of Jesus Christ, who spoke and acted in the very person of God. He spoke of God, but also spoke of his own divinity. While the Old Testament, read in light of the revelation of the Trinity, contains hints and suggestions of this essential dogma (see CCC 237), the Triune nature of God was revealed with the Incarnation, first at Jesus' baptism in the Jordan River.

And when Jesus was baptized, he went up immediately from the water, and behold, the heavens were opened and he saw the Spirit of God descending like a dove, and alighting on him; and lo, a voice from heaven, saying, "This is my beloved Son, with whom I am well pleased." (Matt. 3:16-17)

Then it was further revealed through Jesus' teachings, as when he spoke of his intimate communion with the Father and the Holy Spirit (see Jn. 14:16-26; 15:26; 16:13-15). Jesus commissioned the apostles to proclaim the gospel with authority, saying, "Go therefore and make disciples of all nations, baptizing them in the name of the Father and of the Son and of the Holy Spirit" (Matt. 28:19). There is one "name," but three Persons. The sending of the Holy Spirit after the glorification of the Son "reveals in its fullness the mystery of the Holy Trinity" (CCC 244; see Jn. 7:39; Acts 2:1-4).

Some misconceptions of the Trinity include the belief that it posits three gods, that God appears in three forms or "modes", that there is not a real distinction between the three persons, and that the Son and/or the Holy Spirit are lesser than the Father.

For further reference, see CCC 232-260, 683-86.

MARY, THE MOTHER OF GOD: Lesson 4, Part 1

1. **What was the Annunciation? What was revealed to Mary about herself? About God's plan of salvation? And what was revealed to us about Mary? (CCC 484, 2676; Luke 1:31-33)**

The Annunciation was the announcement to the Virgin Mary that she was invited to be the mother of the Incarnate Son of God. The angel Gabriel addressed her, "Hail, O favored one, the Lord is with you!", revealing that Mary was blessed with the fullness of God's grace—that is, his divine favor. The angel then said:

> *Do not be afraid, Mary, for you have found favor with God. And behold, you will conceive in your womb and bear a son, and you shall call his name Jesus. He will be great, and will be called the Son of the Most High; and the Lord God will give to him the throne of his father David, and he will reign over the house of Jacob for ever; and of his kingdom there will be no end. (Lk. 1:31-33)*

Pope John Paul II, in his encyclical *Redemptoris Mater* (March 25, 1987), wrote, "Mary is definitively introduced into the mystery of Christ through this event" of the Annunciation (CCC 484). The *Catechism* explains that the "Annunciation to Mary inaugurates 'the fullness of time', the time of the fulfilment of God's promises and preparations. Mary was invited to conceive him in whom the 'whole fullness of deity' would dwell 'bodily'. The divine response to her question, 'How can this be, since I know not man?', was given by the power of the Spirit: 'The Holy Spirit will come upon you.'" (CCC 484). This meant that Mary would be the new ark of the covenant, "the place where the glory of the Lord dwells" (CCC 2676).

For further reference, see CCC 430, 484, 490-94.

2. **What are some of the reasons Mary is called a "new Eve"? (CCC 411, 501, 511, 726, 2618)**

Mary is called the "new Eve" because she "benefited first of all and uniquely from Christ's victory over sin: she was preserved from all stain of original sin and by a special grace of God committed no sin of any kind during her whole earthly life" (CCC 411).

Also, because she co-operated fully and freely, in complete obedience, with the will of the Father (CCC 511), she is mother of the new Adam, Jesus Christ, and she is the mother of the Church, the new people and household of God (CCC 726). And she continues to intercede for her children, for her spiritual motherhood extends to all those who are to be saved (CCC 501).

For further reference, see CCC 2618.

3. **If you were asked, "Why do you believe Mary was sinless?", how might you respond? What misconceptions might you have to address when giving your answer? (CCC 490-93, 722)**

It should be emphasized, in giving an answer, that Mary is sinless because she was saved by the grace of God. He desired to prepare a holy and perfect vessel for the reception of his Word, the Son. And Mary's role in salvation was not just confined to giving birth and raising Jesus, but continues for all time, because she is always a mother and she is always a disciple of her son. Her cooperation with the divine initiative was essential; her role in salvation is decisive.

Again, to reiterate the first point, Mary is fully human and so needed redemption just like every man and woman. What is distinctive is not the *if* or *what* of her salvation (she did need to be saved and her salvation could only come from God), but the *how*. Grace, the life of God, is not bound or limited by time; it exists outside of time and can be applied as God wills and directs. By a sort of pre-emptive, redemptive strike, the grace of God removed sin from the Virgin Mary even before the Word became flesh and dwelt among men.

Put another way, Mary did not save herself. She is not a goddess, and certainly not a fourth member of the Trinity! Rather, she is the mother of Jesus Christ, and so she is the mother of God.

For further reference, see CCC 411, 508.

4. **In calling Mary the "Mother of God," what are we saying about Jesus? What is the difference between a "nature" and a "person"? Why is this important to understand? (CCC 466, 481)**

Calling Mary *Theotokos* ("God bearer") is a defense and proclamation of the belief that Jesus Christ is true God and true man. The *Catechism* remarks:

> *Christ's humanity has no other subject than the divine person of the Son of God, who assumed it and made it his own, from his conception. For this reason the Council of Ephesus proclaimed in 431 that Mary truly became the Mother of God by the human conception of the Son of God in her womb: "Mother of God, not that the nature of the Word or his divinity received the beginning of its existence from the holy Virgin, but that, since the holy body, animated by a rational soul, which the Word of God united to himself according to the hypostasis, was born from her, the Word is said to be born according to the flesh."* (CCC 466)

The difference between "nature" and "person" helps us to better understand what the Church believes about Jesus Christ (as well as the Trinity). "Jesus Christ possesses two natures, one divine and the other human, not confused, but united in the one person of God's Son" (CCC 481). The term nature refers to the question: "What am I?", while person answers the question, "Who am I?" Each being has a nature, but not every being is a person since "only rational beings are persons." An inanimate object has a nature, but is not a person.

As Frank Sheed explained in his classic book of basic doctrine, *Theology and Sanity* (orig. 1946; Ignatius Press, 1993), my nature is the source of my actions, but "it is not my nature that does them: I do them, I the person" (p 93). It is in our nature to do certain things, but is not my nature that does them—I do them. So "there is a reality in us by which we are what we are; and there is a reality in us by which we are who we are." The difficulty is that we struggle intellectually to perceive the clear distinction between the what and the who, even though it obviously exists.

Thirdly, while man's nature is finite, God's nature is infinite. And while I have one nature and I am one person, I cannot limit God to the same. In other words, if God reveals (as He has) that He is three distinct Persons with one nature, it goes beyond our full comprehension, but it is not, in fact, contrary to what we can grasp about person and nature. "Thus," Sheed argues, "since the nature of any being decides what the being is, each person is God, wholly and therefore equal with the [other Persons]." And so, since the nature decides what the person can do, "each of the three persons who thus totally possess the Divine Nature can do all the things that go with being God" (p. 97).

If the divine nature of God overwhelmed or consumed the human nature of Jesus, it would mean that Jesus is not truly man, and thus not a fitting representative for mankind. But if Jesus were merely a man with certain divine gifts, he would not truly be God, and thus not be able to bridge the chasm between God and man.

For further reference, see CCC 253-56, 464-78, 487-89.

1. **Does the dogma of the Immaculate Conception indicate that Mary did not need a Savior? Why or why not? How is this dogma often misunderstood or misrepresented?**

   No, the dogma of the Immaculate Conception does not suggest or state that Mary did not need a Savior, but is concerned with how she was saved by her Savior. All who are saved, including Mary, are saved by God's grace. All who are saved are called to lives of faith and holiness. Mary was indeed saved by God's grace, but was kept from original sin from the moment of her conception (thus, she was conceived immaculate).

   In the words of Pope Pius IX, who formally defined the dogma of the Immaculate Conception in *Ineffabilis Deus* (1854): "The most Blessed Virgin Mary was, from the first moment of her conception, by a singular grace and privilege of almighty God and by virtue of the merits of Jesus Christ, Saviour of the human race, preserved immune from all stain of original sin". (*Ineffabilis Deus* par. 18).

   This dogma has often been misrepresented by certain Protestants who claim it states or implies that Mary did not require salvation, or did not need God's grace in order to be kept from sin. Some even insist that it makes Mary into a sort of goddess who is then given worship that is fitting only to God. But such claims go contrary to the clear teachings of the Church and the definitions of the dogmas as expressed in the official texts containing Church doctrine.

   For further reference, see CCC 411, 490-94, 508.

2. **What are some theological reasons for the dogma of the Assumption of Mary? (CCC 964-66)**

   The Assumption is rooted in the fact that Mary had a unique and intimate relationship with her son, Jesus Christ, and the belief that she, the new Eve, humbly accepted the Word of the Lord, embraced the will of the Father, and reciprocated the love of the Holy Spirit. Thus, she perfectly shared in the conception, life, and death of her Son, and so also perfectly shared in his Resurrection. As Pope Pius XII wrote in his Apostolic Constitution, *Munificentissimus Deus* (1950): "We must remember especially that, since the second century, the Virgin Mary has been designated by the holy Fathers as the new Eve, who, although subject to the new Adam, is most intimately associated with him in that struggle against the infernal foe which, as foretold in the protoevangelium, would finally result in that most complete victory over the sin and death, which are always mentioned together in the writings of the Apostle of the Gentiles" (par. 39).

The *Catechism* states, "The Assumption of the Blessed Virgin is a singular participation in her Son's Resurrection, and an anticipation of the resurrection of other Christians: 'In giving birth you kept your virginity; in your Dormition you did not leave the world, O Mother of God, but were joined to the source of Life. You conceived the living God and, by your prayers, will deliver our souls from death.'" (CCC 966). Thus the Assumption is founded on sound biblical and theological principles, all of which point to the mercy, grace, and love of the Father, Son, and Holy Spirit.

For further reference, see CCC 988-1019.

THE INDISPENSABLE MEN: Lesson 5, Part 1

1. **In what ways were Peter and Paul similar to one another? How were they different from each other? (Acts 22:3; 2 Pet. 3:15-16; Gal. 1:18)**

The two great apostles were both first-century Jewish men with a background of serious devotion to the Law, the Prophets, and the Jewish religion. They both possessed strong and stubborn personalities. Both were acquainted with hard, manual labor and both were keenly intelligent; each possessed charisma and were natural leaders. Most importantly, they were both dedicated apostles of Jesus Christ, and they both died for their faith in the Lord, killed in Rome during the reign of Nero in the mid-to-late 60s.

Peter, or Shimeon bar Johannon, was a married fisherman from the northern shore of the Sea of Galilee. Though intelligent, he probably was not well educated. He was a businessman of what might today be called the middle-class. Peter was noted for his stubbornness; he was impatient, direct, often strong-willed and contrary, but also very loyal. He sometimes openly questioned Jesus' teachings and directives, but he also loved his Master deeply. He lived and traveled with Jesus for three years. After the arrest of Jesus, Peter denied his Master three times, but he repented and was publicly reaffirmed by Jesus in his position as head apostle (Jn. 21).

Paul was born Shaul (Saul) in present-day southeastern Turkey. His parents were Jews of the diaspora, and he was born a Roman citizen. He was comfortable with all three of the main cultures of the Middle East of the first century: Roman, Hellenistic, and Jewish. He probably had a solid classical education in Greek philosophy, literature, and rhetoric. But he was first and foremost a student of the Hebrew Scriptures, the Old Testament. He was, he stated before an angry crowd in Jerusalem, "a Jew, born at Tarsus in Cili'cia, but brought up in this city at the feet of Gamaliel, educated according to the strict manner of the law of our fathers, being zealous for God as you all are this day" (Acts 22:3). Gamaliel was arguably the greatest rabbi of the time, which means Paul studied under one of the best Scripture scholars of his day.

A key difference between the two men is that while both were apostles, they had very different roles within the early Church. In the words of Hans Urs von Balthasar, it was the difference "between ecclesial office and the gifted theological writer". Peter, given a unique position of governing authority by Christ, readily acknowledged "the wisdom given" to "our beloved brother Paul" (2 Pet. 3:15-16), while the intellectually gifted Paul, following his dramatic conversion, spent time learning from the head apostle (Gal. 1:18).

For further reference, see CCC 153, 424, 440, 442-3, 551-5.

2. **How is Peter's unique role expressed and evidenced in the Gospels? (Mt. 10:2; Mt. 16:16-18; Jn. 1:42; Jn. 21:15-17; Lk. 22:32)**

His name is first in all the lists of apostles in the New Testament and he is described as "first" in the Gospel of Matthew (Matt. 10:2). Peter was the first to profess the divinity of Jesus (Matt. 16:16), and he alone received a new name, *Petros*, or "Rock," from Jesus (Matt. 16:18; Jn. 1:42). He was appointed by Jesus to be the chief shepherd (Jn. 21:15-17), and he is the only apostle mentioned by name as having been prayed for by Jesus so that his faith wouldn't fail in the face of persecution (Lk. 22:32). Peter's name is mentioned more often in the New Testament than all of the other disciples combined: 191 times (162 as Peter or Simon Peter, 23 as Simon, and six as Cephas). In comparison, the Apostle John is next with 48 mentions.

For further reference, see CCC 153, 424, 440, 442-3, 551-5, 642, 765, 880-2.

3. **What was the meaning of Jesus re-naming Simon? How do the Old Testament images of kings, prime ministers, and keys help us to understand Jesus' words to Peter in Matthew 16? (Mt. 16; 1 Kgs. 4:7-19; Isa. 22:19-23; CCC 551-555)**

Just as God had called Abram and changed his name to Abraham, God called and renamed Simon as an indication of his place and purpose in the plan of salvation. When Peter said, "You are the Christ, the Son of the living God", he confessed both the divinity and kingship of Jesus. He was then addressed singularly by Jesus, who renamed him Petros, (*Kepha* in Aramaic, the language in which they were conversing), that is, "Rock". Jesus, as the *Catechism* explains, "entrusted a unique mission to him" by declaring he would build his Church upon the newly named Rock, granting Peter "the keys to the kingdom of heaven." In this way, Christ, "the living Stone," assures his Church "built on Peter, of victory over the powers of death. Because of the faith he confessed Peter will remain the unshakeable rock of the Church. His mission will be to keep this faith from every lapse and to strengthen his brothers in it" (CCC 552).

After Peter declared Jesus to be "the Christ, the Son of the living God", Jesus appointed Peter to be his prime minister, the head of the Twelve (Matt. 16:16-20), given the power "of the keys" of the Kingdom, which "designates authority to govern the house of God, which is the Church" (CCC 553). The binding and loosing refers to prohibiting and permitting; it also includes the function of rendering authoritative teaching and making official pronouncements.

In the words of *Lumen Gentium*, "in order that the episcopate itself might be one and undivided, [Jesus Christ] placed Blessed Peter over the other apostles, and instituted in him a permanent and visible source and foundation of unity of faith and communion. ... For our Lord placed Simon alone as the rock and the bearer of the keys of the Church, and made him shepherd of the whole flock; it is evident, however, that the power of binding and loosing, which was given to Peter, was granted also to the college of apostles, joined with their head" (pars. 18, 22).

For further reference, see CCC 153, 424, 440, 442-3, 551-5, 765, 880-2.

4. **What is the relationship between the Transfiguration and the Cross? (Ex. 24:9-18; 1 Kgs. 19:8-16; CCC 554, 697)**

While in the desert, Moses the lawgiver had taken Aaron, Nadab, and Abihu with him up the mountain to see God (Ex 24:9). Elijah the prophet had also been in the presence of God on the mountain (1 Kng 19:8). Yet despite having close communion with God, both men experienced rejection at the hands of their own people. Jesus, in taking Peter, James, and John up Mount Tabor, was calling them to a deeper discipleship, to a clearer (and unsettling) understanding of Jesus' identity and calling, and their own identity and calling. They were blessed, but their blessing came by the way of the cross, for the cross is the doorway to communion with God. And the cross was the ultimate rejection of God's gift, the spurning of freely offered grace. On the cross was crucified the New Moses—who had given the New Law in the Sermon on the Mount—and the New Elijah, the great prophet who fulfilled in word and deed all of the prophetic utterances of the Old Testament.

Pope Benedict XVI, in his *2011 Lenten Address*, wrote, "The Cross of Christ, the 'word of the Cross', manifests God's saving power (1Cor 1: 18), that is given to raise men and women anew and bring them salvation: it is love in its most extreme form." The Transfiguration was a foretaste of the power and glory of God; it was a grace meant to shine in the dark night that enveloped the apostles following the crucifixion. It would remind them of their calling, make real their blessing, and keep alive their anticipation.

St. Thomas Aquinas, in considering whether it was fitting that Jesus should be transfigured, observed that since Jesus exhorted his disciples to follow the path of His sufferings, it was right for them to see his glory, to taste for a moment such eternal splendor so they might persevere. He wrote, in the third part of the *Summa*, "The adoption of the sons of God is through a certain conformity of image to the natural Son of God. Now this takes place in two ways: first, by the grace of the wayfarer, which is imperfect conformity; secondly, by glory, which is perfect conformity..." Peter and the disciples had to learn that Jesus' death was necessary so his life could be fully revealed and given to the world.

"The Gospel of the Transfiguration of the Lord," writes the Holy Father, "puts before our eyes the glory of Christ, which anticipates the resurrection and announces the divinization of man. ... He desires to hand down to us, each day, a Word that penetrates the depths of our spirit, where we discern good from evil (Heb 4:12), reinforcing our will to follow the Lord."

CATHOLICISM

For further reference, see CCC 554, 697.

5. **What connections are made in the Gospels between Peter's denial of Christ and Christ's affirmation of Peter? (Jn 18:18; Jn 21:9; Lk 22:61; Jn 1:42; Matt. 16:16-20; Jn 10:1-21)**

A key physical detail that connects Peter's denial and Christ's affirmation of Peter after the Resurrection is the specific reference to a charcoal fire lit by Jesus (Jn 21:9), only the second place in the entire New Testament that a charcoal fire is mentioned. The other instance was the site of Peter's denial, as he stood with the slaves and guards keeping warm outside the gate (Jn. 18:18). Jesus had already confronted Peter, in silence, immediately after that dramatic denial: "and the Lord turned and looked at Peter; and Peter remembered the word of the Lord, how he said to him, 'Before the cock crows today, you will deny me three times'" (Lk. 22:61).

Following the Resurrection, Jesus confronted Peter again—not to put him down, but to build him up and, in doing so, to remind the apostle of his constant need for the Lord's power and grace. Jesus' words were an affirmation of His selection of Peter as head apostle (Jn. 1:42; Matt 16:16-20). They also point to how Peter was called to participate in Jesus' unique role as the Good Shepherd, a role that is emphasized at length in John's Gospel (Jn. 10:1-21; Ezek. 34).

For further reference, see CCC 1429.

THE INDISPENSABLE MEN: Lesson 5, Part 2

1. **What did Paul give up in becoming a Christian and an Apostle? How did his upbringing and education prepare him for his work as Apostle, preacher, missionary, and theologian?**

Paul had studied under Gamaliel, who was one of the best Scripture scholars of his day and who was arguably the greatest rabbi of the time. In addition to being very well-educated, Paul was young, brilliant and intense; he was, in short, destined for a position of prestige and influence within Judaism, a position that would have likely brought both power and comfort.

Paul was well versed and comfortable with all three of the main cultures of the Middle East of the first century: Roman, Hellenistic, and Jewish. This made him perfectly suited to become—through his miraculous and dramatic conversion—an evangelist, preacher, and apostle, taking the Gospel of Jesus Christ and the word of the God of Israel to the nations. His Roman citizenship provided many opportunities that would have otherwise not existed; his knowledge of Greek thought and religion enabled him to proclaim the Gospel to pagans in an effective and challenging manner (see Act 17:16); his deep knowledge of Jewish theology and thought allowed him to plumb the theological depths of the meaning of the life, death, and Resurrection of Jesus Christ in a profound and lasting manner.

2. **Why did Paul put so much emphasis on the Resurrection in his writings? What is the connection between the Resurrection and the new creation? (1 Cor. 15:13-20; 2 Cor. 5:17; Rom. 6:1-9; Rom. 8:15-25)**

Paul seized upon the centrality and vital importance of the Resurrection, understanding that it was the fulfillment of all of God's plans and promises for Israel. All of salvation history was concretized and established by it. All of the covenants, the Law of Moses, the writings of the many prophets, the longing of patriarchs, kings, shepherds, and so many others found ratification in Jesus rising from the dead. The resurrection was the dawn of a new creation, the eighth day. "Therefore, if any one is in Christ," Paul wrote, "he is a new creation; the old has passed away, behold, the new has come" (2 Cor. 5:17).

In his letter to the Romans, Paul emphatically taught that those who have been buried in Christ and his death through baptism will rise again, so that "we too might walk in newness of life" (see Rom. 6:1-9). Through baptism, we are made sons of the Father, co-heirs with Christ, vessels of the Holy Spirit. The risen Lord has conquered death and now rules all of creation—the very created he had brought into being and that had longed for liberation from the bonds of sin, corruption, and decay. Christ is the "first fruits of those who have fallen asleep," and he opened the door for us to everlasting beatitude and communion with the Father (1 Cor. 15:20; Rom. 8:15-25).

For further reference, see CCC 280-81, 349, 638-58.

3. **What is justification? What is its place in the plan of salvation? (Rom. 3:21; CCC 1987-1995, 2019-21)**

Paul was well-acquainted with the Hebrew term *mispat*, which means justice or right order. Mispat was a quality of God—and of those humans who are in right relation to God. The best Greek translation of this term was *dikaiosyne*—righteousness or justice—a word Paul used frequently in his writings.

For Jews, the *mispat* of God was expressed in and through myriad laws, regulations, and covenants. Through these, man became righteous. But Paul knew that Israel, despite having the Law and the covenants, had never kept its end of the bargain; it had always failed to fulfill the requirements of the Law and the demands of the covenant. Jesus changed that through his death and Resurrection; in accepting the Father's will and dying on the cross, Jesus showed that he was the faithful Israel meeting the faithful God of Israel. He was Law and covenant fulfilled, not only in word and deed, but in flesh and blood. This is why Paul could say that we are justified—made righteous and holy—not by the works of the Law, but by the person of Jesus Christ. "But now," he told the Roman Christians, "the righteousness of God has been manifested apart from law, although the law and the prophets bear witness to it…" (Rom. 3:21). It is by mystical participation in Christ that man comes into right relationship with God.

The *Catechism* summarizes by stating, "Justification includes the remission of sins, sanctification, and the renewal of the inner man. Justification has been merited for us by the Passion of Christ. It is granted us through Baptism. It conforms us to the righteousness of God, who justifies us. It has for its goal the glory of God and of Christ, and the gift of eternal life. It is the most excellent work of God's mercy. Grace is the help God gives us to respond to our vocation of becoming his adopted sons. It introduces us into the intimacy of the Trinitarian life" (CCC 2019-21).

For further reference, see CCC 1987-2005.

THE MYSTICAL UNION OF CHRIST & THE CHURCH:
Lesson 6, Part 1

1. **What does the Catechism mean in stating, "The world was created for the sake of the Church" (par. 760)? How is the Church "the goal of all things"? What is the relationship between the world and the Church? (CCC 760, 168-9)**

The rest of paragraph 760 in the *Catechism* provides clues to answering the question: "God created the world for the sake of communion with his divine life, a communion brought about by the 'convocation' of men in Christ, and this 'convocation' is the Church. The Church is the goal of all things, and God permitted such painful upheavals as the angels' fall and man's sin only as occasions and means for displaying all the power of his arm and the whole measure of the love he wanted to give the world: 'Just as God's will is creation and is called "the world," so his intention is the salvation of men, and it is called 'the Church.'"

So the Church is communion with God, the means of participation in the divine life, and the realization on earth of salvation. "Salvation comes from God alone;" the *Catechism* states, "but because we receive the life of faith through the Church, she is our mother…" (CCC 169). If the world is the temporal, natural realm of man's existence, the Church is the communion and body in which man encounters and enters into eternal, supernatural life: The Church is in history, but at the same time she transcends it" for she is the "bearer of divine life (CIC 770). Through the Church we receive the gifts of faith and new life in Jesus Christ through the sacrament of devine life (CCC 770).

For further reference, see CCC 758-69, 772-73.

2. **What are some of the biblical images or names used to describe or name the Church? (CCC 753-757)**

The *Catechism* points out that Scripture contains "a host of interrelated images and figures through which Revelation speaks of the inexhaustible mystery of the Church" (CCC 753). The include images taken from the Old Testament, such as "the people of God," the flock of sheep cared for by the Good Shepherd, and a cultivated field and tilled land from which grows vineyards. Jesus spoke of the reality of the Church as the vines that are given life by the true vine of Christ:

"I am the vine, you are the branches. He who abides in me, and I in him, he it is that bears much fruit, for apart from me you can do nothing" (Jn. 15:5).

The Church is also called the building or household of God (1 Tim. 3:15), "the household of God in the Spirit; the dwelling-place of God among men; and, especially, the holy temple" (CCC 756). Peter draws upon the Old Testament in describing the Church as "a chosen race, a royal priesthood, a holy nation, God's own people..." (1 Pet 2:9). And Paul often describes the Church as the Body of Christ, as when he writes to the Christians in Rome, "For as in one body we have many members, and all the members do not have the same function, so we, though many, are one body in Christ, and individually members one of another" (Rom 12:4-5), or to the Corinthians: "For just as the body is one and has many members, and all the members of the body, though many, are one body, so it is with Christ. For by one Spirit we were all baptized into one body--Jews or Greeks, slaves or free--and all were made to drink of one Spirit" (1 Cor. 12:12-13). Finally, Paul famously describes the Church as the Bride of Christ, "without spot or wrinkle or any such thing, that she might be holy and without blemish" (see Eph. 5:23-32).

For further reference, see CCC 753-57, 781-801.

3. **How is the Church "in Christ, like a sacrament"? (LG 1) What is the relationship between Jesus Christ and the Church? (CCC 774)**

The Church "is in Christ like a sacrament or as a sign and instrument," states *Lumen Gentium*, "both of a very closely knit union with God and of the unity of the whole human race..." (par. 1). This means that the Church participates uniquely in the life and power of Jesus Christ. The term *sacramentum* refers to a sign that makes visible the invisible, hidden reality of spiritual and salvific power. Jesus Christ is the ultimate source of all sacramental power: "The saving work of his holy and sanctifying humanity is the sacrament of salvation, which is revealed and active in the Church's sacraments (which the Eastern Churches also call 'the holy mysteries')." (CCC 774). The seven sacraments spread and dispense the grace and life of God in and through the Church, which is the Mystical Body of Christ. "The Church, then, both contains and communicates the invisible grace she signifies. It is in this analogical sense, that the Church is called a 'sacrament.'" (CCC 774). Since the Church is the Body of Christ and the instrument of his saving work, she brings unity, union, and communion between God and man.

For further reference, see CCC 772-76, 780, 1076, 1114-16.

4. **What are the four "marks" of the Church? How is the Church "one"? (CCC 811-16)**

The four marks, or characteristics, of the Church are that she is one, holy, catholic, and apostolic. "These four characteristics, inseparably linked with each other, indicate essential features of the Church and her mission" (CCC 811).

The Church is "one" because, first, God is one, and also by virtue of her unity in Christ, her head and her source. She is also "one" because of her "soul", the Holy Spirit, the Lord and Giver of Life. This oneness is both interior and exterior in reality. The interior unity is formed by the bonds of charity, while the "visible bonds of communion" are shown in the profession of one faith handed down from the Apostles, common celebration of worship and sacrament, and apostolic succession (CCC, par. 814). And while there is a real and authentic diversity of gifts and charisms, Christians are exhorted to maintain "the unity of the Spirit in the bond of peace" (Eph. 4:3), for there is "one body and one Spirit ... one hope ... one Lord, one faith, one baptism, one God and Father of us all, who is above all and through all and in all" (see Eph. 4:4-6).

For further reference, see CCC 811-822.

THE MYSTICAL UNION OF CHRIST & THE CHURCH:
Lesson 6, Part 2

1. **How can it be said that the Church is holy when there are so many examples of sinful Catholics? (CCC 825)**

This tension and paradox is only possible because the Church is a supernatural institution, founded by God. To believe that the Church is holy is not to deny for a moment that the Church is filled with sinners. We see this in the example of St. Augustine's struggles with the Donatists, during which the great Bishop of Hippo insisted that even unrighteous priests and sinful bishops can validly administer the sacraments. It is God's holiness and grace that guarantees the sacraments, not the moral uprightness of the priest. The *Catechism* explains:

"Christ, 'holy, innocent, and undefiled,' knew nothing of sin, but came only to expiate the sins of the people. The Church, however, clasping sinners to her bosom, at once holy and always in need of purification, follows constantly the path of penance and renewal." All members of the Church, including her ministers, must acknowledge that they are sinners. In everyone, the weeds of sin will still be mixed with the good wheat of the Gospel until the end of time. Hence the Church gathers sinners already caught up in Christ's salvation but still on the way to holiness... (CCC 827)

For further reference, see CCC 823-29, 1425-29, 2044-46.

2. **What does "catholic" mean? In what ways is the Church "apostolic"? (CCC 830-831, 857-63, 865)**

The word "catholic" comes from the Greek terms kata holos, which means "according to the whole." The Catholic Church is a universal church, for God works to gather the whole world unto himself. The Church is "catholic" in two essential ways: "because Christ is present in her" and "because she has been sent out by Christ on a mission to the whole of the human race" (CCC 830, 831).

The Church is apostolic because she was and is built on the foundation of the apostles, she guards and hands on the teachings of the apostles, and she is taught and sanctified by the successors of the apostles in union with the successor of Peter, the Pope. She is also apostolic in her missionary work and the endeavors of her apostolates, which spread the Gospel and advance the Kingdom of God.

For further reference, see CCC 830-38, 857-862.

3. **What is the difference between doctrine changing and doctrine developing? What is the "deposit of faith," and how does it relate to the development of doctrine? (CCC 66, 78, 84-85, 94-95)**

The essential difference is between rupture and growth: change of doctrine would involve a departure from the roots and origins of apostolic teaching, while authentic development of doctrine is a maturation in the understanding and expression of that teaching. True development of doctrine is only possible within the Church, in which the "living transmission" of divine revelation is guided and guarded by the Holy Spirit and through Tradition (CCC 78). While the *Catechism* emphatically teaches that there is no new public revelation between the death of the Apostles and the return of Christ, but states that "even if Revelation is already complete, it has not been made completely explicit; it remains for Christian faith gradually to grasp its full significance over the course of the centuries" (CCC 66).

The "deposit of faith" (or "sacred deposit" of the faith) was entrusted to the apostles and is contained in Sacred Scripture and Tradition:

> *Sacred tradition and Sacred Scripture form one sacred deposit of the word of God, committed to the Church. Holding fast to this deposit the entire holy people united with their shepherds remain always steadfast in the teaching of the Apostles, in the common life, in the breaking of the bread and in prayers (see Acts 2, 42, Greek text), so that holding to, practicing and professing the heritage of*

the faith, it becomes on the part of the bishops and faithful a single common effort. (Dei Verbum, 10; see CCC 84-87)

This deposit of faith can only be interpreted authentically by the "living, teaching office of the Church alone", that is, "the bishops in communion with the successor of Peter, the Bishop of Rome" (CCC 85). The teaching office, the Magisterium, hands on the faith, guards it, expounds upon it, and thus is integral to the authentic development of doctrine down through time.

For further reference, see CCC 65-67, 74-98, 172-75, 888-92.

THE MYSTERY OF THE LITURGY & THE EUCHARIST:
Lesson 7, Part 1

1. **In what ways can it be said that liturgy is "play" or "a sacred game"? What is liturgy not meant to be?**

In the secular realm, proper play and sport are meant to be entered into and enjoyed for their own sake. In the realm of the sacred, to speak of liturgy as "play" or a "sacred game" is to emphasize, first, that liturgy exists for the sake of God and, secondly, it does not serve a "practical" or utilitarian purpose, but so man can contemplate, worship, and love God. This means that attempts to turn the liturgy into a practical program or a "teaching moment" are not only bound to fail, they fail to comprehend what liturgy is since liturgy exists for its own sake. To make the liturgy into a tool or an end to practical means is to ultimately demean and harm liturgy and worship.

Joseph Cardinal Ratzinger explains it in this way: "Play takes us out of the world of daily goals and their pressures and into a sphere free of purpose and achievement, releasing us for a time from all the burdens of our daily world of work. Play is a kind of other world, an oasis of freedom, where for a moment we can let life flow freely." He also noted that liturgy is "a kind of anticipation, a rehearsal, a prelude for the life to come, for eternal life..." (*The Spirit of the Liturgy*, Ignatius Press, 2000, pp. 13, 14).

For further reference, see CCC 1136-58, 2184-85.

2. **How should worshipping and praising God bring harmony and peace? How does it help establish order in one's life? (CCC 374, 1844, 2845; Jn. 14:27; Col. 3:14)**

Worship of God orients us to the source of our physical and spiritual life, and also orients us to our ultimate end, which is, by God's grace, eternal beatitude with the Father, Son, and Holy Spirit. "The first man was not only created good," states the *Catechism*, "but was also established in friendship with his Creator and in harmony with himself and with the creation around him, in a state that would be surpassed only by the glory of the new creation in Christ" (CCC 374).

Jesus, in his great discourse in John 13-17, said, "Peace I leave with you; my peace I give to you; not as the world gives do I give to you. Let not your hearts be troubled, neither let them be afraid" (Jn. 14:27). Harmony and peace, then, are found in and through the person of Jesus Christ. And it is in the Mass and in the reception of the Holy Eucharist, that we partake in the Body of Christ, "the source and summit of the Christian life" (CCC 1324; *Lumen Gentium*, par. 11). This further transforms us and orients us toward full union and final communion with God.

Sacrosanctum Concilium, the Vatican II constitution on the sacred liturgy, states "that every liturgical celebration, because it is an action of Christ the priest and of His Body which is the Church, is a sacred action surpassing all others; no other action of the Church can equal its efficacy by the same title and to the same degree" (par. 7). The *Catechism* expresses this beautifully when it states, "The communion of the Holy Trinity is the source and criterion of truth in every relationship. It is lived out in prayer, above all in the Eucharist" (CCC 2845).

Finally, it is especially in the theological virtue of charity that external harmony and interior order are developed and realized. "By charity, we love God above all things and our neighbor as ourselves for love of God. Charity, the form of all the virtues, 'binds everything together in perfect harmony' (Col 3:14)" (CCC, 1844).

For further reference, see CCC 1324-36, 2184-88.

3. **What is the main point of the Scripture readings and homily? What should good preaching accomplish?**

The readings are meant to draw us into the power and reality of the biblical world and the story of salvation. The many stories, narratives, and events described in the Bible tell the story of God, and are inspired by God, who has given them to his family, the Church. They are an inscripturated expression of God's love, and in hearing them proclaimed in the midst of the Church, we encounter anew the voice of God. "For in the sacred books, the Father who is in heaven meets His children with great love and speaks with them; and the force and power in the word of God is so great that it stands as the support and energy of the Church, the strength of faith for her sons, the food of the soul, the pure and everlasting source of spiritual life." (*Dei Verbum*, par. 21).

The homily "is an exhortation to accept this Word as what it truly is, the Word of God" (CCC 1349). It should, in some way, draw those who hear it more deeply into the world and reality of Scripture. The homilist "unpacks" the readings, and tells of the supremely distinctive character of God himself, who is transcendent speaker and actor in Scripture. By entering into and moving through this world, we learn how to speak, contemplate, speak, and think in a different way.

"But preaching is not speech-giving," writes Fr. Peter John Cameron, O.P. "According to Joseph Cardinal Ratzinger (now Pope Benedict XVI), the aim of preaching 'is to tell man who he is and what he must do to be himself. Its intention is to disclose to him the truth about himself, that is, what he can base his life on and what he can die for.' And that disclosure is not a discourse; it is an encounter." (*Why Preach: Encountering Christ in God's Word* [Ignatius Press, 2009], p. 15). This transforming encounter should take us out of our old world and immerse us in a new world, one vibrant and alive with the word and presence of God.

Pope Benedict XVI, in his post-synodal apostolic exhortation, *Verbum Domini* (Sept. 30, 2010), further explained:

> The homily is a means of bringing the scriptural message to life in a way that helps the faithful to realize that God's word is present and at work in their everyday lives. It should lead to an understanding of the mystery being celebrated, serve as a summons to mission, and prepare the assembly for the profession of faith, the universal prayer and the Eucharistic liturgy. ... The faithful should be able to perceive clearly that the preacher has a compelling desire to present Christ, who must stand at the centre of every homily.

For further reference, see CCC 94, 131-33, 1100, 1122, 2145.

THE MYSTERY OF THE LITURGY & THE EUCHARIST:
Lesson 7, Part 2

1. **What is sacrifice? Why and how is it so central to the liturgy? How is this centrality expressed during the liturgy? (CCC 1323, 1352)**

To offer a sacrifice is to take some aspect or part of God's creation and return it to God as a sign of our dependence upon him for forgiveness, life, and love. God has no need for sacrifice; it benefits us rather than God. Yet it is pleasing to God because it is beneficial to us. And our being increases in the measure that we give it back to God.

The logic of sacrifice and the law of the gift govern the liturgy of the Eucharist. "At the Last Supper, on the night he was betrayed," states *Sacrosanctum Concilium*, the Second Vatican Council's Constitution on the Sacred Liturgy, "our Savior instituted the Eucharistic sacrifice of his Body and Blood. This he did in order to perpetuate the sacrifice of the cross throughout the ages until he should come again, and so to entrust to his beloved Spouse, the Church, a memorial of his death and resurrection: a sacrament of love, a sign of unity, a bond of charity, a Paschal banquet 'in which Christ is consumed, the mind is filled with grace, and a pledge of future glory is given to us'" (par. 47; CCC 1323).

In the Mass, at the saying of the Eucharistic Prayer, "the prayer of thanksgiving and consecration—we come to the heart and summit of the celebration" (CCC 1352). It is the central moment of liturgy, the transformation of the bread and wine into the body and blood of Jesus Christ. We have offered our gifts to God, and since God doesn't need them, they come back elevated and perfected as the very life and existence of Jesus Christ.

For further reference, see CCC, 613-14, 1084-1090, 1328-32, 2099-2100.

2. **What did Jesus mean when he said, "Eat my flesh" and "Drink my blood"? What are some ways in which the language of John 6 points to the liturgy and the Eucharist? (Jn. 6; Ezek. 39:17-18)**

In making those emphatic statements in John 6, Jesus was speaking both literally and sacramentally. If he had been speaking in metaphor (in the Aramaic language, which he was using), he would have been uttering nonsense, referring to self-cannibalism (Dt. 32:42; Ezek. 39:17-18). Instead, he is referring to his true flesh and blood, and to the actual act of eating. Jesus, in fact, emphasized the scandalous nature of his words by moving from the word phago, which means "eat" (6:50, 51), to trogain, which means to gnaw or chew (6:53). In other words, when the Jews objected to the physical realism his language, he intensified the physical realism of his declaration.

An important connection between John 6 and the Mass can be seen in the account of the miraculous multiplication of the loaves and fishes. Jesus took the loaves, gave thanks, distributed the loaves to those present, and then had the disciples gather up whatever was left so "that nothing may be lost" (Jn. 6:11-13). These actions—prayer, thanksgiving, distributing of bread—were clearly meant to set the stage for the coming remarks by Jesus about the Eucharist, as well as foreshadowing the institution of the blessed sacrament. Also, it presents a clear expression of the relationship between Jesus (who gives the bread and will give his flesh and blood), the apostles (who are entrusted to receive the bread/Eucharist from Jesus and give it to the Church), and the whole Church, (which is nourished on the bread from heaven, the very Body and Blood of the Lord). Thus, it is only bishops—who are successors of the apostles—and priests— who assist the bishops as "co-workers", who consecrate and give the sacrament of the Holy Eucharist to the faithful.

For further reference, see CCC 787, 1391, 1406, 1524.

3. **The *Catechism* says the Eucharist and the Cross are stumbling blocks and, "It is the same mystery" (par. 1336). What does this mean? (CCC 1367, 1374, 1413; 1 Cor. 1:18; 1 Cor. 1:23)**

Jesus instituted the Eucharistic sacrifice of his Body and Blood at the Last Supper and "He did this in order to perpetuate the sacrifice of the Cross throughout the centuries until He should come again," states *Sacrosanctum Concilium*, "and so to entrust to His beloved spouse, the Church, a memorial of His death and resurrection: a sacrament of love, a sign of unity, a bond of charity, a paschal banquet in which Christ is eaten, the mind is filled with grace, and a pledge of future glory is given to us" (CCC 47). The Eucharist is the unbloody sacrifice that re-presents "the sacrifice of the cross, because it is its memorial and because it applies its fruit..." (CCC 1366). The *Catechism* states that the two sacrifices are, in fact, "one single sacrifice" and quotes from the Council of Trent:

> *The victim is one and the same: the same now offers through the ministry of priests, who then offered himself on the cross; only the manner of offering is different." "And since in this divine sacrifice which is celebrated in the Mass, the same Christ who offered himself once in a bloody manner on the altar of the cross is contained and offered in an unbloody manner. . . this sacrifice is truly propitiatory* (CCC 1367).

The Cross is a stumbling block because some refuse to believe that the Incarnate Word, the Son of God, could or would suffer and die. As St. Paul wrote to the Corinthians, "For the word of the cross is folly to those who are perishing, but to us who are being saved it is the power of God. (1 Cor. 1:18). But, he added, "we preach Christ crucified, a stumbling block to Jews and folly to Gentiles..." (1 Cor. 1:23). In a closely related way, the Eucharist is a stumbling block because some—including many who accept the Cross—cannot accept that the crucified and resurrected Lord now presents himself—Body, Blood, soul, and divinity—under the consecrated species of bread and wine (CCC 1374, 1413).

For further reference, see CCC 1322-27; 1362-72.

4. **What did Pope John Paul II mean when he wrote that the Eucharist "is truly a glimpse of heaven appearing on earth"?**

The late pontiff, in *Ecclesia de Eucharistia*, his encyclical on the Eucharist and the Church, wrote, "The Eucharist is a straining towards the goal, a foretaste of the fullness of joy promised by Christ (Jn 15:11); it is in some way the anticipation of heaven, the 'pledge of future glory.'" He explained that the reception of the Eucharist, because it is the true Body and Blood of Christ, is a participation here and now on earth in the gift and reality of eternal life: "For in the Eucharist we also receive the pledge of our bodily resurrection at the end of the world: "He who eats my flesh and drinks my blood has eternal life, and I will raise him up at the last day" (Jn 6:54). This pledge of the future resurrection comes from the fact that the flesh of the Son of Man, given as food, is his body in its glorious state after the resurrection. With the Eucharist we digest, as it were, the 'secret of the resurrection. For this reason Saint Ignatius of Antioch rightly defined the Eucharistic Bread as 'a medicine of immortality, an antidote to death.'" (par. 18)

For further reference, see CCC 1130, 1402-05, 1419.

THE COMMUNION OF SAINTS: Lesson 8, Part 1

1. Why is justice considered "the heart and soul of the ethical life"? How is justice in the Catholic tradition different from in the modern world?

A man's justice demonstrates his virtue most openly and obviously, because it is oriented to the good of others, to rendering to them what is rightly due. The German philosopher Josef Pieper, in his book, *Four Cardinal Virtues* (Notre Dame, IN: University of Notre Dame Press, 2003), wrote that "traditional teaching says that man reveals his true being in its greatest purity when he is just; justice is the highest of the three moral (in the strict sense) virtues: justice, fortitude, and temperance. The good man is above all the just man" (p. 64). He refers to the *Summa Theologica*, in which St. Thomas Aquinas states, "Hence, since justice regulates human operations, it is evident that it renders man's operations good, and, as Tully declares (*De Officiis* i, 7), good men are so called chiefly from their justice, wherefore, as he says again (*De Officiis* i, 7) 'the luster of virtue appears above all in justice.'" (II, II, 58.3). Bishop Barron, in *The Priority of Christ*, summarizes the matter by noting that "justice denotes that virtue by which one actually performs what is morally praiseworthy. It is what prudence guides and what courage and temperance protect" (p. 316).

Justice can be misused or misrepresented when it is called or considered "just" to render to someone what is not due them. This can obviously happen in many ways in the realm of material possessions and money. But it can also take place in the moral realm, as when it is considered a matter of "justice" to ascribed moral goodness to a behavior or belief that is not upright or due. Pope John Paul II wrote of this perversion of justice in *Evangelium Vitae*, his encyclical on the "Gospel of Life":

> *Certainly, from the moral point of view contraception and abortion are specifically different evils: the former contradicts the full truth of the sexual act as the proper expression of conjugal love, while the latter destroys the life of a human being; the former is opposed to the virtue of chastity in marriage, the latter is opposed to the virtue of justice and directly violates the divine commandment "You shall not kill"* (par. 13).

To claim the right to abortion, infanticide and euthanasia, and to recognize that right in law, means to attribute to human freedom a perverse and evil significance: that of an absolute power over others and against others. This is the death of true freedom: "Truly, truly, I say to you, every one who commits sin is a slave to sin" (Jn 8:34; par. 20).

> *"The deliberate decision to deprive an innocent human being of his life is always morally evil and can never be licit either as an end in itself or as a means to a good end." It is in fact a grave act of*

disobedience to the moral law, and indeed to God himself, the author and guarantor of that law; it contradicts the fundamental virtues of justice and charity (par. 57).

For further reference, see CCC 909, 1803-05, 1807, 1836, 1867, 2268.

2. **What is "elevated justice"? How did St. Katharine Drexel's life give witness to the reality of elevated justice? (CCC 1803-1804, 1807, 1810)**

A virtue, the *Catechism* explains, "is an habitual and firm disposition to do the good. It allows the person not only to perform good acts, but to give the best of himself" (CCC 1803). These human or natural virtues, including justice, "are firm attitudes, stable dispositions, habitual perfections of intellect and will that govern our actions, order our passions, and guide our conduct according to reason and faith ... they dispose all the powers of the human being for communion with divine love." (CCC 1804). When these natural virtues are taken up and filled, as it were, with divine grace and life, they are elevated: "Human virtues acquired by education, by deliberate acts and by a perseverance ever-renewed in repeated efforts are purified and elevated by divine grace. With God's help, they forge character and give facility in the practice of the good. The virtuous man is happy to practice them" (CCC 1810).

"Now what happens," writes Bishop Barron in *The Priority of Christ*, "to the virtue of justice when it is transfigured by the love that is the divine life? It becomes radicalized, absolutized, elevated, perfected, turning into a total gift of self, a willingness to render to the other beyond what is merely his due."

There are many specific examples of elevated justice in the life of St. Katharine Drexel, including her charitable giving, her pursuit of missionary work, her entrance into the religious life, and her tireless work on the behalf of the material and spiritual wellbeing of minorities throughout the United States.

For further reference, see CCC 1803-1813, 1833-41.

3. **What are some examples of prudence? Of "supernatural prudence"? How did Thérèse model this supernatural prudence? (CCC 1806; Mt. 10:16; 1 Cor. 12:31)**

"Prudence", wrote St. Augustine in his treatise, *On Freewill*, "is the knowledge of what is to be sought and avoided." And St. Thomas Aquinas defined the virtue of prudence as "the application of right reason to moral practice" (*Disputations Concerning the Cardinal Virtues*). And the *Catechism* explains that "it is not to be confused with timidity or fear, nor with duplicity or dissimulation" (CCC 1806). Jesus touched upon the virtue of prudence when he told his disciples, "Behold, I send you out as sheep in the midst of wolves; so be wise as serpents and innocent as doves" (Matt 10:16).

So answers to the first two questions can vary, depending on one's experience and background. Examples of prudence can often involve very ordinary tasks: decisions made in the course of working, raising children, studying, and going about one's everyday activities. Is it prudent to stay up late to finish a project or to get up early? Is it prudent to work long hours when you have a wife and children at home? This use of practical knowledge and wise decision-making directs how we speak to others about sensitive matters, how we handle tensions in relationships, conflicts in the workplace, the use of talents and abilities, and much more.

When the natural virtue of prudence is transformed by grace, the supernatural life of God, explains Bishop Barron, it is "elevated into supernatural prudence, which is to say, a moral sensibility radically in service of the love of God. ... A feel for the expression of divine love in concrete situations is infused or supernatural prudence" (*The Priority of Christ*, p. 299). An example of such prudence is how a person uses the spiritual gifts they are given for the glory of God and the good of the Church. But this isn't just limited to one's gifts, but extends as well to our trials and sufferings.

At the heart of Thérèse's "little way" is the prudence to know—in every situation, great and small—what is the path of love, willing the good of the other. Thérèse desired to do everything that the saints and heroes of the faith had done throughout Church history: to be a priest, a martyr, an evangelist, a missionary, a doctor. But she knew that she wasn't capable of such things. Then she read the magnificent passage from St. Paul's first letter to the Corinthians: "But earnestly desire the higher gifts. And I will show you a still more excellent way" (1 Cor. 12:31). She realized that love was the form of all the other virtues, the quality shared by every single saint, the dynamic supernatural power that makes possible the work of the missionary, the martyr, the doctor, and the priest. And so she resolved that her vocation would be to love. This was demonstrated in little acts of charity; it was also evident in how she faced death at an early age. "She was convinced," writes Bishop Barron, "that her final illness was a gift from Jesus, a final opportunity to live, the last step on the little way of elevated prudence" (*The Priority of Christ* p. 315).

For further reference, see CCC 1803-4, 1806, 1780, 1788, 1833-6. 2088.

4. **Why do you think Thérèse's approach to the spiritual life became so popular and widespread? Is it completely unique, or is it rooted in basic Catholic spirituality? Explain.**

There are several possible answers to the first question. Pope John Paul II touched on many answers in his 1997 Apostolic Letter, *Divini Amoris Scientia*, in which he proclaimed St. Thérèse to be a Doctor of the Universal Church. He noted that the humility and lowliness of Thérèse is appealing because it demonstrates how God works through and "has continued to reveal himself to the little and the humble..." (par. 1). Her approach is also appealing because its holiness is so evident, rooted as it is in a profound love for God and desire to live out the Gospel: "As if in imitation of her precocious spiritual maturity, her holiness was recognized by the Church in the space of a few years. ... Her message, often summarized in the so-called 'little way', which is nothing other that the Gospel way of holiness for all, was studied by theologians and experts in spirituality. ... The Pastors of the Church, beginning with my predecessors, the Supreme Pontiffs of this century, who held up her holiness as an example for all, also stressed that Thérèse is a teacher of the spiritual life with a doctrine both spiritual and profound, which she drew from the Gospel sources under the guidance of the divine Teacher and then imparted to her brothers and sisters in the Church with the greatest effectiveness" (pars. 2, 3).

John Paul II wrote that "Thérèse discovered"—in her own words—"new lights, hidden and mysterious meanings" and "received from the divine Teacher that 'science of love' which she then expressed with particular originality in her writings" (par. 1). But this newness and originality was not due to a departure from Catholic teaching and spirituality, but resulted from her complete gift of self to God and to others. "The Pastors of the Church," wrote John Paul II, "beginning with my predecessors, the Supreme Pontiffs of this century, who held up her holiness as an example for all, also stressed that Thérèse is a teacher of the spiritual life with a doctrine both spiritual and profound, which she drew from the Gospel sources under the guidance of the divine Teacher and then imparted to her brothers and sisters in the Church with the greatest effectiveness" (par. 3). And:

> Her teaching not only conforms to Scripture and the Catholic faith, but excels ("eminet") for the depth and wise synthesis it achieved. Her doctrine is at once a confession of the Church's faith, an experience of the Christian mystery and a way to holiness. Thérèse offers a mature synthesis of Christian spirituality: she combines theology and the spiritual life; she expresses herself with strength and authority, with a great ability to persuade and communicate, as is shown by the reception and dissemination of her message among the People of God. (par. 7)

Thérèse's teaching expresses with coherence and harmonious unity the dogmas of the Christian faith as a doctrine of truth and an experience of life. In this regard it should not be forgotten that the understanding of the deposit of faith transmitted by the Apostles, as the Second Vatican Council teaches, makes progress in the Church with the help of the Holy Spirit: "There is growth in insight into the realities and words that are passed on... through the contemplation and study of believers who ponder these things in their hearts (cf. Lk 2:19 and 51). It comes from the intimate sense of spiritual realities which they experience. And it comes from the preaching of those who have received, along with their right of succession in the episcopate, the sure charism of truth" (*Dei Verbum*, n. 8).

For further reference, see CCC 2011, 2684, 2687, 2692-3.

THE COMMUNION OF SAINTS: Lesson 8, Part 2

1. **What are some of the differences between natural courage and supernatural, extraordinary fortitude? (CCC 1808, 2473)**

Courage, or fortitude, the *Catechism of the Catholic Church* explains, "is the moral virtue that ensures firmness in difficulties and constancy in the pursuit of the good. It strengthens the resolve to resist temptations and to overcome obstacles in the moral life. The virtue of fortitude enables one to conquer fear, even fear of death, and to face trials and persecutions" (CCC 1808). Pieper explained that fortitude "is basically readiness to die or, more accurately, readiness to fall, to die, in battle" (*Four Cardinal Virtues*, p. 117). Natural courage, then, can be displayed in a willingness to die for one's country and countrymen in battle, or in putting oneself in danger of injury or death in protecting an innocent person from physical attack or harm.

Pieper also notes that the "essential and the highest achievement of fortitude is martyrdom, and readiness for martyrdom is the essential root of all Christian fortitude. Without this readiness there is no Christian fortitude" (pp. 117-8). Supernatural fortitude is therefore deeply rooted in faith and in the hope of eternal life, as well as the conviction that it is better to die than to renounce Christ and the Christian Faith. It is willing to give up a good—one's life—for the greatest good: God, the giver of both natural and supernatural life. "Martyrdom is the supreme witness given to the truth of the faith: it means bearing witness even unto death", states the *Catechism*, "The martyr bears witness to Christ who died and rose, to whom he is united by charity. He bears witness to the truth of the faith and of Christian doctrine. He endures death through an act of fortitude. 'Let me become the food of the beasts, through whom it will be given me to reach God'" (CCC 2473).

For further reference, see CCC 1805, 1808, 2471-74.

2. **How does Edith Stein's journey to the convent differ from that of Katharine and Thérèse? What similarities are to be found? Why was she so willing to accept her death at the hand of the Nazis?**

Unlike Katharine Drexel and Thérèse, Edith Stein was not raised as a Catholic, but as a Jew. In addition, by the time Edith was thirteen, she no longer believed in God. This lack of faith lasted until she was twenty-one. By then she was pursuing a life in academics, intent on making her mark as an intellectual and philosopher. She struggled for quite some time with despair and great loneliness, grabbling with a "struggle for clarity" that "went on amid great internal suffering".
Upon visiting the widow of a good friend and mentor who had died in the war, Edith was surprised at the woman's serenity, which the widow attributed to her Christian faith. "It was my first encounter with the Cross and the divine power that it bestows upon those who carry it," Stein explained, "For the first time, I was seeing with my very eyes the Church, born from its Redeemer's sufferings, triumphant over the sting of death. That was the moment my unbelief collapsed and Christ shone forth—in the mystery of the Cross."
It was a momentous change in perspective for the analytic philosopher, who soon began reading the New Testament and started to seriously ponder whether to convert to Lutheranism or Catholicism.

Her conversion, befitting her careful and studious ways, was not sudden and dramatic, but—much like the conversions of Augustine and Newman—was gradual, interior, marked by much intellectual wrestling. She struggled to take the final step of conversion, and she underwent a long period of profound interior struggle and pain—a "spiritual night"—as she wrestled with God's persistent pursuit.
She was received into the Church on January 1, 1922, but did not enter the convent at Carmel (a choice inspired by Teresa of Avila) until 1933. Like Katharine and Thérèse, Edith had a profound love for Christ and the Eucharist, as well as a desire to live humbly in service to others.

CATHOLICISM

In 1939, facing the inevitable fact of persecution and possible death, Sister Teresa Benedicta of the Cross wrote the following in her will:

Even now I accept the death that God has prepared for me in complete submission and with joy as being his most holy will for me. I ask the Lord to accept my life and my death ... so that the Lord will be accepted by His people and that His Kingdom may come in glory, for the salvation of Germany and the peace of the world" (June 9, 1939)

On August 2, 1942, Sister Benedicta and her sister Rosa were arrested and taken away; they arrived at Auschwitz a week later. They were most likely killed immediately. "The elevated fortitudo of Edith Stein," writes Bishop Barron, "was visible in her willingness to accept the full implications of that solidarity and that union" (*Priority of Christ*, p. 297). Her final (and unfinished) work, *The Science of the Cross*, a study of St. John of the Cross, contained this statement: "The nuptial union of the soul with God is the goal for which she was created; redeemed by the cross, accomplished on the cross, and for all eternity signed and sealed with the cross."

For further reference, see CCC 1805, 1808, 2471-74, 2506.

3. **In light of the *Catechism's* definition of temperance—"[it] is the moral virtue that moderates the attraction of pleasures and provides balance in the use of created goods"—how was Saint Teresa of Calcutta a great exemplar of this virtue? More to it, why is she an example of "elevated temperance"? (CCC 1809)**

The *Catechism* states, "temperance is the moral virtue that moderates the attraction of pleasures and provides balance in the use of created goods." Mother Teresa found her good in living for the poor and caring for their needs, both spiritual and physical. She did not allow the desires that would deviate her from that good lead her away from carrying out her vocation. In particular, she embraced a life of poverty, chastity and obedience. In all those ways, she accepted less so that others could have more. She went above and beyond the natural virtue of temperance by the commitment of her religious vocation in which she made the entirety of her self a gift to the Lord. She held nothing back and gave everything.

PRAYER & THE LIFE OF THE SPIRIT: Lesson 9, Part 1

1. **What are the basic types or forms of prayer? What is the most common type of prayer found in Scripture? Provide some examples. (CCC 2568-2622, 2625-2649; Eph. 6:18)**

The *Catechism of the Catholic Church* first speaks of prayer as a gift, as covenant, and as communion (CCC 2559-65). It teaches that there are several forms of prayer, including prayers of blessing and adoration, prayers of petition, prayers of intercession, prayers of thanksgiving, prayers of praise, and prayers of contemplation. Of these, the three most basic types are prayers of adoration, petition, and contemplation. Prayers are petition are the most common type of prayer found in the Bible:

> The vocabulary of supplication in the New Testament is rich in shades of meaning: ask, beseech, plead, invoke, entreat, cry out, even "struggle in prayer." Its most usual form, because the most spontaneous, is petition: by prayer of petition we express awareness of our relationship with God. We are creatures who are not our own beginning, not the masters of adversity, not our own last end. We are sinners who as Christians know that we have turned away from our Father. Our petition is already a turning back to him (CCC 2629).

Some examples of this include the Lord's Prayer, which asks of God, "Give us this daily bread and forgive us our trespasses..." and "lead us not into temptation, but deliver us from evil". Jesus himself, in agony in the garden, offered a prayer of petition to the Father: "And going a little farther he fell on his face and prayed, 'My Father, if it be possible, let this cup pass from me; nevertheless, not as I will, but as thou wilt'" (Mt. 26:39). Jesus exhorted his disciples to persevere in prayer; he tells us the same: "Ask, and it will be given you; seek, and you will find; knock, and it will be opened to you. For every one who asks receives, and he who seeks finds, and to him who knocks it will be opened" (Matt. 7:7-8). And Paul, writing to the Christians in Ephesus, said: "Pray at all times in the Spirit, with all prayer and supplication. To that end keep alert with all perseverance, making supplication for all the saints..." (Eph. 6:18).

For further reference, see CCC 2623-49, 2697-2724, 2746-51.

2. **What were some of the obstacles that Thomas Merton had to address and overcome in his journey toward the Church? How did Merton's misconceptions about God hinder his spiritual life?**

Merton, who was a very well-educated and highly intelligent young man, held the arrogant view (common among intellectuals of his time) that belief in God is ridiculous, assuming that God was a "noisy mythological figure," and religion the stuff of neuroses and projections. His concept of God, in reality, was seriously shallow and crude, as he realized upon reading Etienne Gilson's *The Spirit of Medieval Philosophy*.

In reading that book, he discovered the concept of *aseitas*, which, he wrote, "can be applied to God alone, and which expresses His most characteristic attribute..." Merton learned that God does not require any justification for existence, for his very nature is existence: "And to say that God exists *a se*, of and by and by reason of Himself, is merely to say that God is Being Itself. Ego sum qui sum." (SSM, 209). He also realized that God is not one being among many, but ipsum esse subsistens—the sheer act of being itself. He came to understand that God alone IS, as the *Catechism* states: "The revelation of the ineffable name 'I AM WHO AM' contains then the truth that God alone IS. The Greek Septuagint translation of the Hebrew Scriptures, and following it the Church's Tradition, understood the divine name in this sense: God is the fullness of Being and of every perfection, without origin and without end. All creatures receive all that they are and have from him; but he alone is his very being, and he is of himself everything that he is" (CCC 213).

Merton also had to address several moral issues in his life, including several improper relationships. Writing years later about his conversion, Merton lamented that he has not embraced the truth years before, making mention of his grave sins: "What scores of self-murdering and Christ-murdering sins would have been avoided—all the filth I had plastered upon His image in my soul during those last five years that I had been scourging and crucifying God within me?" (SSM, 253)

For further reference, see CCC 39-43,198-231.

3. **How can our appetites, desires, and interests hinder our prayer life? What did St. John of the Cross teach about this problem?**

Our appetites, desires, and interests can compete for our attention, distract us from the necessity of prayer, cause us to form improper priorities, weigh us down with cares and worries, and otherwise keep us from entering into conversation with God. St. John of the Cross saw that in order for prayer to nurtured and flourish, man needs to rightly understand who he is before God. In describing the essence of St. John of the Cross's theology, Fr. Jordan Aumann explained that, first, "God is All and the creature is nothing" and, secondly, in order to arrive at perfect union with God, in which sanctity consists, it is necessary to undergo an intense and profound purification of all the faculties and powers of soul and body."

In *The Living Flame of Love*, John wrote of how "the deep caverns of feeling"—referring to intellect, will, and feeling—were "once obscure and blind" because of sin and distractions. Our will desires infinite goodness, and it will not rest until it rests in the absolute good of God, and the emotions ache with an infinite longing, because they are ordered to the infinity of God. We are restless and dissatisfied when we try to fill these infinitely deep caverns with the illusory and petty goods of this world, with pleasure, sex, power, praise, and comfort. But these sinful roads often lead to addiction as we try more and more of these unsatisfying goods. Or we live in a completely superficial way, ignoring the depths within our deepest being.

In order to fulfill these intense longings, we must undergo a purging process—the "purgative way." This is how we rid ourselves of attachments to the many and various substitutes for God, what John calls idols, or false gods. This requires two steps. The first is a complete and practical opposition to idolatry, what John called the "dark night of the senses". This teaches us to not seek ultimate satisfaction in sensible and sensual things, but to let go of them and fast from them. The second step is the "dark night of the soul", during which we let go of even those most rarified things that substitute for God, the concepts and images of the mind. When these purgations are complete, we are ready for the journey into God—that is, to receive the divine and holy gift that God wants to give.

For further reference, see CCC 2683-90, 2709-2719, 2725-45.

PRAYER & THE LIFE OF THE SPIRIT: Lesson 9, Part 2

1. **What is the "interior castle" that St. Teresa of Ávila described? What are some of the methods or techniques she employed in order to pray more deeply?**

The "interior castle" is, as Fr. Thomas Dubay has written, a place of "intimate sharing between friends" and "a being alone with God Who loves us". It is rooted in prayers of adoration; Teresa is an exceptional exemplar of the prayer of adoration, which can be described as the prayer of the center. When we adore God, we allow God to take his place at the very center of our lives and hence to become the organizing principle of our lives. St. John of the Cross referred to the center as the "inner wine cellar," the place of intoxication and the lifting up of the spirits. Teresa referred to it as "the interior castle", and wrote an entire book focused upon describing it.

St. Teresa's prayer life flowed from her complete trust in God, an awareness of her complete reliance on God's strength and grace, and a patient reliance on God's goodness. This is evident in her poem, "Bookmark"—a prayer uttered from the security of the interior castle:

> Let nothing disturb you,
> Let nothing frighten you,
> All things are passing away:
> God never changes.
> Patience obtains all things.
> Whoever has God lacks nothing;
> God alone suffices.

For further reference, see CCC 2626-38, 2709-19.

2. **In what ways is the "Our Father" a prayer of petition? Why did Jesus give his disciples that prayer? If prayer cannot change God, what is prayer really meant to accomplish?**
(CCC 2629, 2632, 2761-62, 2771)

Supplication is common in the New Testament, the *Catechism* explains, taking on different shades of meaning: to "ask, beseech, plead, invoke, entreat, cry out, even 'struggle in prayer'". Most often, supplications are expressed in the form of prayers of petition, in which "we express awareness of our relationship with God. We are creatures who are not our own beginning, not the masters of adversity, not our own last end. We are sinners who as Christians know that we have turned away from our Father. Our petition is already a turning back to him" (CCC 2629).

The "Our Father," like all prayers of petition, begins with a request for forgiveness, which indicates our humility and trust, as well as our desire to be in right communion with God. It is centered on the Kingdom: "Thy Kingdom come, Thy will be done, on earth as it is in heaven". Thus, "we pray first for the Kingdom, then for what is necessary to welcome it and cooperate with its coming. This collaboration with the mission of Christ and the Holy Spirit, which is now that of the Church, is the object of the prayer of the apostolic community" (CCC 2632).

Jesus gave the disciples this prayer, first, because they asked, "Lord, teach us to pray, as John taught his disciples" (Lk. 11:1). In giving the prayer to them, Jesus also entrusted it to the Church. It is, said Tertullian, "the summary of the whole gospel" and St. Augustine stated that all the prayers of Scripture are "contained and included in the Lord's Prayer" (CCC 2761-62).

The "Our Father" contains seven petitions (in St. Matthew's longer version; St. Luke's has five petitions), beginning with "Thy kingdom come" and concluding with "deliver us from evil". This "fundamental prayer" is intimately connected with the Holy Eucharist:

> In the Eucharist, the Lord's Prayer also reveals the eschatological character of its petitions. It is the proper prayer of "the end-time," the time of salvation that began with the outpouring of the Holy Spirit and will be fulfilled with the Lord's return. The petitions addressed to our Father, as distinct from the prayers of the old covenant, rely on the mystery of salvation already accomplished, once for all, in Christ crucified and risen. (CCC 2771)

By praying the "Our Father" and by receiving the Eucharist, we are further transformed by grace and conformed to the image and likeness of Jesus Christ. As St. Teresa of Avila wrote, "All that should be sought for in the exercise of prayer is conformity of our will with the divine will, in which consists the highest perfection."

For further reference, see CCC 2626-38, 2759-2772, 2803-06.

THE LAST THINGS: Lesson 10, Part 1

1. **What are the four "last things"? What is the difference between general eschatology and individual eschatology?**

    The four last things are Death, Judgment, Hell, and Heaven.

    The study of these four is called eschatology, which comes from the Greek word, *eschata*, meaning "the final things." Traditionally, eschatology is divided into two parts: individual eschatology and general eschatology. The latter is what might be called the cosmic perspective—the big picture about history, the end of time, and the manifestation of the new heavens and new earth. Individual eschatology, as its name indicates, focuses on what awaits each man after his death.

    For further reference, see CCC 1020-60.

2. **What is the theological basis for Dante depicting the Devil stuck in ice in the very bottom recesses of hell? What other details are based upon Catholic teaching about hell? (CCC 1033-1037)**

    Dante doesn't describe Hell as filled with flames, but as a dark world filled with beings trapped in ice: "It was/where the shades are all covered up in ice,/and clearly seen, like wisps of straw in glass." This is a dramatic representation of how sin, carried to its end, entraps and "freezes" the sinner so that he is completely caved in upon himself: "Some souls lie prone and some stand straight; of those/some have their heads up, other have their soles,/and some bend over, face to feet, like bows." In the words of C.S. Lewis, in *The Great Divorce*, "Every shutting up of the creature within the dungeon of its own mind—is, in the end, Hell." This means that those who are in hell have chosen to separate themselves from God. The "state of definitive self-exclusion from communion with God and the blessed is called 'hell.'" (CCC 1033).

    Dante also portrays Satan has having great wings. Satan once flew in the service of God, but having rebelled against his Maker, he is completely weighed down by sin and evil. And Dante also writes, "I saw three faces in his head, how great a marvel it appeared to me!" These three faces are a perverted mimicry of the Three Divine Persons, the Trinity. Satan dared to grasp at godliness, to ascend the throne of heaven, but of course failed.

    In *The Inferno*, tears come forth from Satan's six eyes: "With his six eyes he wept, and down three chins/dribbled his tears and slaver slick with blood." This points to the immense sadness that weighs down the unrepentant and self-absorbed sinner. When Virgil and Dante approach Satan, the fallen angel doesn't even notice them—such is the total self-absorption of Hell. In Hell, there is no relationship and no communion, just complete isolation from real live and love.

For further reference, see CCC 633, 1022, 1033-37.

3. **What is the relationship between love, free will, and hell? (CCC 1036-37, 1057)**

Love cannot be forced or coerced; by its very nature, love is rooted in free will and the giving of oneself to another. *Gaudium et Spes*, the Second Vatican Council's Pastoral Constitution on the Church in the Modern Word, expressed this truth in this way:

> *The dignity of man rests above all on the fact that he is called to communion with God. This invitation to converse with God is addressed to man as soon as he comes into being. For if man exists it is because God has created him through love, and through love continues to hold him in existence. He cannot live fully according to truth unless he freely acknowledges that love and entrusts himself to his creator* (par. 19).

If man is free to entrust himself to God and to love God freely, he is also free to reject God as well. And that rejection, carried to its ultimate end, is Hell. That state of damnation is not the condemnation of man by God; rather it is man's condemnation of himself. It is the state of those persons who reject a right relationship with God and insist upon their own autonomy from God and turn their back on his supernatural life. This rejection of supernatural life and love is the embrace of supernatural anguish and death. The *Catechism* states:

> *The affirmations of Sacred Scripture and the teachings of the Church on the subject of hell are a call to the responsibility incumbent upon man to make use of his freedom in view of his eternal destiny. God predestines no one to go to hell; 620 for this, a willful turning away from God (a mortal sin) is necessary, and persistence in it until the end. (pars. 1036, 1037)*

Various theologians and mystics have noted that the "fire" of Hell is the divine light and burning love of God that has been rejected by those in Hell. While the fire of God's divine love animates those who receive it, it torments those who reject it. Or, as the *Catechism* states, "Hell's principal punishment consists of eternal separation from God in whom alone man can have the life and happiness for which he was created and for which he longs" (CCC 1057).

For further reference, see CCC 1033-37, 1056-58.

4. **What are three faulty understandings of purgatory? What are three correct metaphors or descriptions of purgatory? (CCC 1030-1031)**

Some of the faulty understandings and representation of purgatory include:

- Purgatory is a second chance. Not so. As the *Catechism* says, "All who die in God's grace and friendship, but still imperfectly purified, are indeed assured of their eternal salvation; but after death they undergo purification, so as to achieve the holiness necessary to enter the joy of heaven" (CCC 1030). Put another way, those who are in purgatory are on their way to heaven.

- Purgatory is a part of hell. No, again. While there is a sort of suffering in purgatory and hence a superficial similarity, it is the joyful suffering of those being completely cleansed and sanctified so they can enter heaven. This is in direct contrast to the eternal torment of Hell, which is due to man's free rejection of the mercy, life, and love of God.

- Purgatory is a place of gloom and despondency. On the contrary, as noted, the suffering in purgatory is a joyful suffering, because it involves the final cleansing of those impurities that keep man from full and final communion with God. The sixteenth-century bishop Jean Pierre Camus wrote, "If purgatory is a species of hell as regards suffering, it is even more a species of paradise as regards heavenly love and sweetness" (*The Spirit of St. Francis de Sales*, 6,6)

- Purgatory has nothing to do with God's saving work. In fact, it has everything to do with God's saving work, for it is the Father, the Son, and the Holy Spirit alone who redeem, justify and sanctify. It is the completion of man's sanctification. St. Catherine of Genoa likened this work of purification by God to the purification of gold: "In a like manner, the divine fire acts on souls: God holds them in the furnace until every defect has been burnt away and He has brought each in his won degree to a certain standard of perfection" (*Treatise on Purgatory*, 10).

Some correct metaphors or descriptions of purgatory include a purifying fire, a final spiritual cleansing, a washroom or anteroom to heaven, and a seven-storey mountain.

For further reference, see CCC 1030-32, 1987-2029.

5. **How is purgatory a continuation and fulfillment of Christ's work of salvation? What Scriptural evidence is there for a belief in purgatory? (CCC 1987; 2 Macc. 12:40-46; Mt. 12:32; 1 Cor. 3:12-13, 15)**

The *Catechism* states, "The grace of the Holy Spirit has the power to justify us, that is, to cleanse us from our sins and to communicate to us 'the righteousness of God through faith in Jesus Christ" and through Baptism...'" (CCC 1987). The final cleansing of purgatory is the justification and sanctification gifted by the grace and power of the Holy Spirit, made possible because of the saving death and resurrection of Jesus Christ. Purgatory is the final act in the drama of salvation, made possible through the Cross of Christ.

The idea of purgatory is a logical one, based on Scripture and reason. The belief in praying for the dead is evident in 2 Maccabees (2 Macc. 12:42-46). This would not make sense unless the souls being prayed for were in a state in which prayers could help them in some way. Jesus stated, "And whoever says a word against the Son of man will be forgiven; but whoever speaks against the Holy Spirit will not be forgiven, either in this age or in the age to come" (Matt. 12:32). The "age to come" is likely the afterlife, suggesting that some sins can be forgiven and cleansed after death.

St. Paul, in his first letter to the Corinthians, wrote of good works and the foundations upon which they are built. "Now if any one builds on the foundation with gold, silver, precious stones, wood, hay, straw," Paul declared, "each man's work will become manifest; for the Day will disclose it, because it will be revealed with fire, and the fire will test what sort of work each one has done" (1 Cor. 3:12-13). The fire will, in some cases, burn up a man's work and "he will suffer loss, though he himself will be saved, but only as through fire" (1 Cor. 3:15).

For further reference, see CCC 1030-32, 1987-2029.

THE LAST THINGS: Lesson 10, Part 2

1. **What are angels and how are they different than human beings? Can a human become an angel after he/she dies? (CCC 329-330; Heb 1:14)**

Angels are supernatural beings created by God with a spiritual, not human, natures. They have intelligence and will. They are "personal and immortal creatures, surpassing in perfection all visible creatures" (CCC 330). Angels are servants and messengers of God as it states in Psalm 103, verse 20:

Bless the Lord, all you his angels, mighty in strength, acting at his behest, obedient to his command.

A human being cannot become an angel after death as we retain our human nature, albeit changed and perfected by the grace of God in heaven. While both creatures, our nature is different than the nature of angels, which is spirit, and the nature of the Creator God, which is divine.

2. **Who leads the fallen angels and what is his power on earth? (CCC 391-395)**

Satan (the devil) leads the fallen angels. The Church teaches that "Satan was at first a good angel, made by God: 'The devil and the other demons were indeed created naturally good by God, but they became evil by their own doing.' " (CCC 391)

Satan exercises limited power on earth. He is still a creature, but he is powerful on earth because he is pure spirit endowed by God with the nature and capabilities of all angels. "Although Satan may act in the world out of hatred for God and his kingdom in Christ Jesus, the action is permitted by divine providence which with strength and gentleness guides human and cosmic history. It is a great mystery that providence should permit diabolical activity." As Christians, we believe that God will banish Satan and his followers to eternal punishment in Hell at the end of the world.

3. **What are some descriptions of heaven found in Scripture? In Tradition? How would you explain the term "beatific vision"? (CCC 1024-27, 1045, 1326)**

Heaven is a sharing in God's Trinitarian life, the life of perfect love. Heaven is love, love in the fullest sense—love completed. "This perfect life with the Most Holy Trinity—this communion of life and love with the Trinity, with the Virgin Mary, the angels and all the blessed - is called 'heaven.' Heaven is the ultimate end and fulfillment of the deepest human longings, the state of supreme, definitive happiness" (CCC 1024).

Heaven is life with Jesus Christ and with all those who love him. "To live in heaven is 'to be with Christ.' ... Heaven is the blessed community of all who are perfectly incorporated into Christ" (pars. 1025, 1026). Heaven is never experienced alone. To love God is to love all those things and people loved by God. The Church is the "household of God," (1 Tim. 3:15) and in heaven the Church triumphant is like a glorious and bustling household.

Heaven is also experienced here on earth, in a real way, at Mass and in the reception of the eschatological sacrament, the Eucharist. The Mass is an opening into heaven, the door through which we gaze into the eternal worship of the angels and the saints in heaven. As we sing, "Holy, holy, holy", we join our voices to those of the angels: "May our voices be one with theirs." For "by the Eucharistic celebration we already unite ourselves with the heavenly liturgy and anticipate eternal life, when God will be all in all" (CCC 1326).

The *Catechism* further notes other images of heaven: "Scripture speaks of it in images: life, light, peace, wedding feast, wine of the kingdom, the Father's house, the heavenly Jerusalem, paradise: 'no eye has seen, nor ear heard, nor the heart of man conceived, what God has prepared for those who love him." (CCC 1027).

The beatific vision is the vision—the ultimate reality—that makes us finally and fully happy: that is, God himself. "The beatific vision, in which God opens himself in an inexhaustible way to the elect, will be the ever-flowing well-spring of happiness, peace, and mutual communion" (CCC 1045, 1028).

For further reference, see CCC 163, 1028-29, 1042-50, 1052-53, 1090.

NOTES

NOTES

NOTES